INTO THE WILDERNESS

One Woman's Extraordinary Journey through Corruption, Lies, and Betrayal

Karen Marie Dion

Published by
WSA Publishing
301 E 57th Street, 4th fl
New York, NY 10022

Copyright © 2019 by Karen Marie Dion

All rights reserved. No part of this book may be reproduced or transmitted in any form or by in any means, electronic or mechanical, including photocopying, recording, or by any information storage and retrieval system, without the written permission of the Publisher, except where permitted by law.

Manufactured in the United States of America, or in the United Kingdom when distributed elsewhere.

Dion, Karen Marie
    Into the Wilderness: One Woman's Extraordinary Journey through Corruption, Lies, and Betrayal
    LCCN: 2019914584
    ISBN: 978-1-948181-78-5
    eBook: 978-1-948181-79-2

Cover design by: Tanja Prokop of BookDesignTemplates.com
Author cover photo by: Behold Photography
Interior layout and design: Claudia Volkman
Proofreading: Jennifer Rothman

Disclaimer: Although this is a true story, many of the names have been changed out of respect for privacy.

www.kmdion.com
www.knewspring.com

For my beautiful, delightful children

PROLOGUE

Gold Coast, Santa Elena Province, Ecuador

In *Out of the Orchard: The True Story of Me,* I inadequately told the story of my controversial beginnings in this life and the ways in which I "reasoned" myself into acceptance. Reasoning was hackneyed as a coping mechanism for the things that were just too painful to endure without some end in sight, or as means of keeping me tolerant of my abusers and oppressors. I felt powerless, and so I sanctioned the feelings with the device of noble reason.

As any good communication coach will tell you, any strength overused becomes a weakness. In my case, I had reasoned my way into an enabling personality where codependency flourished; my abusers were cared for, but my emotional well-being was dying a slow death.

Though by the end of *Out of the Orchard* I was aware—and ending—the vicious cycle of codependency I had been trapped in for decades, it takes time to replace those convenient, familiar coping mechanisms with new ones. New choices feel foreign, and even cruel, when first exercised. There are plenty of upset bystanders and participants in this life to tell you how wrong and mean you are when you start exercising healthy boundaries.

It takes courage to look in the mirror and realize that however noble you thought you were, you were wrong because you sinned against yourself. There is a time and place to put others ahead of yourself, but enduring abuse is not one of them.

ONE

Sometimes saying "goodbye" is better than asking "why."

THERE'S AT LEAST ONE bite in every life that tastes bittersweet. Like the moment in the sky where the sun setting looks as if it could be rising. You only know which it is if you've marked the time, followed the day through to its ephemeral end, or passed the dark hours waiting for light. That is the precipice upon which I sit now; times past being swallowed up as if the last possible morsel, the one I've pushed around my plate in contemplation, my stomach already full.

Life is full of things that are hard to digest. Pain leaves its mark; trauma its wounds, whether seen or unseen. They are keenly felt, often resented.

Glancing at my hand, I am amazed that though no ring has been around my finger for some time, there is yet a demarcation, no matter what I do it seems to linger. It is the telltale sign that I was committed to someone for an era; that I at least thought I was loved . . . initially. Was I completely deceived? Or was there some truth that shriveled up and blew away, like chaff in the wind? What was the moment that turned the sweet to bitter? Looking back, it was the first morning we were husband and wife, when he sat aloof and wondered aloud, all those years ago. That was the moment when I tasted the bitterness of his soul, the poison that permeated our entire life together.

No. Instinctively, because of the way the truth finally came out, I knew there was nothing I could have done differently. Bob had been dealing with his issues since early childhood. I remember his reaction when his cousin was ultimately found sitting in his parents' attic, drunk, his hulking football player frame squeezed into a woman's dress, makeup on his face smeared with tears of self-absorption, oblivious to what he was putting his wife, Sue, and children through. Bob was not stunned as I had been; he seemed to be curious in a jealous sort of way. Even then, I didn't get it. I could not put myself in Sue's shoes. I had such compassion for what she must be going through, such sorrow as she grieved and moved on alone. I had no idea that would be me soon.

I asked Bob one day when he was in a sincere state of mind, "If you have always dealt with this, why did you marry me?"

"Because I thought it would fix me," he responded succinctly. "I adored you. You represent the perfect woman to me. I thought if I could have you, I would be whole."

That about summed up our relationship. I was a possession to him. I was the trophy, counselor, coach, friend, and rock. It was not reciprocal. Ever.

Now I am happy to own hard-fought truth, if nothing else. I am happy, in a gruesome sort of way, that my worst fears have been realized; nagging thoughts vindicated. I am not crazy; I was right, after all. I was lied to. I was deceived, and I was used. I was lied about, publicly humiliated, physically abused, emotionally blackmailed and yet, I am free now, wiser. I am no longer a captive to mendacious circumstances. The future lies ahead clothed in hope while forgotten possibilities are awakening in my heart.

I surprised myself at how easy it was to move on but realizing the entirety of our seventeen-year marriage had been a sham, an absolute fraud, helped. Sure, it stung. It cut to my core at first, but as I grasped it all through the lenses of 20/20 hindsight and truth, I felt my confidence return, and my self-esteem rise. Why had I distrusted my own instincts all those years? Why didn't I stand up to him sooner? That too, became easy to understand when I looked at how my family had abused me first. My father conditioned me to accept lies as truth, to second guess and doubt myself always, and to never fight back.

Then there was the early childhood trauma I had drowned out of my consciousness for decades. When I said "No!" to my abuser and he forced himself on me anyway I learned that no matter what I said, no matter what I wanted, I was powerless. It has taken me a lifetime to unlearn that; to regain my power.

All that is past now; an epic tragedy on which the final curtain has dropped. All that is left to do is begin anew, seize the day and appreciate new adventures ahead. I felt I had survived the worst of times; life could only get better as I neared the end of four decades on the earth. I was not looking for a new relationship since, for the first time in nineteen years or so, I felt free and content. There was no one to care for other than my children, and they were a joy to live with, especially now that I didn't have a need to protect them from a monster living under the same roof. It was a pleasant realization to me that they were better off without their father in the home. I hadn't known about his manipulative behavior behind my back, or the lies he told them because we were just trying to survive his abuse and narcissistic rage. I had hung in there for so long because I thought it was best for them, among other reasons, and now joyfully, I accepted that removing him from our lives was healthiest for all of us. I got them into counseling to debrief and give them some support for the adjustment; what came out in those sessions only solidified my conviction that the right choice had been made.

But old habits die hard. A part of me listened to the church people and ignorant know-it-alls who claimed that I must give Bob a chance, give the children time with their father. Even though Bob never wrote his desired visitation schedule, nor retrieved his belongings, I felt compassion for him and would pile boxes of his things into my vehicle, load up the kids and go for a visit from time to time.

He was living in old officer housing on the former Plattsburgh Air Force base. One Saturday morning Jonathan and Katlyn took turns ringing the door bell, simultaneously helping me unload boxes and putting them on his porch. It must have been about five minutes before he opened the door; by then we were getting back in the car to drive away.

"Dad!" Katlyn yelled as I took off my seatbelt again. The kids ran to hug him. As I approached him the smell of alcohol and heavy body order smacked my senses. He looked like he had been ill and probably dropped about thirty pounds since I saw him last, two or three months previous.

"Are you okay?" I queried as the kids shoved past him into his apartment.

"I'm great," he stated, ushering me in with some embarrassment. "Please excuse the mess. I am kind of hungover . . . wasn't expecting anyone this morning."

"I had to come to Plattsburgh to do some errands. I thought I'd bring some things you might want," I told him, eyeing the mudroom floor as I walked by. It was littered with vodka bottles and SlimFast cans. "SlimFast? You're not eating?"

"I am trying to lose some weight," he said with irritation in his voice. "I've lost twenty-eight pounds so far."

"I can tell. You want to lose more than that?"

"Yeah, another ten pounds, I think." His dark eyes were darting around the kitchen and living room, watching the kids as they meandered curiously in his place. "Want to see the rest of the place?"

"Sure. C'mon kids," I called, following Bob up the narrow stairs.

"I don't really need all this space," he offered with that unmistakable nervousness in his tone I had come to know so well. "So, I rent two of the rooms from time to time . . . people who travel to the area for business a few times a month. This room belongs to Kristy . . . she's not here right now . . . kind of left it a mess." I noted the makeup askew on the bureau, just below an antique mirror and the negligee hanging in the open closet with a wig above it on the shelf.

"Kristy, huh?" I nodded, realizing no woman gone for more than a day would leave her makeup behind.

"Is that your girlfriend?" Katlyn asked.

"No! No," Bob blurted quickly. "I don't have a girlfriend. She just rents a room from me when she's in town. And the other room gets used by my friend Bruce when he has to come here on business." He opened the door to a perfectly neat and tidy room that looked like it hadn't been used in years. "So, that's about it."

"Dad, how come you don't call us?" Jonathan asked.

"And how come you never come to see us?" Katlyn added. I fidgeted nervously.

"I've just been so busy with work," Bob glanced in my direction with a plea in his eyes. As if I would make excuses for him anymore! "Maybe you could come next weekend for a sleepover. Um, would you like that?"

"Can I bring a friend?" Katlyn asked innocently.

"I thought you wanted to spend some time with me?" he retorted. "We'll go play miniature golf and then pick up a pizza and watch movies. How does that sound?"

"Okay," Jonathan and Katlyn agreed in unison. Plans set for the following Saturday night, we left as Bob thanked me for bringing the rest of his belongings. I admit, there was a selfish motive as well in that as much as I wanted him to have them, I wanted them out of my house for good.

Driving home, the kids expressed regret and anxiety about promising to spend the night. I knew he wouldn't do anything foolish around them at this point, but their anxiety was real.

"We don't really know him," Jonathan said eerily. Since he was so much younger than Katlyn, I realized he was right. By the time he was five years old, Bob had been so detached and aloof from us that he was nothing more than a violent figure who lived in our home and sometimes participated in family activities. The final year or so of our "marriage," Bob mainly stayed in the basement and was either gone or sitting with a laptop watching porn or surfing for hookups.

"I will be there with you, Jon," Katlyn offered. "He's still our dad. But Mama?"

"Yes?"

"If we change our mind . . . don't want to spend the night, will you come get us?" she asked warily.

"Of course I will! All you have to do is call me and I will come right away," I reassured them. "If you just want to go play mini golf and have pizza, that's fine, too."

"Why don't you come play mini golf with us, Mama?" Jon asked eagerly, his brown eyes wide as he leaned forward, peering in the rearview mirror so I could see him.

"Sweetie, I don't think your dad would appreciate that. He wants to spend some time with just the two of you. Isn't that what you wanted?"

"Maybe," he replied.

I picked up the phone to dial Nana, but there was no dial tone. "Hello?" I said, thinking I might have to dial again.

"Wow, you answered fast," she said with a laugh on the other end. "I just dialed!"

"I just dialed you," I said, snickering. "I thought I didn't have a dial tone and was going to try again!"

"How many times do you think we've done that?" She continued giggling. "I get a kick out of it every time! We're so connected!"

"That we are!" I smiled, wishing I could be in her kitchen rather than across the lake. Still, I was very happy to be only an hour away as opposed to the ten or twelve hours away I had been for so many years.

"I was wondering how the kids made out with Bob last night? They've been on my mind all night," she said sobering up a bit.

"Well, they called me repeatedly, but they did stay overnight. I don't think they rested well."

"No? Were they upset?" she worried. I could just see her freckled face in my mind, soft hazel eyes brimming with love.

"Katlyn confided in me she was sure that 'Dad has an ugly girlfriend. Her picture is on the mantle, and she looks like a man pretending to be a woman.'" I said, giggling.

"I bet! It's probably a picture of him!" she said with disgust. "Or do you think he really does have a girlfriend?"

"No, I don't think so," I half-wondered. "I bet it is a portrait of his alter ego."

"Well, I wouldn't be upset if the kids decided never to spend the night again," she said with a sigh. "Poor babes. I used to think it was good for families to stay together but now I know that's not always the healthiest option. Thank God you finally saw that," she said determinedly.

TWO

Sometimes eccentricity is authentic; at other times, it's a cunning disguise.

WHEN I FIRST MET Don Lorry, he struck me as an eccentric fellow without any particular smarts. However, not soon enough, I came to learn his eccentricity is more craftiness and his scheming brain is disguised by his frumpy character. "Never trust an old man with a ponytail," someone once told me. I thought to myself, *How judgmental!* Well, since that guy was speaking of Don at the time, I should have paid more attention.

Don is the sort that is always looking for an easy ride and the high life all at once. He once bragged to me about how he came into possession of his property portfolio—a lack-luster group of properties in the vanquishing village of Keeseville and Town of AuSable. It was during a meeting about his screen-printing business, run by his son Tom.

"Carolyn's first marriage was a disaster," he stated with some glee. "Roland was a drunk, and he relied on her as a workhorse. The $75,000 in legal fees I spent for her divorce was a bargain since I ended up with all his properties," he smirked.

I had been consulting since moving to the Adirondacks and now with money issues Bob was creating, I was hoping to pick up more work again. The events of September 11th, 2001, put a huge dent in the work I had contracted to do, primarily because the thrust of consulting dollars from that day on for several years shifted to disaster preparedness, which was not my bailiwick. I lost about $75,000 in contracts for the next eighteen-month period. That is in part why I decided to focus on smaller, local contracts, along with being closer to the kids.

"I'd like you to help my son get a financing proposal together. The screen-printing business is doing great, but he needs to make some upgrades. Then he can buy me out, so I can retire," Don said wryly. "It's time for Carolyn and me to simplify." He was restating what Tom had already told me; I met him that day because Tom sent me. I had all sorts of projections from Tom, along with the paperwork required by the Small Business Administration and other potential financing agencies, but Don was still an owner. After touring the dilapidated shop and office on Route 9, I could see that Tom did need to upgrade. Furthermore, any proposal would have to include Don's financials as well since he was still on title and listed as an officer. However, it had been nearly an hour of listening to Don ramble on about this thing and that person, his antiques and the place on Ausable Street, before I could finally get him to focus on the purpose of our meeting.

"I've spoken with The Development Corporation, and they are willing to look at the proposal, so I need your financial information and signatures to complete that application," I explained. "Now, if you can just list your assets and income on this financial statement—"

"Why the hell do they need my income? I'm not gonna repay the loan, Tom is! The business is. . . ."

"Because you are listed as an officer and a primary in the business—"

"That's bullshit! They don't need my personal info. They can do this without it."

"I'll tell you what, I will talk to them again to be sure, okay? Meanwhile, maybe you can pull it all together? I mean, copies of your tax returns for the past two years, income verification, all the typical paperwork."

"Just go talk to, what the hell's his name . . . Carolyn! Carolyn!"

Carolyn came urgently from the other room, worriedly looking over the top of her reading glasses, mug in one hand, phone in the other. The drab house was dark for the middle of the afternoon, and her billowy figure seemed to emerge from its shadows.

"What the hell's the guy's name—he owes us a big favor—at Glens Falls bank? Italian? You remember?" Don impatiently prodded, but Carolyn just stared like a deer caught in headlights.

"I don't know," she said quietly. "*Um* . . . is it Tony?"

"That's it! Tony Parillo. Take the damn proposal to Tony. Tell him I sent you. Remind him how I helped him get his job."

"I'm afraid that sounds a bit like you're asking for a return favor. He will still need the right paperwork. $250,000 is not a simple handshake and this is not the 1950s!" I said with a laugh.

"Well, these things are done right if you know someone, if you network," Don recoiled. "I don't know who's at The Development Corporation anymore."

"Adore Kurtz," I informed him.

"Oh, well, is there a guy there, too? She doesn't seem to really know us. If there's a guy there, talk to him. And go see Tony at the Plattsburgh branch—on Margaret Street, Glens Falls National Bank." Lifting his pointer finger and narrowing his eyes, he said, "Who else are you gonna take this to?"

"No one unless I have a complete package," I stated. "Evergreen Bank? So, when can I get your info?"

"Nah, I don't want this stupid local bank to know all of our business. How about you work on what Tom has given you and come back at the end of the week? We've gotta get ready to go now. We're meeting our friend for dinner; he's a chief of the Akwesasne tribe, like family really. Isn't that right, Carolyn?" She had settled herself into the wing-back chair next to me, and seeming to not have a voice of her own, simply nodded and sipped her tea, her furrowed brows raising up in unison as she widened her crinkly, hazel eyes. "So, we'll hit the casino and have some fun. Be back in a couple of days." I think he wanted me to be impressed, but I wasn't. Gambling never appealed to me.

Handing me his notes, which were more like pointed instructions, he stood to his feet and we made our way to the door. I was disappointed my time was not very productive but figured I would go back to Tom with his part completed anyway. Setting a day and time for the end of the week, I was off.

Tom continued to feed me his projections, accounts receivable, accounts payable and more. His timing was of a far more urgent nature. On a glorious April morning, once the kids were in school and I was on with my day, I went back to his ramshackle operation to follow up.

"Did you get everything from Dad? I've gotta get this done!" he said as he pushed through papers with one hand and slurped coffee from an over-sized mug with the other. His unusual eyes darting back and forth, he was practically dancing in his chair. I wondered if he should really be having another cup.

"Your dad is reluctant to share his personal info with the SBA, or pretty much any financial info, really. He said I could come back at the end of the week, but he wants—"

"End of the week? You've gotta be fucking kidding me." Tom was up and prancing now. "I'll call him. I'll talk to him. He can't have it both ways."

"Good idea. Meanwhile I just need to update the numbers you've given me this morning in the narrative and get your paperwork signed. I will be presenting this to Brian at The Development Corporation as soon as I get your parents' info and signatures. What exactly do you mean by 'both ways'?"

"Who the hell is Brian? What about that A—what's her name? I can't remember, it begins with 'A' . . . unusual, sounds like 'a door' or something." His bicolor eyes seemed to finally stand still as he wondered aloud. Tom has what is called heterochromia iridium, a genetic condition where one individual has two different eye colors. In his case, one is brown and the other is a blue-green. I had never encountered it before, so I kept finding myself paying attention to his eyes, wanting to focus on either one or the other at a time.

"Adoré (Ador-A). Your dad said she doesn't really know you, and he prefers that I deal with Brian. How do you know Adoré? She's a nice woman, very savvy. I've worked with her before," I said, curious to hear his take.

"I think Dad didn't like her is all. He used to rent some space from them when we first expanded to Plattsburgh, he never got along with her. Want a coffee?" he asked, raising his mug.

"Sure." He led me to the back room, still talking as he poured.

"The thing is, between you and me, my eff'in' brother really screwed me. He was dealin' drugs right out the back door here and spending all his time on the basketball court or the golf course. You can't be dealing in front of employees, in broad daylight, outta the back of the business! That's all kinda crazy." I could almost see his blood pressure going up as he talked.

This is Don junior you're talking about, right?" I had seen him around the elementary school and at the kids' mini-mite soccer games with his ever-tired-looking wife.

"Spike. Yeah, he's Don, junior, but we all call him Spike. You can't be on the basketball court or golf course everyday an' spending money like it's water. Eventually people wonder where you get your money. And it's not fair to me. I work my ass off around here!"

"So, that's why you need the money—to buy him out?" I queried, upset that such a seemingly good father of young children could be dealing drugs in broad daylight.

"I already bought him out! That's what's fuckin' killin' me here! Last fall I told him we were done. We worked this business together since high school. Before us, Dad didn't do trophies, he only did screen-printing. We did that, me and Spike, we brought that part in. An' then he started screwin' with it—actin' like he could just be some CEO or something and everything would just take care of itself. It doesn't work like that."

"So, he doesn't own the business anymore? What does he do?"

"That's just it, right now, nothin'! He works his wife like a bitch, but he plays all day and deals drugs and I don't want anything to do with that," Tom stated flatly.

"Does your dad know this? Your mom?" I queried, aghast.

"Carolyn's not my mom, she's my stepmom. Yeah, Dad knows; that's why when I went to him and said I needed to get rid of Spike he worked it out with us. I told him he would ruin us both if we didn't. Spike wasn't too happy, but he likes money a lot more than work, so. . ."

"So, you and your dad bought him out and now you need to buy your dad out so it's all yours?"

"Payback's a bitch. My old man is not as generous as he comes across. But I really do need to make some repairs and upgrades here. I'm carrying a full load, business is good, but I can do better with better equipment and some facade improvements will make this place more appealing from the road. A lot of traffic goes by here—you'd be surprised. I plan on opening a shop in front and keeping the orders and work area in back." The phone rang as he sat back down in his squeaky, 1970s desk chair. "Hello, this is Tom . . ."

I wandered around the office, taking in all that needed to be done. Stacks of boxes lined the perimeter, while racks of shirts—mostly team shirts in all sizes—stood in the center of the room, blocking the flow. The windows were old and dusty; the paneled walls and thin, worn carpet tasteless.

"That consultant I told you about," I heard him say to whomever was on the line. "Yes, she's a woman, but—" His eyebrows raised, he half got out of his chair, motioning as if the person on the other end of the phone could see him. "I am telling you she is not that kind of woman. It's all business. I'll be home for lunch. Love you."

As I watched, I could not help but wonder why he was so unkempt. His hair was all greasy and a mess, and he smelled as if he could use some deodorant. Then again, since I arrived in Keeseville and the surrounds, I had already been surprised many times by the ambitious amateurs in business I kept running into. It struck me that none of them could survive business in Philadelphia without major personal overhauls.

"Maybe I should get going. You can just let me know when you've had a chance to talk with your dad."

"Get the whole thing ready. Make it the best damn proposal you've ever done. I want a quarter of a mil to get my dad off my ass an' this place up to the potential it has," Tom replied determinedly.

Going home to check email and get in touch with the mortgage company, I prayed for some breathing room. For some reason, I had not thought to ask Bob for his debit card back when I changed the bank account from a joint account to an individual one. I guess I just didn't believe he would stoop as low as he had been doing lately, or that it would still work. Because I had no regular job when we moved to the area and he did, the mortgage was in his name only, my name was added to the property title. He was supposed to execute a warranty deed to me under the terms of our agreed upon divorce settlement; I had two years to get the mortgage refinanced into my own name. Meanwhile, I paid the ABN AMRO mortgage. My lawyer assured me that with an on-time payment history of six months or more, wherein I could prove my income and that I had been paying, refinancing into my own name would not be an issue. One night about four months after our official separation, Bob went to six different ATM's and took out the maximum allowable cash of $200 at each. In one night, unbeknownst to me, my checking account was down $1,200. This caused my mortgage check to bounce. I didn't put the pieces together until several days later when I received a notice in the mail.

Of course, I called ABN AMRO right away, but they would not speak to me because, as the long-awaited real person on the other end of the phone said in her best broken English, "You are not the mortgagor." Though I tried to explain and asked for a supervisor, it ultimately got me nowhere except incredibly frustrated. I called Bob who feigned an apology and claimed to have some major expense that had to be met. I demanded the card back, but he refused. I explained that he had to call ABN AMRO and give them permission to speak with me, on the record. I demanded it in writing. Then, I told him I was calling my lawyer about the $1,200.

"I'll pay it back," he said sheepishly. "It was urgent. I figured you'd at least be compassionate."

"Compassionate, yes, but not stupid!" I retorted. "What on earth makes you think I have that kind of extra money lying around? You don't even pay alimony or child support on time!"

"I promise, I'll pay it back," he sounded only sorry to be caught in the act.

"I've had enough of your promises, Bob. You've never kept them. I am disappointed that you don't have more respect for me and the kids. This is our well-being that you are undermining." I had given all for him; my career, my savings, even my reputation in the eyes of most people who had no idea what he was up to in secret all those years. I was judged harshly for the divorce. Why shouldn't I just tell the world the truth about him now? Yet, I kept my silence because he asked me to and for the sake of the kids. This is how he repays my kindness? "What on earth was so urgent?" I sighed.

"I needed to pay a security deposit, but I get paid Friday and I will pay you back," he assured me yet again. "I can meet you and give you cash, if you want."

"You didn't think to call and ask if I had anything I could loan you? You just took it and made the mortgage check bounce?" I was incredulous, anxious.

"I'm sorry. That was kind of dumb, I guess. Want me to meet you Friday?"

"Yes. I want it in cash, along with your debit card. Meanwhile, you will call ABN AMRO and write out a statement authorizing them to speak with me and sign it. Fax it to me by the end of the day." I demanded.

"You got it," he promised again. I wasn't so sure I could believe him, but what else could I do?

THREE

There is a vast gap between the spirit of a law or regulation and the understanding of those who carry it out like zealots.

DON FIDGETED WITH HIS pen as he read the forms I had just placed in his hand. Carolyn sat quietly nearby, sipping from a mug again, like a loyal dog awaiting a command from its master. The leather chair crunched as Don shifted his weight and lifted his briefcase to his lap.

"I am just going to cross some things out." Using his briefcase as a desk, he began editing the forms mandated by the financing companies. "They don't need to know everything."

"Well, they need to have facts to base their decision on," I replied as politely as possible.

"They have plenty of information. I don't want them snooping in my affairs. They don't need blood and my firstborn. Bureaucracy, that's what it is. Too much red tape. Big banks and government want their hands in my pockets. What they don't know won't hurt 'em. Isn't that so, Carolyn?"

She nodded on cue. "Yes, the amount of paperwork they want is ridiculous," she obliged.

"For instance, why do they need to know about all my properties?" he queried rhetorically. "Why do they need to know about my income? I'm not personally going to repay this, the business is!"

"I understand, but you are a principle in the business. The properties go to your assets and viability. If the business can't pay, then you and Tom are personally responsible."

"Well, at least, I want you to see if there's a way that we can do without the tax returns. They don't need to know—it actually may hurt us 'cause we don't claim much of the laundromat business. It's all cash, ya know. All cash. Good business to get into. But I'll list the properties." He scribbled some notes in one of the columns. "It's a good write up, you did. Very professional. I guess Tom has you writing up a piece for the website, too? Do you need me for that?"

"No, I'm all set, thank you." As I watched him alternately scribbling and stroking his chin, wire-rimmed glasses encircling his eyes, I wondered about his motivation. It seemed that Don wanted to take ownership of everything but didn't want the responsibility, or maybe he really was getting tired and old, like he told me early on. *Does he just need to feel important?* I couldn't decide.

"Can we get you something? Coffee, maybe? I think there's some coffee, or tea? Carolyn?"

"Yes, what would you like?" she offered, sitting forward in her chair.

"Well, if it's not too much trouble—"

"No. No trouble," Don replied while Carolyn stood to her feet.

"Then I would have some tea, thank you."

"What kind? I have some herbal tea and some regular . . ." Carolyn's voice trailed off as she rounded the corner into the kitchen.

"Herbal sounds great, thanks."

"Do you ever drink coffee?" Don asked.

"Yes, but I've had plenty of it this morning already. So how long have you lived here?" I asked, trying to make conversation.

"Carolyn, how long have we lived here?" he bellowed to be heard in the kitchen.

"About fifteen years." She stuck her head around the corner. "Do you take anything in your tea?"

"No thank you, just plain herbal tea."

"Yeah, we had a fire and we redid everything, smoke and water damage, ya know." Don stopped scribbling and handed me the SBA forms.

"Oh, is that the fire that Tom mentioned? I thought it was downtown—" A wave of sympathy swept over me as I pondered the losses and trauma.

Don broke in, "No, that was *another fire.*" Carolyn returned to the living room, handing me a mug, her face looking wrought at the mention of fire. "That was in our building, last year. Where the laundromat is."

"Oh, so you had *two* fires?" I couldn't fathom that much trouble coming on one family. Recalling my Aunt Shirley and Uncle Tom's tragic losses from fire during the Ice Storm of '98, I was moved with compassion for them.

"Yes, the house just got finished from all the repairs a couple of years ago—takes forever, ya know, fighting with insurance companies. Carolyn, you should give her a tour of the house."

Carolyn nodded, "It's not something I want to live through again; the mess, the loss. We had trash bags full of stuff we tried to save, but we ended up having to throw so much out. But the people were so nasty—the tenants . . ." I had not seen her so animated until this moment. My heart went out to her.

"It must have been horrible. You had tenants in your house and they—"

"No, in the building" they said in unison.

"And they tried to sue us, but it wasn't our fault," Carolyn lamented, her voice cracking with anger.

"What Carolyn means is, we had a lot of losses when our house burned. When the building burned, we understood how the tenants must have felt, but there was nothing we could've done." Don sat soberly back in his chair, having just placed his briefcase on the floor next to him.

"They left a candle burning . . . someone left a candle burning in one of the apartments and something caught fire and it just spread." Watching her become agitated, I thought it might be best to change the subject.

"Oh, that's awful! I am so sorry. I can't imagine."

"Yeah, it's really sad. That's why we are ready to put things in order and just try to enjoy life," Don said wearily.

"But those people at that office on the river—what's that place called?" Carolyn was still disturbed. "Anyway, they were horrible too. I got all the info together for them; they seemed so sympathetic and understanding, and we went through all this work—"

"The Friends," Don interrupted.

"That's it! The Friends of the North Country. Well, anyway, they had us go through this whole process to get approval. All this paperwork and stuff they really didn't need to know—"

"A lot of red tape. Typical bureaucracy," Don interrupted.

"—and then we get to the meeting and she, oh! What's her name? The one that heads it up?" Her face pinched in thought as she grabbed her forehead.

"Something with two last names," Don answered. "She thinks she's so damn high society with two last names."

"Yes, Ann, I think, with two last names, yeah. Anyway, she stood up and gave our proposal and then said she didn't recommend they approve it! Can you believe it? How embarrassing. I was so mad. I still am."

"So, you already applied for financing for the fire damage?" I asked, trying to sort out the facts of two different fires and keep up with the details in my mind.

"Yup. For the Front Street property, after the fire. This is for the screen-printing business. Two different things," Don adamantly leaned forward, his finger lifted to point in that direction.

"Yes. We were going to fix up the Front Street building after the fire. We still run the laundromat out of one side, but the insurance company didn't give us enough money for the losses. There's a program, somehow the Friends has this money for the Village—"

"Yes, I understand." I nodded.

"—and they get to say who gets it and who doesn't. It's not fair at all, really." Carolyn's anxiety over the whole situation permeated the atmosphere.

"Well actually, The Friends . . ." I tried to explain, but Don was hopping mad.

"What Carolyn means is," Don expertly explained, "the loan fund. The Friends monitor a HUD program for the Village. It's a low-interest loan for economic development. We applied and the two-faced woman who started it—"

"The fund?" I asked.

"No, she started—Ann with two last names—she started the Friends. When it came to a vote of the board of trustees, she told them she didn't think we were viable, so she didn't recommend the loan. Since the insurance company didn't give us anything but a pittance after the fire, we haven't been able to put a roof back on the building or do anything really. But that is separate from this. It was a pissing contest is all. She's a little high on herself. Wish we'd known before we put in all the work." Don's sad expression was only matched by his determination.

"I am familiar with the Friends. I was on the Board of Directors for a little while. I didn't get too familiar with the fund, I was involved in other aspects. I respect what Ann has done there. They are all pretty good people as far as my experience can tell," I offered.

"That was our retirement," Carolyn added, heaving a sigh. "That building and the tenant income, that was our retirement. Now it's sitting there getting ruined. I get a headache just thinking about it."

"Well, let's see if we can get *this* headache finished up and out of your way," I summoned. "Let's see . . . you have listed the properties as A, B—"

"Yeah, they don't need to know the addresses." I couldn't help but think of how much like my own father he was, one minute friendly and intelligent, the next I'm wondering how he can function in society.

"Why don't you give me the addresses just in case?" I knew they would need actual addresses. "Are they all in Keeseville?"

"Well, most of them, there's some in AuSable—ya know, this whole thing with the two towns and the village, so there's the laundromat building on Front Street, the one that burned. We really gotta do something about that," he said, looking at Carolyn wistfully, his voice trailing off. Watching them lock eyes over such sadness moved me again. After a moment, he launched into a history lesson of the Village and how it is split in half by the Town of Chesterfield on one side of the river, and the Town of AuSable on the other, which led him into a political discussion that left me desperately trying not to smirk. *The politics of Keeseville? They should try to get out more!*

"Okay, so we have property A at Front Street," I interjected. "That's Chesterfield; then where is property B?"

"That's the one on AuSable Street, we've got a bunch of stuff stored in there and an apartment we rent out," Don commented.

"You've got to get that garage cleaned out, Don, so we can put the Ghost in there," Carolyn scolded.

"Yeah, I've just been so busy," he agreed.

"Ghost?" I couldn't help myself. I had to ask.

"One of my antique cars . . . it's a . . ." He rattled on describing it, but I was beginning to feel like this meeting had turned into part reminiscing session, part family pow-wow. As I glanced at my watch, Carolyn noticed.

"Don!" she said. "We need to get back to business here and let her get on with her day." I was grateful. It's not that I wasn't sympathetic. I was very sympathetic, it's just the only thing I could do to be helpful at that point was to get on with the business at hand. We wrapped up our conversation, finally. I had the list of properties, was promised copies of tax returns and pretty much everything else I needed.

"I will be in touch as soon as I have all forms finalized for your signatures. In the meantime, please get back to me if you would like to see any changes to the draft proposal I've given you today. I plan on submitting this by the end of the week, okay?" I knew Tom was very anxious, and I was glad to be able to give him something concrete, as well as to be out from under being the family financial go-between.

"Tom has to sign, too," Don declared emphatically.

"Yes, and it appears that Carolyn and Betty will have to also."

"Well now, I want to keep Carolyn out of this; she doesn't need her name on this." Don turned squeamish again. Stroking his goatee, his neck outstretched, he pondered something foreign to me.

"Is she on title to the properties? The business?" Don continued to stroke his goatee but said nothing. "Well, let's just see what it looks like when I finalize these forms and have the criteria of each potential lender in front of me, sound okay?" I stated more than questioned, as I stood to leave.

"Well, we have to give you a tour of the house," Don rose from his chair.

"Yes," Carolyn chimed in. Obligatorily, I followed her around the tiny, dimly lit, split level. It was not my taste, but I understood how proud they were of it and especially how pleased they were to have their home "fixed up" after such a long, drawn-out ordeal.

As I made my way back home again, I picked up the mail to find my payment to ABN AMRO, the one I sent to replace the check Bob caused to bounce. It was returned to me with a note that read, "You are not the mortgagor."

FOUR

Everyone needs a new beginning sometime, conveniently or not.

"GOOD MORNING, THIS IS Karen Marie."

The shrill ring of the phone interrupted the serenity of the morning. I answered just before it went to voicemail, still gazing out my window at the gorgeous panorama. Fog was lifting from the valley as the sun rose just above Mount Trembleau, the only obstacle between me and Lake Champlain, and my beloved Nana on the other side. I daily took comfort in knowing I could be home in an hour or so, depending upon the ferry schedule.

"What a sexy voice you have. . . . Damn, you make me wanna do things!"

"Who—? Tom?" I recoiled, recognizing his voice.

"Ha-ha! See! You want me, admit it!" He laughed out loud.

"Well, I will say that I recognized your voice and only admit you caught me off guard."

"Seriously, hasn't anyone ever told you that you have a sexy voice? Somebody's told you by now, I'm sure."

"Not that it matters," I stated, a little flummoxed.

"Ah! So, you *have* been told! Well, if my wife ever heard your voice I'd be in trouble! Ha! Let alone if she ever saw you! As it is she won't let me shave and shower before work, says it makes me too attractive to other women." Tom's voice has a certain raspy quality to it, I noted as he talked, while scanning my brain for a way to change the subject and simultaneously trying not to gag.

"You should stop talking to other women like this and give her less to worry about. Anyway, I'm assuming you called for business reasons?" I returned my gaze to the valley below, wishing I hadn't answered the phone.

"Yeah. I guess we can get down to business." His voice dampening, he continued: "Just wondering when the proposal will be ready. Dad's getting ready to go out of town and I'm lookin' at a stack of bills."

"It's pretty much done. I just need to double check with Brian that I have all the forms the Development Corp is requesting, then I will need all your signatures and tax returns from Carolyn and your dad. Will you all be available later today?"

"Me and Dad, ya mean?"

"All of you—Carolyn and Betty need to sign, too."

"I will make sure of it. You wanna call my Dad, or should I?" Tom was completely about business now.

"I can. I will set a time for this afternoon then swing by the shop afterward to get your signature," I volunteered.

One would think I had requested state secrets when I asked for the tax returns and other financial forms from Don and Carolyn, so it was ironic to me that when I finally picked them up they were handed to me in a plastic shopping bag.

"Now, ahem," Don started, clearing his throat. "You know that these figures on the taxes, well, they are not the actual income from the laundromat. I mean, it looks pretty bad on paper, but it's a cash business so. . ." His eyebrows raised, he tilted his head as if to request some acknowledgment from me. I tried to remain neutral while wishing I could remain ignorant.

"This decision is not up to me. I am only the facilitator between you and the financing opportunities. You have to sign and acknowledge according to your conscience and their terms."

"Yes, well my conscience doesn't bother me one bit since the government has their hands in too many things. We pay enough taxes. Cash is hard to report, ya know. Are you interested in a good business? 'Cause eventually we're gonna wanna sell the laundromat. It's a cash cow. No one pays by credit card, very few checks, all cash."

"No, thank you, not interested. Maybe something else down the road, but I do have some acquaintances in Pennsylvania who own a couple of laundromats. They say it is really good business." I was being completely sincere, although the thought of running a laundromat didn't appeal to me at all.

"It is!" Don brightened at the acknowledgment. "I'm tellin' you, we make at least four times what we report! There's no way of tracking it, so the bottom line is what we say it is." Smiling broadly, he reached for the pen I held out.

"As long as what you are telling me is truthful, I mean the parts I wrote out in the proposal and the forms I filled in." He nodded agreeably. "Are you happy with the proposal? Do you have any questions or comments before you sign it?"

"Everything looks good. You do real nice work, doesn't she, Carolyn? Carolyn didn't get to read the whole thing, but. . . "

"Yes. Don't forget to mention about the marketing thing," Carolyn interrupted.

"Oh yeah! I was talking to Tom earlier, and he said he's asked you to do a write up for the website, something about the history of the business, to drum up sales and give people the background, you know. So, you might wanna interview me for that, since I started it. I had contracts with the Air Force and everything. If you wanted an Air Force blanket, I was the one with the contract for the actual emblem—no one else." As he finished scrawling, I took the papers and handed them to Carolyn. Glasses perched half way down her nose, she peered at them only long enough to find where to sign.

"Well, if Tom lets me know what he wants as far as marketing, I will get back to you and we can set up a time, okay?"

"Okay. That'll be fine, except we're headed up to Akwesasne tomorrow."

"Again? Weren't you just there recently?" I was curious.

"Yeah, well, we are good friends with one of the tribal leaders, a chief. We like to go spend some time up there," Don replied smugly.

"Is there anything much to do up there besides gamble? I'm not a gambler, so I have never given much thought to going up there."

"No, the casino is the big draw, but they have other things, good food and drinks . . . it's quiet. We mostly enjoy the casino and spend some time with our friend."

"It's nice to get away from Keeseville," Carolyn added, handing me the papers and my pen.

Having submitted the financing package to The Development Corporation and a couple of banks, I turned my attention to what else I might do to drum up business and settle the mortgage issue once and for all. I had faxed in the statement Bob provided, along with a copy of our divorce order which stated that I was to pay the mortgage and had up to two years to refinance. I also resubmitted the payment that had been returned to me, this time, by cashier's check, including a late fee, along with the next month's payment. Bob never returned the debit card though, so about once a week I emailed him and asked for it.

Before the divorce, I had begun a theatre group using the facilities of the local Nazarene church we attended. Strangely, despite our extensive theatre background together, Bob was so separated—although he was still living in our home at the time—and so into his addictive behaviors that he wanted no part in it. It was during this time that I met a troubled young woman by the name of Sara. Her twin sister had been a part of a couple of productions and asked me if I would allow Sara to help me out; since she was very introverted and troubled, she thought it might help her. I agreed and Sara came to the next audition. I was not prepared for her to be drunk on arrival, but we tried to include her, in between her multiple smoke breaks.

Sara was not your typical-looking twenty-year old. She had a spiky, green mohawk, too many piercings to count, and several tattoos. I soon came to learn that she had just come out of Saint Joe's Rehab in Saranac Lake for drug and alcohol addiction, but they did nothing about her severe anorexia, or some of her other issues. Obviously, the drinking was still going on, and her family was beside themselves not knowing what else to do for her. She got involved a little in the next show and thrilled to be named "stage manager". She rose to the occasion and was a huge help. It seemed that having a job, a purpose, spurred her onto better things and drinking was less of an issue. She looked forward to rehearsals, in between she would often come to my home and work on sets in the workshop, or shop for props with me and the kids. But when that show ended, it was only a couple of weeks before she was back into a severe depression.

It was just after dinner one night when the phone rang. The familiar voice of Shelia, Sara's mom, was on the other end.

"Hey! How are you?" I asked, happy to hear from a new friend.

"Well, not good," she replied somberly. "I have a huge thing to ask of you . . . and, I hope you know, as a mother, I—" Her voice cracked with emotion. I sensed her pain keenly.

"Is everything okay, Sheila?"

"I think it will be eventually, but . . ." As her voice trailed off, I wondered what could be going on. I only knew Sheila to be a strong and courageous woman. "We're at the hospital. Sara tried to kill herself."

"Oh no!" My heart sank; tears welled up in my eyes.

"She's okay, it's actually been a couple of days now and they're going to release her, but . . ." She fumbled for the words, sighing heavily. "She won't come home with us, and she can't be released to live alone again."

"Oh, I'm so sorry. How can I help?" I wondered aloud.

"Well, she is adamantly refusing to come home, and when we explained to her that she cannot go back to her apartment she said 'Call Karen Marie, she'll take me in. She loves me.'"

"Oh—" The weight of her words hung thickly in the air.

"I know I am asking a lot, but as a mother, you must know the humility and desperation I feel at this moment. You don't have to agree, but you've made such a difference with your acceptance of Sara—she really believes you would take her in . . . so I had to at least call." Sheila wept openly now. I thought about my own children and what kind of influence I would be subjecting them to at their young ages. I also thought about the gravity of Sara's request.

"Sheila, can I set some ground rules? I mean, my children are so young and impressionable, and I want to help, but—"

"Of course! Ground rules would be very good for Sara, and she loves your children, so she would adhere to them; she gets it."

"Please tell her that I will call you back in a little while, okay? I need to discuss this with the kids and Bob." Even though Bob was not really participating in our family life, he was still in the house at the time.

We had a family pow-wow, and I asked Bob if he would mind. I explained to the kids that I was asking for their input because Sara was a needy person right then; they were happy to open our home to her as well. Bob's only statement was, "This is what you do; you help people. If you set some ground rules, and it doesn't work out, she can go home to her parents, right?"

"If she will." I called Sheila back and within a couple hours, they brought Sara over. I asked Sara to agree to some simple rules. "One, when it's mealtime, you must participate and eat with the family. That means you must eat, and not purge or skip. Second, no smoking in the house. Third, no drugs or alcohol. Be mindful that my children are watching you, they look up to you, so you must set a good example."

"Of course," she replied thoughtfully. "I love you and your kids. I don't want to do anything to hurt them in any way. I just need a supportive environment to move on . . . thank you!"

Sara's arms were bandaged up and down, from the hands and wrists. She was on thirteen different meds to keep track of, and thinner than I had ever seen her. She enjoyed our hugs and got settled in for the night.

The first few meal times were extremely challenging for her, but she kept her promise and sat through the entire meal, forcing herself to eat. She joined in mealtime conversation and helped with dishes. The first few times I changed her bandages, I waited until after Katlyn and Jonathan were in bed. Those were times of deep conversation about life, the past, and what was underlying her depression. She smoked less and less, and though she was afraid of the horses at first, eventually got involved in our daily horse chores, even grooming them. It took much longer for her to be interested in riding one of them, though. By the time we were ready to begin the next production, Sara was a little more outspoken and willing to take on a small role as well as being stage manager. Her transformation in just a few months was truly impressive. When show time came, the whole community was talking about it.

Because of this and my consulting expertise, I considered being a franchisee of a counseling agency focused on helping people overcome past trauma and abuse and developing new life skills. Since I didn't personally have all the credentials needed, I would have to work with a local psychologist or pastor accredited in counseling. Nana and Papa were very encouraging in this direction. Pastor Dave was also open to the idea after seeing Sara's transformation and hearing about the experiences of others in the theatre company. (Furthermore, he had eventually come to see that he should never have told Bob of my whereabouts once I confronted him with the truth and sought safety for a few days. To his credit, he apologized.) I was approved by the agency; all that was needed was for the church board to approve the use of their facility and provide the franchise fee. By this time, Bob was long gone and Sara was still living with the kids and me. When it finally came to a vote before the church board, I was one vote shy of approval. The reason some of them voted against it? I was told by the pastor and a deacon, "It would be helping a woman to be established and successful without a man and we can't have that."

Immediately, the kids and I started attending a different church up in Plattsburgh. I no longer ran the theatre group, which dissolved into nothing.

FIVE

Look! Don't be deceived by appearances—men and things are not what they seem. All who are not on the rock are in the sea!
WILLIAM BOOTH

KATLYN AND JONATHAN SEEMED to be doing very well adjusting to life without their dad. He hadn't seen them since that sleepover and having Sara around was a lot of fun for them. Nana and Papa came over frequently to spend a day, or even overnight. Papa spent lots of time teaching Jonathan how to golf. Nana enjoyed spending time with Katlyn and me in the garden or even walking the horses. We always ended the day with a meal together, making plans for next time. Sara also doted on the kids, enjoyed rough-housing, playing soccer, or helping us with gardening. She was doing very well, too. One night she asked if we could have a bon fire, which we did occasionally, roasting marshmallows, singing songs, just enjoying the beauty of nature around us. This night, however, she had an ulterior motive.

"I want you kids to help me do something," Sara announced with a smile.

"What is it?" Jon queried, his adorable little face looking up to her as if in one big curiosity question mark.

"You'll see," she told him, as we lugged some cardboard and fallen pine boughs to the site. Once the fire was roaring and we had sung a song or two, she pulled her cigarettes out of her army jacket. "C'mon guys, help me burn these. I'm done with smoking as of today!" Handing them a couple of cigarettes each, they threw them in the fire one at a time. "This is very unhealthy for my body," Sara continued. "It's not good for you, either. You promise you'll never smoke and that is my motivation to never pick up a cigarette again."

"I won't," Katlyn chimed in.

"I won't either," Jon told her. "I think they make people stink." Then realizing he may have offended, "Uh, sorry, Sara."

"You're right, little buddy," she laughed, tousling his hair. "I am done with stinking living!"

It seemed she was. In the past few months, she had been not only eating three meals a day, but also a healthy snack in between at times. After the kids were asleep in bed most nights, she and I would sit in the living room and talk.

"Sara," I called as I came down the hall and into the living room one evening. "Would it upset you if I had a glass of wine? Is it too much for you?"

"No," she said sincerely. "I noticed the last time Nana and Papa were here you each had a glass of wine with dinner . . . it seemed so strange to me to see people stop after one or two glasses. I have never seen people drink in such moderation—without getting drunk."

"Okay, thanks," I replied, going to the kitchen to pour a glass of Cabernet Sauvignon. I had not had a glass except for that dinner she referenced in the first six or so months she was with us, for fear of it being more than she could bear. Nestled in my favorite chair, slowly enjoying each sip, we began to talk about what makes people run into addiction.

"I am not really sure what it was for me," she confided, slinging her feet up on the end of the couch and pulling an afghan around her shoulders. "I feel stronger now, like I have some perspective, but still don't understand why some people can enjoy a glass of wine and that's it, but others can't stop until they're wasted. What do you think?"

"I wish I knew. I sometimes wonder about it from Bob's perspective. I mean, how can some people be exposed to porn and think 'I'm not going there,' and others, like him, just go deeper and deeper, until it swallows them up in a fantasy life, so they can't even cope with the real world anymore." I stretched my legs out on the ottoman in front of me.

"I still can't believe he would leave his family behind for a fantasy sex-life, and then lie about it to everyone. That must really hurt you." Sara's eyes softened. In recent months she had begun getting her empathy back, another sign of emotional health.

"I can't believe it either sometimes," I acknowledged. "But it is what happened. There's more going on than meets the eye. He just isn't the person I thought I married. I have finally accepted that I was deceived from day one. I just feel badly that it took so long for me to realize, especially that the kids have suffered as a result."

"Do you think you'll ever get married again? What about that hunk in the Plattsburgh church who's been calling you lately?" She grinned deviously.

"Brian? I have to admit, he's a beautiful man," I was a little embarrassed at my own reaction. "But I am in no hurry to get into a relationship again. I remember what it's like to be attracted to someone when he's around but . . ." I sighed, "looks and a suave disposition aren't enough to make me jump. I have not been as content and happy as I am now in a long, long time. I am enjoying life and focusing on my children."

"But he has called you quite a bit lately," she prodded with a giggle.

"Yes, and I have not committed to even a date at this point," I reminded her. "It's too soon, and he is very forward, which kind of turns me off since that's how Bob was! "

"But would you, I mean, eventually . . . would you date again?"

"It would depend on the man and on whether it would bother my kids. I am not in a hurry. But how about you? You're a beautiful young woman."

"Ahhh! Yeah. I am curious about someone, but need to stay focused on making progress," she replied smartly. "And, I have been having some, I think they're called flashbacks . . . have you ever had a flashback?" Her tone shifted somberly, she leaned forward as she asked.

"Yes, I have." I thought about the severity, the debilitating way they had snuck up on me in the past and how important it was for me to get closure. "Do you have any idea what they stem from?"

"I wish I did." Her voice was earnest, with an urgent quality to it. Her face strained as if searching the vast, secret places in her own brain. "It's making me kind of crazy. I remember before I started drinking and using drugs; I had flashbacks then, but only fragments. Bits and pieces of a scene of—" Her voice lagged as she searched for the right description. "Some sort of violence; I was very young."

"Have you ever asked your parents about it?" I had only known Sara's parents for a few years but recalled that Sheila told me they had a rocky past when her husband was in the Navy, many years previous.

"Yeah. They don't talk about it, except to say they were different people when I was young," she replied wistfully.

"Have you ever prayed about it? I mean, asked God to make it clear to you?" I recalled my own experience, with no one to turn to.

"I have, actually," she said, surprised that I asked.

"And?"

"And, I get nothing. It's like, I feel like God wants to help me, deep down, like He wants to help me see it, so I can let go of it, but—" She halted, closing her eyes a minute, and placing her hands on her heart. "Something's blocking it, in here. Maybe I'm afraid. Or, maybe I just don't know how to hear in my heart."

"Well, how about asking again?" I queried, feeling a sense of warmth in my chest; a knowing that timing is important. "Maybe you weren't ready to deal with it before."

"How about this," Sara said as she sat back against the couch. "How 'bout you ask God to show you, then tell me if He shows you something? Maybe, you can hear more clearly than I can." We agreed to pray together for a few minutes. We sat in silence except for each of us taking turns at first asking for God's direction for Sara and for her understanding so that she could release whatever past trauma was holding her back. After a few minutes, a scene unfolded in my mind's eye and the impression of words written over the scene read: *She feels responsible, but it was never her fault. She was just a small child. She was never to blame. She is free.*

When I described the scene to Sara, she slid to her knees onto the floor, crying. "I remember! I remember!" she wept.

"You are not responsible," I told her firmly, making my way to her and wrapping my arm around her shoulder. "It was never your fault. You were just a small child. You were never to blame. You are free." She turned and hugged me tightly.

"Say it again," she whispered, her face wet next to my ear.

"You are not responsible. You were just a small child—never to blame. You are free. You are loved. It's time to let it go, Sara. Let it go, sweetie."

"Yes," she said aloud. "I'm letting it go." After a few minutes, she pulled away and wiped her eyes and cheeks. "I let it go. Thank you for your help."

Within months, Sara had a consistent part-time job again and was dating the guy she had been curious about. Her hair had grown out and she decided she liked her natural color and waves. What's more, she was down from thirteen meds to just one by the end of the first year she lived with us, and instead of counselling appointments several times a week, she went once. She was part of our family. We were so proud of her, as was her own family, whom we came to love and appreciate.

During that year, Don Lorry approached me about his building on Front Street, the historic one that had been all but condemned by fire, in which they still ran their little laundromat out of one section at the street level. The financing proposal I had put together for him and Tom had been approved by The Development Corporation and one bank, but the required disclosures and collateral left Don feeling uneasy. He refused the terms, with no further explanation. I had no idea what they decided beyond that, since my job was done, obviously done well. Tom expressed frustration at his "old man" but did not let on about what they intended to do beyond that. I finished the marketing work he had requested and had begun working on a long-term leadership and communication development contract I had negotiated with a regional, multimillion dollar restaurant and hotel corporation.

"I was talking with Tom the other day about what to do with this building," Don relayed over the phone. "He told me that you have expressed an interest in setting up a bed and breakfast at some point."

"Well, I have always thought about it," I answered candidly, "but I am not so sure this is the time. My kids are young, and, what I told Tom is I can envision some real change for Front Street, if only we could revitalize and dress it up a bit."

"You've done real well for us," Don said patronizingly. "I bet you would do real well for the village. Why don't you come down and take a tour of the building? There's that revolving loan fund you could apply to—to fix it up and start your B&B."

"That's a lot of work, and risk—and my kids are so young. I am not sure I have that kind of time." I was curious about the building and felt badly about the eyesore it was in the center of the village but would not kid myself about the work involved. "Besides, I don't have money to invest right now."

"That's the beauty of the fund," he prodded. "If you're low income, or a woman, or tying to promote economic development, then you get a low three percent interest rate, and sweat equity counts for your contribution. It's a HUD thing. HUD programs work, I had those apartments up there, on the second floor, five of 'em. I got paid whether the people were deadbeats or not."

I remembered our condo outside of Philly, and how the neighborhood went downhill once investors came in and bought up properties in bundles during the recession, turning them into Section 8 or "HUD homes". I got off the phone that day having said "thanks, but no thanks." Three days later, I got a call from the mayor, Ed Bezio.

"I am wondering if I can interest you in a business proposition," he stated abruptly. "I want to see something done with that burned-out building on Front Street. Don Lorry, and a few others from Friends of the North Country think you're just the person to handle it. Have you ever heard about the Village Revolving Loan Fund?"

SIX

A blast from the past isn't always worth the effort.

I MET MAYOR BEZIO and Don at the building, 1709 Front Street, on a balmy June day. The entrance was boarded up, except for the little side storefront area, 1707, where Don and Carolyn continued to run their laundromat. After being formally introduced to Mayor Bezio, and discussing the fund for a while, he assured me that he would recommend approval of my application if I was indeed interested, then left, leaving Don to show me around.

"So, pretty much nothing has been done in here since the fire?" I asked, peering through sheet plastic which had been draped over a gaping hole in the brick between the small and large storefronts.

"Nothing. I guess you heard that two people died in the fire," Don stared solemnly. "We couldn't bring ourselves to do much and, I had heart surgery. . . . We're just tired, Karen Marie," he sat down wearily and looked at the mess around him. "We've had our time. It's someone else's turn."

"I hadn't heard. That's so sad." I sat down across from him for a few minutes, listening to his tale of woe, watching Carolyn intermittently as she nodded along, clucking her disgust in sighs and groans here and there. Eventually, he got up and found a cordless drill behind the front desk. Motioning me to follow him, we went outside again and around to the boarded-up entrance, where he proceeded to remove the screws from the plywood so we could enter.

The main floor was filled with furnishings I had seen before the fire in the Lorrys' self-titled "Gift Emporium." I had been in the store looking for a birthday gift for one of Katlyn's friends, but was disappointed in the cheap goods, mostly marked up tchotchkes, poorly-made, imported from China. There were also remnants of wood, and some appliances that were out of place. It was quite large, and very dark since almost all the windows were covered or boarded up. I noted that there were no stairs from that level to the second floor, but there was a set of rickety old stairs going down to the basement in the back, as well as a wider set in the front.

The building was built in 1840, with massive stones as a foundation, at least three feet thick, and large, flat rocks set into the basement floor. The property backed up to the AuSable River, which could be accessed by the original door, complete with iron bars and hasps to lock it. There were little alcoves at the end of long passageways in the front, which appeared to be under the Front Street sidewalk, beyond the stone of the basement, framed and fitted with bricks apparently locally made, back in the day. Black, cast iron pipes ran the length and width. There were more cheap goods in boxes there, as well as stacks of clothing, fabric rolls, and old carpeting. Spider webs hung everywhere, and there was no shortage of dust or mildew.

Finally, we went back outside, making our way to the boarded-up entrance to the second story. A massive set of stairs was framed by chipping plaster, and splintering old wainscoting, that had obviously been painted dozens of times, in varying hideous colors. Atop the flight, I noted a playpen frame next to a pile of ash as tall as me.

"Playpen?" I whispered, as tears rolled down my cheeks uncontrollably.

"Yes," Don soberly acknowledged. "What's left of it."

"Did the baby—"

"No. He didn't make it." Don motioned me beyond as I wiped my eyes repeatedly.

There were tarps hanging in some areas to keep water out, as well as sheets of plywood. I walked through piles of debris and ash, noting how high the ceilings were, wondering about the massive bundles of cords and wires stretching from the worst area, back through a cast iron door frame and under suspended ceiling tiles in the next section. There had been five apartments, some larger than others, all with very outdated appliances and countertops. In some places the plaster covering the old brick had been scorched or burned off. Other places had horsehair plaster and lathe badly burned. Since there were so many layers of flooring over the past century and a half, much of the old plank flooring with original square nails was exposed again, so that I could see the potential of restoring it. Don told me of the old nail factory above the bridge, and brick factory that used to be in the mill along the other side of the river. They were part of the Industrial Revolution, some of the village's first successful businesses.

"It needs a roof before winter," Don gazed up the sixteen feet or so to where bricks had even been removed from the cornices, leaving gaps between the tarps and plywood atop, and the walls below. "If you're interested, we'll get a roof on right away, you can put together a proposal for the funding. If I were you, I'd get HUD apartments in here—worked well for me."

"If I were to do this, I would utilize the space as a bed-and-breakfast inn, with maybe one full apartment," I noted soberly. "The one that's already a studio—in the far corner. But that's a huge 'if'."

"Well, give it some thought. I mean, you could buy the laundromat, too and have all that camp business as well as a bed and breakfast. All those lake front camps fill up for the summer, an' they're not allowed to have washer run off—that's a lot of business; to say nothing of the kids' camps we contract with. Did I ever tell you about the time Carolyn and I stayed in a B&B in Vermont?"

"Not that I recall," I was overtaken with sadness at the loss of life. "Can we head out?"

"Sure," he said as he shoved the cast iron door open again and motioned me to go through. "We stayed in an old converted carriage barn, the owners didn't even stay. We were the only guests for the entire night—had the place to ourselves."

"Well, my children are young and active. I only live a mile and a half away. I would do exactly the same thing . . .*if*."

"I think that's nice, really. I mean, guests have privacy and the host is close by if needed. We enjoyed it." Don reached the bottom of the stairs and turned to board up the entrance again.

"Thanks for the tour," I told him. "I better get going."

"Wait! Do you think you're interested?" urgency apparent in his voice.

"I'm interested but would have to do a lot of research and be ready to work hard. This is a big undertaking. On top of that, I would have to be guaranteed the work would be done in time for the next tourist season, or it's too big a risk." I had grave concern.

"Well, give it some thought," he said somberly. "Carolyn and I can recommend good carpenters and we're willing to finance your purchase of the building itself. You can get the financing to do the work, get your business up and running, and pay us off down the road. We're gonna put a roof on right away, so that's one less thing," he stroked his goatee and tilted his head to the left, making eye contact. "Don't forget the laundromat is a cash cow, we could negotiate that into the deal, too."

"I'm not interested in biting off more than I can chew. I will give this some thought, but don't hold your breath. It's a lot of work," I said earnestly. To me, it was a pipe dream.

Still, for some reason when Nana called me later, I couldn't help but run the idea by her.

"It's just such a big undertaking, but then, it could be a great opportunity, too," I said, desperately wanting her advice. "Then I think about that horrible 'C' I got in interior design, and . . ."

"I told you then you were ahead of your time, babes," she earnestly encouraged. "That professor should have long been retired. You've got a knack. You've always wanted to run a bed and breakfast."

"Maybe, but it is a big undertaking," I sighed.

"Give it some thought," she offered. "Better yet, talk to God about it. I'll pray on it, too. It would be good for you to have a business of your own; you'd be flexible with the kids that way."

"I know, that's what appeals to me," I agreed. "It's just—I wish you could see how much work would be involved. I need to be sober about it . . . and there's no guarantee I would get the financing."

"Pray about it, babes," she said confidently. "I have a feeling if God's in it, things will fall into place."

I did pray about it. I wondered about it a lot. Then, I let it leave my mind within a few days in the busyness of life.

Along about September, I received another call from Don, as well as an application in the mail from the new director of Friends. In her cover letter, she introduced herself and explained that in her recent meeting with Mayor Bezio he had suggested I was interested in applying to the fund, as well as noting my prior status on the Board of Directors. She invited me to meet with her and at least discuss the possibilities. Having done that, when Bob called in early October, I mentioned it.

"I haven't heard from you in a long time. Is everything okay?" I sincerely wanted to know.

"Yeah, things are okay, it's just . . ." his voice trailed off in that familiar, things-are-not-really-okay-way I had come to know well in twenty years. "Well, I need to talk with you. Even after the divorce and all, you're still the best friend I have."

"What about all your new friends?" I was mindful we had an approaching anniversary of sorts, in a few days. He was probably just feeling blue and nostalgic.

"They're not the type—I mean, they just don't know me well and you do. Plus, you have always given me good encouragement, you get me." He whined into the phone.

I couldn't help but feel compassion for him. He had chosen his way and I was glad to be relieved of a one-sided, fraud of a marriage, but I still cared about him as a person. "Sorry, Bob. It's tough, isn't it?" He rambled on about his job and situations with new roommates, his family, and eventually got around to asking about the kids.

"Yeah . . . so, how are the kids? What's' new with you?" He seemed sincere.

We chatted a little about Jonathan's soccer and Katlyn's developing friendships then I told him about seeing the Lorrys' building on Front Street.

"The last time I was down that way, it was still boarded up," he exclaimed with surprise.

"It still is," I told him. "I think it's a lot of work, but I might be willing to consider it since I lost so many consulting contracts due to 9/11. I would be happy to have more work nearer to home, where the kids are close by; they can even get off the school bus there if need be."

"It's your lifelong dream to run a B&B . . . maybe you should try," he replied, much to my shock.

"Really? I mean, I don't have the funds for an architect—just to draw up my plans to apply for the funding! How could I do that?"

"I can do it for you," he offered, again to my growing disbelief. "It's the least I can do."

"What? Are you serious? You would do that for me?" I was genuinely overcome.

"Sure," he said without hesitation. "Why don't you set up a time to take me through the place and tell me what you would do. I'll put it all down in plan format for you."

The fact that Bob even sounded willing to do something like that for me was amazing, so I decided to take him up on it before he changed his mind. As if the universe was aligning, Don called me the next day to ask if

I had thought anymore about the building. Thus, having arranged things with Don, I met Bob at the building a few days later. We spent the better part of an hour going from room to room, up and down. I relayed my desire to have five suites plus an apartment on the upper floor, along with a parlor, two dining areas, and a large kitchen. In addition, I wanted each room to have its own en suite bath. Downstairs, I insisted I had no desire to buy the laundromat, but was not opposed to the Lorrys, or some other person, running it on site. On the larger portion at street level, I desired an office, sitting area with gas fireplace, and antique and gift shop. The two floors comprised over six thousand square feet, excluding the laundromat and basement, which I envisioned as an art studio and workshop in the future.

When Don returned to lock up, we were on the main floor taking note of a large, old, cast iron safe on rollers.

"Hey Don, what's the deal with this modern metal plate on the side of this antique safe?" I asked.

"Funny story," he grinned. "When we first bought this place, it was in a dark corner of the basement. I was sure it must have old money, or valuables in it. No one could pick the lock, and so we decided to blast the damn thing open, but first," he raised his eyebrows and stuck his finger in the air, "we had to get it up the damn stairs!" He let out a belly laugh before continuing. "It took six of us grown men and a lot of leverage, but we eventually got that sucker up the steps, blasted it open, and guess what was inside?"

"I don't know, what?" I curiously leaned over to see it more closely.

"Not a damn thing!" He shook his head in disgust. Bob laughed heartily. "I hope you appreciate it. If you buy the building, it stays with it. We're not moving it again!"

SEVEN

When everything around you is a question mark in time, remember that life is fleeting, and love is its most solid foundation.

IT HAPPENED AGAIN. IN early January 2003. Bob withdrew another $600 from my checking account. It had been so long, I had forgotten he still had a debit card. I feared that my mortgage check would bounce again. In the previous ten months, I had resubmitted that one cashier's check multiple times from the same type of episode in December 2001. Although I was sending regular payments by check each month, for some reason, the cashier's check being only in my name—although it had the mortgage account number on it—was not acceptable to ABN AMRO's reps. Given my expertise as a paralegal, I was sure if I could just talk to a live person who had a grasp of the English language and the situation, the whole mess would be straightened out in a heartbeat. I finally got a hold of a woman by the name of Vicki Lester, an officer of ABN. She claimed to understand but wouldn't budge on the accrued fees and interest. Nevertheless, now that Bob had pulled this stunt a second time, I needed to get more money in my account in a hurry, or it would happen again, compounding the issue.

In addition, Bob wasn't paying alimony or support on time. I initially agreed not to have his wages garnished if he would pay in a timely manner, but as he sunk further and further into his fantasy world, the cost of his props and tranny junkets sky-rocketed. His priorities were all that mattered. I tried to reach him unsuccessfully by telephone, so I wrote an email to him on the eighth of January. I demanded the card back, as well as the cash, then contacted my bank a second time about blocking the card. By this time, I found someone sympathetic to my plight and the card was terminated.

"Hello?" Bob sounded weary.

"Bob! Where have you been? Why haven't you returned my calls or email? I need you to pay me back right away!" I was so frustrated. It had been several days since I sent the email and left repeated voice messages.

"I was in Las Vegas," he said. "I guess I just didn't check until I got home around midnight . . ."

"You're behind on alimony and child support, you stole $600 from my account, yet you can afford to go to Las Vegas?" Incredulous, I paced the floor, trying not to raise my voice too loudly.

"I'll pay you back. It was sort of an emergency," he whined. "Jeez, can't you think of anyone but yourself?"

"No emergency constitutes theft! You could have called. As it is, if I don't get that money back by today you will be responsible for bouncing another mortgage payment," I fumed. "I already sent it out, on time!"

"I can't give it to you til Friday." I heard him fumble with the phone, then say something quietly to someone at the other end. "Or maybe Thursday, at the earliest."

"That is not acceptable, Bob. I am calling my lawyer and having your wages garnished. Furthermore, I will call the police about you stealing money out of my account—"

"Okay, wait, wait—" Again he spoke in hushed urgency to someone else.

"Who are you talking to?" I demanded.

"Kris," he stated. "I'm asking to borrow the money."

"Kris? You mean Kristy?" I wondered.

"No! This is, I mean, my roommate, Cranberry Kris she likes to be called." He fumbled the phone again, "Just a minute."

Cranberry Kris? It sounded like the name of a porn actress to me.

"Okay," he got back on the phone. "I'll bring you the money tomorrow, just don't garnish my wages or call the police."

"I am not making any promises," I told him. "Call before you come down so I am sure to be here."

But it was too late. The mortgage payment bounced, exacerbating my issues with ABN ABMRO. I sent in a cashier's check directly to Vicki Lester, by certified mail, along with a copy of the former paperwork I had sent in numerous times, and a copy of the email to Bob about him stealing money out of my account. I couldn't afford to pay my lawyer another retainer, so I contacted Child and Family Services and was told

I could be represented by one of their staff attorneys at a marginal rate, based upon my ability to pay. I asked them to send me an application, so I could move forward with garnishing Bob's wages and collecting back alimony and support.

By this time, I had been in negotiations with the Lorrys to buy the building on Front Street and had submitted a business proposal and financing application to Friends of the North Country. They were happy to work with me, since I had spent time working with them in the past, and they believed I had a grasp of what it would take to bring some revitalization to the Village of Keeseville and surrounds. During our negotiations the mayor and the village board of trustees were involved. I contacted numerous contractors to obtain bids. I still wasn't sure I would be able to go forward with the project, but if the price was right and the timing was right, I was happy to do so. The supervisor of the Town of Chesterfield sat down with me as well, since that section of Keeseville was in the town, as Don had described when I first met him. Gerry, the town supervisor, was also my neighbor and was happy to support my undertaking.

"Just watch your back," he told me as I sat in his office one day. "I don't trust Don Lorry to look at him. If you have any doubts, feel free to ask me, I can check into things for you." I noted his candor as he sat back in his chair, folding his hands over his plump mid-section. His black hair slicked back neatly, contrasting his crisp white dress shirt.

"Should I pursue this, Gerry? I mean, if he's that bad?" I wondered aloud. "I know he's rather eccentric . . ."

"Eccentric, like hell!" He laughed heartily, then leaned forward, hands still clasped, pushing them across the desk toward me and meeting my gaze. "He's an old, washed up wannabe. But my point is, he's a liar, so get everything in writing. And no matter what he says about the laundromat, don't buy it."

"He has continually asked me to buy the laundromat, but I am not interested," I replied thoughtfully. "I'm not interested in the least, but I have no objection to them leasing the space from me and continuing to run it."

"You'd be better off the farther away they are, but get a lease, and you're doing well. It will go right to your own mortgage payment," he winked and smiled at me. "They leave for Florida part of the year and the employee runs it anyway. I think your proposal is thorough and one of the best I've seen. I took the liberty of writing you a letter of recommendation. You should go see Stephen, over at Architectural Heritage, he'd be happy to support your plans, too. I don't want you dependent on that bastard, Bob anymore."

"Thanks Gerry," I was touched by his concern. "I appreciate that. Stephen is a friend, I've already spoken with him."

"I remember that night a few years back, when Bob offered to take all those blocks off my hands . . . we loaded them up and took them around to your place. The bastard yelled at you like you were his slave. I lost all respect for him, then what he did since. . . . No. I've got no respect for him. I wish you all the best." He stood to give me a hug, arms outstretched.

"Thanks, Gerry. I really appreciate it," I said earnestly, appreciating the hug. "I'll keep you posted."

"Please do and call me anytime. I can go to board meetings, or whatever, show my support."

In the weeks that followed, I was approved by the Village Board after glowing recommendations from the Friends, Gerry, and Adirondack Architectural Heritage, among others. The only caveat was that they would not allow Don and Carolyn to hold the mortgage on the building and that the Lorrys must provide a warranty on the roof. My plan had included a demographic study, current Adirondack and related tourism trends, sweat equity proposal, and signed agreement between the Lorrys and myself along with bids and proposals from subcontractors for plumbing, electrical, and carpentry. Having already confided in one of my colleagues at the Friends, Brigette, about the lack of trust in Don's reputation, she was ready when the trustees convened.

"We would submit that your concerns about the Lorrys can be easily addressed if the Village is willing to finance the whole package through the Revolving Loan Fund," she stated succinctly. "There are enough funds available, and so long as the Lorrys sign a lease to rent from Karen Marie, provide the roof warranty, and sell for no more than the current appraised value, we would support that heartily."

After significant discussion, the Board issued its conditional approval unanimously, with notably one abstention, Mayor Bezio. While that confused me, Brigette assured me that he was just ornery and unpredictable, then asked me to order an appraisal. Given the backwards people I had met since I moved there in 1999, I had to agree. We scheduled another meeting to tie up loose ends.

When the appraisal came in, it was $2,000 less than Don and Carolyn had asked for, and previously agreed to. Don, true to his reputation, began asking me to pay it to him privately, or take it off their rent. I would not. Negotiating a lease with him became an even bigger task. I asked for $800 per month, which was even below the going rate, but given the condition of the property, I felt was fair. I also asked for heat and air conditioning, as well as electric to be metered separately and paid on top of rent. At first Don seemed to agree it was fair, but wanted the rate tied to the consumer price index and a term of five years. He claimed that he would prepay if I gave him a lower rent, giving me an infusion of cash to start business with. Then he asked me if I was willing to take a reduced rent in exchange for them doing the repairs and improvements in the adjoining laundromat space at 1707 Front. I agreed to consider it if I could review plans, talk to contractors, etc.

"I think it's all going to come together, Babes," Nana told me one afternoon as we had tea. "When are they saying the closing will happen?"

"By the end of February," I replied with a nervous sigh. "I told them I will not go through with it if it's any later. I need to be open by mid-May to make ends meet the first year, based on my projections. As it is, it's a pretty aggressive work schedule."

"That's smart. I'm proud of you," she winked at me, patting my hand softly. "You have to know what your boundaries are, or you can get sucked in."

"Yes, I've learned that the hard way. Still learning, actually but getting there." I wondered about whether the deal would really go through. How is it possible I could be so close to putting my lifelong dream into action? "I have talked to several out of work carpenters, they're all happy to have work in the winter time, except one has backed off. I'm not sure why."

"Is that the one that's your friend's husband?" Nana sipped her ginger-peach tea and sat back with eyebrows raised.

"No. It's a well-known restoration carpenter, Rene Guyette. He apparently can't stand Don Lorry, and even though Don will not be involved, he muttered something about it not being a good situation. I haven't been able to reach him since. Anyway, there are a few others who are available, and my friend's husband, Jeff, is very skilled; he was just laid off. He restored their house and built a beautiful addition."

"I think I've been there—we went to pick Jonathan up there, one afternoon, on the lake, right?"

"Yes, he did a great job," I replied.

"He did," she said. "Nice family, too."

"Yes. And, I have the plumbing and heating contractor with a not too exceed estimate, and electricians' estimates, so the rest is bargain hunting. I am trying to do this at or under budget." I finished my tea and got up for another cup. "More?" I asked, holding out my hand for her mug.

"You know, the Canadian dollar is down right now; you should do a lot of shopping up in Montreal," she said, handing me her mug for a second cup. "I think we save about forty percent, when you figure it out, plus get your taxes back at the border."

"I've been looking into it." I sat down again, wrapping my hands around my mug for warmth. "There are so many more choices up there, too. But my main thrust at first is buying supplies at the best price possible and cleaning it out. The Lorrys are supposed to remove all their belongings right away, and they have put a roof on. I'm sure it won't seem as daunting once they get all their junk out of there."

"Did you decide on a lease?" she asked soberly, then leaned over to breathe in the aroma and steam of her tea.

"Not quite, but I did meet with the contractors who are going to do the improvements on their rental portion. So, we should settle on a rent soon. I had a lease drafted and they don't like it—said they'd pay to have their lawyer draw one up if I agreed. I'm waiting to see it."

"Get everything in writing, honey. I know you're smart that way, but just be sure." Jonathan and Katlyn emerged from their game-playing with Papa just then. "Here they come!" Nana said in her high-pitched, loving tone. "Come here and get your hugs and kisses!"

They giggled as she smothered them each, hugging and kissing her right back. With all that had gone wrong the previous years, if nothing else, I was thrilled to have a sane family life, and eternally grateful to be near Nana and Papa again.

EIGHT

We can manage to protect ourselves legally, but we cannot account for the illegal motives of others.

FEBRUARY 27TH, 2003, THE day of the closing, was bitterly cold. In the couple of months since the whole deal had been sorted out, Don and Carolyn had left for Florida for the winter, leaving their lawyer, Evan Tracy, with power of attorney to finish up the loose ends and closing. Just a few weeks previous, my dearest friends, Linda and Sonny and Marie and Tim, had come up with all their kids for our annual President's Day weekend snow-fest. We typically had a bon fire going for the kids, hot cocoa and tea ever at the ready. The kids would sled all day long, even us big kids. But this year, I also asked them to go through the building with me and give me some feedback. They were very encouraging; Tim and Sonny even listened in on a planning meeting I had with subcontractors and had some good advice for me. They were all very supportive even before they arrived, as we had been in constant contact anyway, however, having fresh eyes on the situation, they caught my vision and really boosted my confidence.

Don and Carolyn gave me permission to start the process of clearing out items and getting a dumpster in place prior to closing, so that I could be sure to meet my time frame. There were many out of work that winter, thus finding labor was not difficult. Jonathan and Katlyn even got involved in helping to get junk into the dumpster, although I had to repeatedly get on the Lorrys to have their junk removed, or just get it out of our way. Mayor Bezio had become rather hostile, which all attributed to a falling out he had with Don and the fact that he was an old-school chauvinist at heart. It was decided that Deputy Mayor Robarge would attend the closing with me, and an Oversight Committee/Liaison was also established so that I would not have to deal with him directly: the deputy mayor,

Doug Robarge, and Brad Knapp, one of the trustees, an acquaintance of mine as well.

I got to the offices of Piller & Tracy on Cornelia Street in Plattsburgh a few minutes early. John Clute, the Village Attorney was already there, and Deputy Mayor Robarge arrived shortly thereafter. Evan Tracy, however, was not. We went forward with our formalities anyway, since Evan's role was to represent the Lorrys in the closing after my settlement transaction with the Village. There were a few places that Mr. Clute had made changes to the building agreement and the drawdown structure, which we went over thoroughly. Initially, The Friends were asking him to draft the papers, but he kept sending them blank forms, and finally told them, "I assume the Village pays you to do something pertaining to administering the fund." Having had enough of the back and forth, Brigitte finally called me one day and asked if I could stop by. When I did, she handed me his forms, a copy of my credit report, and a list of what they needed, asking me if I would draft it myself. I was happy to do so, as well as to point out what was mine and what was not mine on my credit report (there was a woman with the exact same name in Vermont who had two mortgages and a bankruptcy showing up on my credit.)

Consequently, I signed off on a mortgage and note, with a renovation loan agreement, complete with drawdown schedule for everything, including business start-up. This gave me the $55,000 to purchase the historic, dilapidated building, and $90,000 to complete the work, while I had to put up at least $10,000—which could be sweat equity, or a combination of things. Repayment would not start until I was open for business, in June.

"You know that old train station where my offices are now?" John Clute asked me, his large frame lurching over the table toward me.

"Yes, it's adorable," I replied.

"Well, I renovated that, I mean, I contracted to have it done," he said, clearing his throat gruffly. "It cost me $300,000 and it was in better shape than this Front Street property," he offered. "I have gone over your proposed budget and I can't imagine that you won't run into cost overruns somewhere."

"I have 'not to exceed' clauses for the subcontractors—electrical and plumbing, as well as the two gas fireplaces. The rest is bargain hunting, salvaging and repurposing, buying in the off season, when people are happy to make deals," I told him. "Also, the apartment didn't get burned much at all, so I will rent that out, plus the Lorrys are renting the laundromat space, so that covers the mortgage."

"But, what about the workers, the main contractor?" he asked seeming sincere, his pen tapping the table. "We had union workers, it costs us a bundle."

"I have out of work contractors, who are happy to find work in the winter. Was your project a seasonal one?" I queried, watching the surprise spread across his face.

"You've really thought this through," he exclaimed. "I should have hired a single mom to go over my budget! Yes, it was during peak season, which is also why it took longer than expected. The main contractor had accepted way too many jobs at the same time, in my opinion, anyway."

"I am trying to get the most out of every dollar, that's for sure," I was extremely nervous, but I was sure hard work and perseverance could pay off and I was committed to do just that. "Is Evan here yet?"

"He should be," John said, looking at the bulky watch on his wrist. "Maybe he got tied up in court, or something. In any event, I am going to stick around for a few minutes, if you have any questions. . . ." Turning his attention to the woman entering the room, he nodded. "Is Evan back yet?"

Evan's paralegal, Dawn, shook her head negatively, as she set a small stack of papers in front of me on the table. "He says I should be able to go over everything with you for now."

Annoyed at his absence, I went through the closing paperwork with Dawn.

"Here are the papers to begin signing on the purchase . . . the Agreement of Sale has already been signed, so—"

"No, actually, it hasn't," I stated. "The one you are looking at is invalid. The Village would not allow me to pay more than the appraised value, which is $55,000, not $57,000, and more importantly, they require a warranty on the roof, which is not in this voided version. Here's the new one." I handed her a new Sales Agreement which had been approved by the Village and Friends noting that John Clute had risen from the table and was standing nearby chatting with Deputy Mayor Robarge.

"Well, I have no authority to sign this," Dawn stated, surprised. "This is news to me."

"If it isn't signed, we have no closing," I told her, then turned to address

John and Doug. "Gentlemen, can you advise Dawn of the Agreement of Sale and roof warranty, please. She says she didn't know about it, so . . ."

"The Village's position is very clear," Mr. Clute stated authoritatively, "The purchase can be for no more than $55,000 and the Lorrys must provide a warranty for the roof they put on. Evan agreed to sign the new sales agreement."

"He didn't say anything about it to me, and I can't reach him right now," Dawn replied with some exasperation.

John looked at his watch. "I have another meeting across town in a few minutes. Why don't you get the Lorrys on the phone and they can authorize the change for you. Meantime, you know what our position is, unless Karen Marie is willing to do differently, but then she might be in violation of our agreements."

"No, I am not willing," I thought about the ramifications, having had just enough insight as to the Lorrys' unprofessional behavior. "The new one gets signed or the whole deal is off."

"You've put a lot of work into this already. You would walk away just like that?" John Clute asked, sincerely surprised.

"Yes. There must be some healthy boundaries, or it won't work. I am not willing to take too many chances."

Leaving Dawn and I alone, John and Doug exited the conference room, as she picked up the phone to call Don and Carolyn. Don was out and Carolyn was unsure if she should agree to any changes. When she failed to comprehend what Dawn was proposing, I offered to talk with her.

"Hi Carolyn. I hope you're enjoying Florida—"

"Thanks, yeah, we are."

"Remember when we went over all of this before you left? We were at the meeting of the Village board?" She mumbled about remembering but being uncertain of the facts. "The bottom line is, the Village is requiring you and Don to warranty the roof you put on or there's no deal. I'm sure you remember about the appraised value because Don kept asking me to pay it to him on the side."

"Yeah. I remember that. He's just mad because that appraiser would not have been the one we chose, ours would have said $57,000," she relayed with confidence.

"Well, this new agreement lists the $55,000 purchase price and the roof warranty, and it must be signed, or we cannot move forward," I told her earnestly. Dawn made a motion toward the speaker button on the phone, and I nodded affirmatively.

"Carolyn, this is Dawn. We're both on with you now. The thing is, she's right. Mr. Clute was just here, and he confirmed it."

"Oh, well, okay but—" her voice trailed off a little nervously. "If only Don were here. He'll be so mad if I make a mistake. You better wait 'til he gets here."

"Carolyn, we don't need Don at all since you are the only owner on the title. Your signature is all we need," I told her, as Dawn looked at the deed.

"Can I speak with Evan?" she wondered.

"He's in court right now. But it's true, Carolyn. I thought it was both of you, but she's right. You are the record owner. Don's name is not on the deed at all. Maybe because you got this property in your divorce settlement. So, do I have your permission to go forward with this? If so, Evan will sign it when he gets here." Dawn fidgeted, looking at the clock hanging above the desk.

"So, if I don't agree then the whole deal is off?" she said, sounding worried.

"Yes," Dawn and I said in unison.

"Okay, then, tell Evan to sign it for me." We exchanged goodbyes, and she hung up.

"When *will* Evan arrive?" I asked her pointedly, recalling that New York state treats paralegals more like glorified secretaries and does not endue them with the authority and scope of responsibility I was accustomed to in my former career in Philadelphia. "I'm still waiting for him to sign the lease on their behalf as well."

"I'm not sure," she answered honestly.

I was annoyed that he was not present but having secured the proper agreement of sale with warranty, we went forward with executing the rest of the closing documents. On the way back to the building I picked up sandwiches and hot coffee to take to the crew who had already begun working.

I breathed a prayer of thanksgiving as I made my way up the long flight of stairs. The bustle of activity going on up there was gratifying; almost all the debris had been removed from the floor on the worst side.

"That looks like hot coffee!" Jeff rounded the corner, covered in dust from head to toe. "Are we looking at the official owner?" The rest of the motley crew gathered round as I set the sandwiches out on a piece of board set over two sawhorses in the former kitchen.

"Yes, you are!" I smiled. There was a chorus of congratulations and well wishes, even some hugs and high fives. As they dug into the sandwiches, I thanked them for their efforts and laid out the priorities we faced, including what I hoped we could accomplish by the end of the week. Then, I put on my work clothes and got to work chipping plaster off brick.

NINE

Progress is not always a smooth road, but one must keep traveling on it.

"I'M SO EXCITED FOR you, Babes!" Nana's voice emanated love from the other end of the phone, as usual. "When are you coming over to Burlington again? I'll treat you to lunch!"

"I'll be there Saturday with the kids, shopping for toilets and sinks," I said, reveling in her joy. "And I thought about going down to the restoration warehouse in Montpelier."

"Count me in!" she laughed.

Thus began a flurry of trips to Burlington, Montreal, or elsewhere if needed, with Nana sometimes coming along, other times just pointing me in the right direction, or supporting my efforts. I had been making the trip to Burlington at least once a week, usually helping her with some household chore, sometimes cleaning the house for her, or working on the landscaping, but now my time was limited, and she completely understood. Our daily chats never let up, though, and she followed my progress eagerly. Sara moved in with her new boyfriend, so it was just the three of us at home again.

One day in mid-March the Lorrys' employee, Nancy, came up the stairs looking for me, claiming there was someone I had to meet, a possible tenant for the apartment. She raved on and on about what a nice guy he was, saying he had frequented the laundromat since arriving in Keeseville a year or so before.

"Don't be mad at me, now" she looked at me deviously, smirking. "But I gave him your phone number. He's *really* cute, and so nice. You just have to meet him!"

"You gave him the number here, right?" I had grown tired of the locals trying to fix me up with someone by now. Every week there was someone new "just stopping by to meet the new owner" who happened to be single a guy, around my age, and always asking me on a date before leaving, while the crew lingered close by to listen in and offer their opinions afterward. Even Brian had begun dropping in unannounced. I had given more thought to going out with him, but then changed my mind again.

"I gave him ALL your numbers," Nancy beamed. "Trust me! He's so cute, and so, so nice. You're gonna thank me!"

"Nancy! I really don't want my personal numbers given out to just anybody!" I sighed loudly. And I don't need to be fixed up!"

"Trust me, Karen," she laughed and patted my shoulder. "You'll be glad I did. There aren't many guys like him around here."

"We'll see about that. While you're here, what's going on with the Lorrys? Evan still hasn't signed the lease, when will they be back?"

"Carolyn says they'll be back at the end of the month," she replied. "I don't know nothin' about the lease."

"The next time they call, please tell them to call me right away," I asked her, grimly thinking of how they had stopped responding to emails and not returned my calls.

A day or so later I got an email from Don which read:

What happened to our sweet, innocent, Karen Marie? Why are you so upset about the lease? I have not authorized Evan Tracy to sign it, and we disagree with the amount. This can be settled when we get back. We don't want to rack up a big legal bill while we're gone.

I replied that the lease needed to be signed, and that I had others interested in the space, if not, which was true. Apparently, someone had been in negotiations with Don to purchase the laundromat and had approached me about leasing the space. He did not quibble with my lease one iota, which encouraged me. I also told Don that I was still waiting for my signed copy of the agreement of sale and needed him to remove the rest of his belongings which were in the way of our work.

I was beginning to feel the pressure of everything and long for some comfort. A strong hug at the end of the day, a kiss, a meaningful conversation with an adult after the kids had gone to bed. As if the Lorry issues were not enough, I was still dealing with ABN AMRO, and every time I tried to pursue Bob for back support and alimony, he would pay up quickly so further action would be pointless. Additionally, when we finalized the divorce, Bob had been driving an old Oldsmobile he had taken over from Granddaddy, since he was by now dangerous behind the wheel. Under terms of our agreement, I took on some of his debt, but he promised to keep paying on the Jeep Cherokee I was driving until it was paid off, in plus or minus two years. After he protested about it, one year into the agreement, I offered to switch vehicles with him so that at least if he was paying for the Jeep, he could drive it. All I cared about was not having a car payment.

"That's a trap! You're trying to trick me!" he snarled. "I know how much you hate driving that Oldsmobile!"

"What? I don't get it?" I marveled at how his critical thinking skills were skewed by hate and wondered where his 'you're still one of my best friends' disposition had gone. "I just can't afford a car payment, right now. You're not paying support and alimony on time, so . . ."

"I'm gonna talk to my lawyer about this; it seems too good to be true," he said.

"Okay, run it by your lawyer. That's fine. I was just offering, since you have to pay the payment under terms of our divorce decree." As an afterthought, I added, "While you're talking to him, get that warranty deed you're supposed to have signed already so I can go forward with my house financing."

A week later he called me back saying that it was "no deal," and still complaining that he had to pay the car payment.

"Look, you've only got another year to pay," I sighed. "I don't know what to tell you, I gave you my best offer. I was just trying to be nice about it."

"My lawyer says that no one would do something like that unless they had to, so there must be some trick—you're up to something!" he fumed venomously.

"Really? Who's your lawyer?" I wondered.

"Evan Tracy," he shot back quickly. "He said that you must be up to no good. No one in their right mind trades a Jeep Cherokee that someone else is paying for, for an old Oldsmobile—that you used to refer to as 'the boat'! I know how much you hate that car!"

"If I were you," I said and cleared my throat of the rising anger, "I would get a new lawyer. I was just trying to work things out win-win. Your loss. I did my best."

But it turned out to be my loss, because Bob stopped making the payments and the car went into repossession status. When the loan company called me about it, I was able to show them where they had double charged interest, which bought me a couple of months, but eventually, I had to give the car up. They worked with me about a suitable time frame, while I hunted for something else to drive, nevertheless, I was stressed out over it. My mother called one day to catch up and I confided in her how stressful and bizarre the whole thing was. The next thing I knew, my father was calling me.

"I hear you're having some issues with a car," he said right away.

"Hi Dad. How are you? I haven't talked to you in a while," I answered, realizing it had been at least a year.

"I'm okay. Busy. So, what's the deal about the car?" he asked with urgency.

"Well, Bob stopped paying and it's going to be repossessed. I offered to trade vehicles with him, but he thought it was some sort of a trap." I heaved a sigh. "Now I am in the market for a new vehicle. I think I would like to lease, since I'm not terribly mechanical. I found a Jeep at Racine's. The payments are good, but due to my lack of formal employment the last few years and the divorce, they want a co-signer."

"Yes, leasing would be the way to go if you can. I don't understand why Bob should have to pay for your car anyway," he remarked snidely. "What's the price?"

"Because, I gave up a career for him, and paid a fortune of his debts, all the while he was living a double life and having affairs behind my back, for starters." I had a feeling trying to defend myself was pointless, but I tried to do it anyway.

Eventually we launched into a discussion about the whole scenario, and he kept insisting he could get a better deal, or make the franchise use only my signature. In the alternative, I should buy a used vehicle. I didn't want a better deal as much as I wanted a solid, reliable car. I had researched the price, checked out the reviews, and even price shopped locally. I lived a long way from family, in a rural area, with two children where the winters are harsh. Reliability and safety were huge issues for me. However, by the time he called the salesman and insulted him, the deal was blown.

"We're gonna get you a used car," Dad told me when he called a few days later.

"Dad, what did you do? What did you say to that salesman?" He ignored me.

"Nothing, it's just . . ." He said something to my mother out of ear shot, then got back on the phone. "I found an old station wagon; I can get it for $1,500, you can pay me back as you can."

"I don't want an old station wagon, but thank you anyway," I replied, annoyed.

"Well, who cares what you drive as long as you have wheels," he said snobbishly.

"I do. I want a safe, reliable car, preferably with four-wheel drive, and if I must make payments, I want to get some good credit standing out of it. It will help me with my mortgage financing." He had scarcely been in touch for a few years, except to blame me for Bob's sexual preference, which was totally inappropriate, so why he would butt in on my decisions as I approached forty years old was beyond me. In the end, he again told me how wrong I was, and how unappreciative. When I told Nana about it, she was incredulous, and apparently mentioned it to my Uncle Frank, who is good buddies with another local franchise owner. He called me and offered to co-sign if necessary, telling me to call his friend and have him get what I wanted, in whatever color I wanted. Once again, the contrast between his real love and concern as opposed to my dad's desire to look like the savior, and dictate the terms was stark, yet welcome.

True to their long-standing love and care, Aunt Mimi and Uncle Frank asked me to be sure and pick up the car when they could take me out to lunch and catch up. When the dealer drove the striking royal blue Liberty Sport to their house, Aunt Mimi remarked, "Oh good! It matches your eyes!"

David was looking for an apartment in the area because he thought it was so beautiful and peaceful, not because it was close to work. He had driven through one sunny day taking photographs of the stone arch bridge, the stately architecture, AuSable River and, the rural scenery. His current apartment was just too cold, and too noisy, however, and the lease would be up soon. He called me to discuss the apartment in the building, and I declined to show it to him because it was not finished. He was very disappointed, but I explained that I was afraid he would not be interested in its current state.

"I hope you don't mind me asking, but where are you from? Obviously, the South. You have a strong accent."

"Tennessee," he answered in a twangy drawl. "I've been up here about three years or so, I really like it. Have you always lived here?"

"No, I just came back up north a few years ago myself. I'm a native of Burlington, but I spent about 19 years in the Philadelphia and Washington D.C., areas."

"I was gonna say, your accent isn't the same as people around here," he answered. "Why'd you come back?"

This launched us into a conversation about families, divorce, and getting on in life alone. He told me that, originally, he had come to the area to be nearer the Canadian border because of a woman he had met online and started seeing. She lives in Montreal. He explained it was a rocky relationship, on and off, and now it was done. Before I knew it, we had been on the phone for forty-five minutes.

"Well, listen, I hope you don't think I'm being too forward or anything, but—" He paused a second and I heard him let out a deep breath. "You seem like a very nice lady and I am wondering, if I can't see the apartment, can you at least meet me for a cup of coffee?"

"Well, I—" I was surprised and strangely comfortable with the idea. "I suppose, I mean . . . I have never done that sort of thing before . . . I mean, with someone I have not met yet, but . . ."

"I just don't have a lot of friends here and you seem so nice. We have a lot in common, too." He paused briefly, and I tried to catch my breath. "You pick the place. Make it somewhere you're comfortable, around people you know. I totally respect that this may be awkward."

"Okay then, maybe the Riverbend," I replied. I had never been in there but knew the owner and it was close by.

"That's great! Thank ya," he replied happily. "You just made my week! How about tomorrow around six?"

"I drop my children off at youth group at six and could be there at 6:15."

"Okay. I'll be waitin' on you," he said. "What do you look like?"

"Well, I am about five two. I have blonde hair, and I'll be driving a blue Jeep," I replied.

"I am about five eight or nine, maybe taller . . . I don't know actually. Well, anyway, I have blue eyes and I am balding a bit on top, but I'll find you. I'll be there early."

That night I said a prayer asking God to keep me from another disaster but asking Him to give me the courage to eventually love again.

Above all, I only want a reciprocal relationship. Help me to recognize what that is and what it isn't. I'm not so sure I'm ready to date again, but I'm not getting any younger, and I still long for what I've always wanted and only had before I was old enough to realize it.

As I prepared to go to bed, I thought about calling David and putting him off, until I realized I didn't have his phone number.

TEN

*Attraction is fine, and conversation is pleasant,
but a person's soul takes time to know.*

AS I WALKED UP the steps toward the entrance, Trudie, the owner of The Riverbend came out of nowhere to greet me. I knew Trudie because as part of my effort to be sure I could make a success of my business, I wanted to use my expertise to help other businesses in the community be successful as well. Everyone yearned for revitalization to the little, historic downtown. They were mostly mom and pop enterprises, many of them with only a high school education, many others having never been out of the region. Along with my friend Ericka, who owned the local wine shop, I had begun an organization called Rural Entrepreneurial Support & Training (REST for short). So far, we had coordinated marketing campaigns, scheduled a village clean-up day, even planned a fall festival, as well as improvements to the Riverwalk and free concert series beginning in the spring.

"It's about time you start getting out again!" she smiled, then winked. "You look great!"

"Does the whole village know about this?" I asked her, incredulous, but serious.

"No, but the guy you're meeting, he told me you were coming, asked if I knew you well." Then as if she had to prepare me, "He's really cute, and very nice. Just give me a sign if you're uncomfortable or anything."

"He is?" I was nervous. *Why did I agree to this?* "Thanks, Trudie, but I think I can handle a cup of coffee." I pushed past her into the reception area, squinting to adjust my eyes from the sunlight outside. As I did, he stood to his feet beside the table, pulling out a chair for me.

"You must be Karen Marie. I'm David," he said, a look of great pleasure on his face. Indeed, he was handsome, I had to admit. His pale blue eyes shone brightly, set off by the pale blue V-neck shirt he wore very well. He smiled broadly, exposing neat, very white teeth and a few laugh lines in the corners of his eyes. He was balding on top, but his brownish, bushy eyebrows seemed to make up for that somehow. "I'm very pleased to meet ya."

"It's nice to meet you, too," I replied, taking a seat. "I hope you haven't been waiting long."

"Not too long," he motioned to Trudie who was already bringing the coffee. "Menu?"

"I'll just have coffee, thanks, but go ahead and order if you'd like." My stomach was in knots, and as I asked for coffee, I wasn't sure I should drink it.

"Well, tell me about yourself," he said letting out a deep breath, leaning over to look me in the eyes. I felt myself being appreciated in that gaze. I hadn't experienced that in a long time; it made me more nervous.

"Well, I have two gorgeous children, whom I am so grateful for. Katlyn is fourteen, and Johnathan is nine. As you know, I'm renovating the building on Front Street. Uh, I'm not sure what else you'd like to know, I guess." I sipped my coffee, hoping my hand wasn't visibly trembling.

"I'm real impressed by what you've done so far," he responded genuinely. "I love kids, maybe I could meet yours sometime. I mean, I hope I'm not bein' too forward or anything."

"Yeah, you might meet them. So, tell me more about yourself." I was more accustomed to listening and felt that maybe something he said could be a better conversation starter.

"Well, I guess I told you that I came up here a few years back. I work at a company up in Beekmantown. I am a Quality Control Manager. I'm in the National Guard, and former Navy. I spent five years in the Navy when I was young. Didn't know it then, but that's what eventually destroyed my first marriage." He sat back a little, watching me intently as he spoke.

I was struck with his sincerity, or at least I thought that's what it was. I asked him more about the first marriage, if he'd ever married again, did he have children?

"I wanted children, badly," he said with some angst. "My first wife, she kept tellin' me it must be me—that she wanted kids, too. I went to doctors . . . but then, I discovered after almost ten years that all my suspicions were true. She was cheatin' on me while I was away, and takin' birth control pills all those years. Kicker is, when it was finally over, she and her boyfriend had a baby about a year later—she brought the baby around to show it to me."

"That's awful." I could relate to being cheated on, lied to. I told him a little of my story. We talked about his Navy years, the places he's been in the world and my travel lust, his drawing and photography hobbies, and the fact that he dabbled in writing children's stories.

"Really?" I was surprised at how much we had in common. "I've written a few children's books, and studied art, too. And, I understand how frustrating it is when you're giving your best to someone and they are lying to you . . . I'm sorry. Is that why you never married again?" He looked me deep in the eyes, pregnant silence in the air.

"I never married again because, even though I've tried, I've never found anyone who wanted to love as deeply as I love. I always wanted a marriage that was equal, reciprocal." A chill ran down my spine and my tummy fluttered. *He used that word! Reciprocal!* His eyes never left mine; I could not break away from his gaze. I hoped he could not see how intensely that touched me. "I get the feelin' you know about that, too."

"Yes," I whispered, lacking the voice to speak any louder in that moment. He waited for me to say more, but I could scarcely breathe. After a long pause, I finally exhaled. "Sometimes you just wonder if that really exists. My ex-husband always told me I was unrealistic, but I had that in the past, a long time ago."

"I think it exists, at least I hope it does." He kept watching me, I was still a bit uncomfortable, though I wasn't sure if it was him, or the topic.

"What time is it?" I asked, fumbling for my cell phone, realizing we had been talking a while.

"It's 7:30. Do you need to get your kids?" he asked, looking at his watch, then back at me.

"Wow, we've been talking a while!" Again, the time seemed to slip quickly. "No, they are being picked up by a friend and taken out for ice cream."

"Well, are you hungry? Can I buy you some dinner?" His brows raised as his eyes expressed eagerness.

"I am a bit hungry," I admitted. He motioned to Trudie who had been not so inconspicuously in and out of the dining room repeatedly, pretending to be busy with odd jobs, eyeing us and winking at me from time to time. There were barely any patrons in the restaurant, mainly in the bar.

"Can you bring us some menus?" When she went to retrieve them he asked me, "How's the food here?"

"I honestly don't know," I told him. "I've never eaten here."

We ordered the shrimp alfredo, salads, and a glass of wine. It was terribly disappointing: over-cooked spaghetti noodles sitting in a pool of warm milk with canned baby shrimp thrown on top. Later, he asked me if I liked the food.

"Umm, well, thank you very much for dinner," I answered. "It was very sweet of you."

"Haha! I didn't much like it either!" He laughed heartily. "So, do you want to try the desserts?"

"No, thank you. I had better be going," I smiled. "The kids will be back soon."

"Well, can I see ya again?" he wondered.

"That would be very nice," I told him, just as Trudie brought the check to the table. He reached in his pocket to pull out his wallet. Suddenly a horrified look came over his face. "Is everything okay?"

"Oh no!" His face flushed red. "I cannot believe this—"

"What's wrong?"

"I went home to shower and change after work, before meeting you." He squirmed. "I left my wallet in my work pants. Can you wait here? I can be back in about twenty minutes or so . . ."

"No worries. I'll get this," I told him, pulling my purse off the chair next to me.

"I'm so embarrassed," he said with a grimace. "I'll pay you back. It's an awful thing to ask a woman to dinner and then not pay for it!"

"It's okay. No need to pay me back." I paid Trudie, who found the whole episode quite amusing.

"It's not okay. If you won't let me pay you back, then let me buy you a *proper* dinner," he said under his breath as she walked away. "I want to see you again. What do you say?"

"Sounds nice," I agreed. Once outside, he walked me to my car.

"I'm not gonna really kiss you, 'cause I'm a gentleman, but . . ." He gazed at me intently, once again, mostly over his embarrassment. Taking my hand in both of his, he raised it to his lips, gently kissing it, then held it at his chest, never leaving my eyes. "I really enjoyed getting to know you a little. I am grateful that you said 'yes'."

"I am, too. Thank you." I felt awkward, but excited at the thought of seeing him again.

Once at home, Katlyn and Jon were dropped off within fifteen minutes. We settled into our night time ritual of stories and prayers. I sat on the couch between them, an arm around each, and they took turns turning the pages of the book. Sometimes Katlyn read—she is an avid bookworm, but Jon was more interested in trucks and soccer, and anything military or Indiana Jones. We snuggled and talked about the day, made plans, and then we either prayed together, or I would pray with Jon as I got him into bed. Katlyn stayed up later, and sometimes I would just chat or pray with her a little as she read before dozing off to sleep.

I had continued in my daily reading and prayer time, too, and around this time revisited the story of Ruth. I was curious about her loyalty to her mother-in-law, even after the death of her husband. In fact, the bond they shared made me think of the relationship I have with Nana. But what also struck me was the way she went about meeting Boaz, her future husband, at the direction of her mother-in-law, Naomi. I could not fathom the directions Naomi gave her, but I could so appreciate that God Himself is my "kinsman redeemer"—the One who creates a place of rest and comfort, provides for and establishes me. Regardless of the actions, or manipulations of my father, or Bob, I had wonderful people in my life that I thanked God for, people who loved and supported me. I would rather freeze in a big empty bed than share it with an enemy. Thus, my reminder to be grateful and trust became an evening ritual where I would throw an afghan on the side of the bed I slept on, and say aloud, "Thank you for spreading your garment over me, Lord." This night, as I did so, the phone rang.

"Hello?" I answered quickly and quietly so as not to wake the kids.

"Hi. I'm sorry if I'm calling too late," David said soberly. "I didn't think about the time 'til after I dialed."

"It's okay," I told him as I crossed the room to close my bedroom door.

"I just want to thank you again for meeting me. I had a real nice time tonight," he said in his unmistakable accent.

"I did, too. Thank you." I sat on the bed and pulled the afghan over me.

"Sorry about the wallet thing," he drawled sheepishly. "Can I stop by tomorrow to visit ya at the building?"

"Seriously, don't worry about it. Um, sure. I'll be there all day. Jon is getting off the school bus there. I've got a lot to accomplish tomorrow," I told him sobering at the thought.

"Okay then, I'll see ya tomorrow. I get outta work about 4:00, so on my way by, I'll stop in." He paused, then earnestly, quietly spoke again. "You really made my week—make that my month. You're a sweet lady, and I hope we get to know each other better."

"Thank you. That's very nice of you to say," I could feel my face flush. "I'll see you tomorrow."

"See ya tomorrow. Good night."

"Good night."

ELEVEN

*Being wiser is not enough, you must be proactive
with your newfound wisdom.*

OVER THE NEXT FEW weeks, David stopped by frequently, almost daily. He watched the progress on the upstairs, what was the bed and breakfast inn portion of my building, with lots of encouraging comments. He offered to help me by taking pictures for the website I was having created to launch the business. In 2003, most bed and breakfasts relied on the paperback version of Lanier's Guide to Bed & Breakfasts, but I could see the trend moving to online reservations and wanted to be ready. Many people still preferred to book by speaking with 'the owner' but being online would mean wider access by guests from anywhere in the world. The electricians were all but finished and finishing carpentry had begun. The plumbing and heating was for the most part also completed. I had gone from shopping for toilets and sinks to making color choices and choosing room themes. I ran into a snag when it was discovered that the kitchen cabinets were not salvageable like we originally thought. Since the kitchen was crucial, and very large, I worried about where to get quality cabinets that would look nice and not cost a fortune. I also looked for what I could cut out of the budget to pay for them.

In those few weeks, the apartment was also nearing ready to rent, but by now David had decided to stay on where he was month to month through the nicer weather. His old flame in Montreal had been in touch, and he had gone to see her, which meant their relationship was somewhat on again, though he complained about it a lot. Brian had been pursuing me more, as well. I agreed to have lunch with him one day, and he began calling me more after that. Even still, David stopped by daily and we frequently had great conversations. We became close friends, even offering each other relationship advice. He also got to know the kids, especially Jon, since Katlyn was usually involved with friends after school or extracurricular activities, but Jon enjoyed helping me at the inn and shop.

The village code officer had been coming to my building almost daily, scrutinizing every little thing, although I had valid permits, he seemed to enjoy making me squirm and pushing his weight around with the crew a bit, then he would act like he was doing me a favor before making an appreciative comment about the work being done, or my creativity. I found him to be an enigma. Mayor Bezio, also stepped up his chauvinism and outright meddling. Though he was supposed to leave me alone and deal with my liaisons, instead he would stop by and yell at me that he didn't like the way I was doing things. "You're just a stupid woman! What the hell does a woman know about renovating a building anyway!" He interfered with my drawdowns on more than one occasion, causing me to send crew home for a few days while I waited for Doug and Brad to meet with him and get Mr. Clute involved. If I couldn't pay them on time per the drawdown schedule, I didn't have it to cover on my own.

As if all of that were not enough, the Lorrys still had not signed a lease, although they had been fully operational in the premises since our closing in February. Evan Tracy had still not given me the sales agreement, and now he was shoving a lengthy and ridiculous commercial lease at me. The Lorrys kept claiming it was fair, but it wasn't fair. I finally gave them notice to quit the premises by May saying I had another offer. This resulted in a more serious lease discussion with Evan, wherein I outlined that the Lorrys could pay for heat and electric separately, but only as long as the boiler supporting their portion of the premises was sound. Once it became unusable, I would be connecting the 1707 premises to the new commercial boiler I just had installed. There were various other provisions I insisted on, but eventually, I agreed to accept $400 per month at first, provided they do all the restoration and repair as discussed and reviewed, then $800 per month, with additional provisions for water, electric, heat and air conditioning.

Stress and fatigue were taking their toll on me as Bob continued to play his games with support and alimony, and I repeatedly logged calls to ABN AMRO to try and get the excessive fees and interest reduced. I frequently wrote to Ms. Lester, who reassured me that if I continued to pay timely, I would have no trouble switching my home mortgage over to my name by assumption. I prayed often. I even prayed that God would help me find the best possible deals on provisions, even the kitchen cabinets. The time had come to install them, and I didn't have any, so in addition to praying, I went to Gregory Supply in Plattsburgh. Discussing the dimensions and showing the layout I desired to the kitchen designer there, I was met with a whopping price tag. By now I had figured I could shake $2,000 out of my budget, but she assured me there was no way I could expect to pay any less than 7,000. I was ready to give up there and move on but breathed a prayer as I wandered the store. *I don't have time to waste, nor money. Is there anything here, Lord? Where should I go?* I had the sense there was something I had not seen yet, like a nagging feeling. I went back over to her station.

"Are you sure I've seen all there is to see? Do you have any overstock, or discontinued cabinetry?"

"No," she shook her head, then stopped suddenly. "Actually, we have some hickory cabinets that were custom ordered; I didn't even think about those. But they're—the customer ordered them and swore he wanted them unstained, but when they came in he didn't like them and wouldn't pay or take delivery. I tried to tell him about the contrasts in unstained hickory, but he wouldn't listen . . ."

"I understand, but can I see them, please?" I knew they must be for me.

"Sure." Rising to her feet she quipped "Follow me. I don't know why I didn't think of them sooner." We made our way to the back of the store, through a hidden doorway into a storage area. "They're in these boxes, we'll just get someone to lift a section out . . . but they've been in the way so long, months now."

"This box looks torn. Do you mind if I—"

"Just tear the rest of that off, you'll get a good look for yourself," she interjected, coming toward me as I did so. "Do you see what I mean about the hickory?"

"Yes, I like it." Immediately I knew these were very expensive cabinets. They were solid wood, and like she said, had been custom ordered. "If I could see a few more—see how the streaking patterns look? They must have cost a pretty penny."

"Yes!" She picked up a telephone and dialed an extension. "Can I get some heavy lifting help back in storage, please? Okay. Yup. Thanks. This is a big configuration, and they are solid wood, custom work. The customer was supposed to pay more than $8,000. He lost his deposit but . . ."

"Do you have a diagram of the configuration?"

"No, but, let's take a look at yours and see if we can make these work," she offered. With help lifting many of them out of their boxes we were able to form my configuration with one section to spare.

"This is a big configuration. How much would you take for it?" I asked.

"I'll have to ask the boss. I'm sure he'd be happy to get them out of the way and recoup some of his outlay," she paused. "What would you suggest?"

"I'll give you $1,800," I told her.

"All I can do is ask," she replied walking toward an office area. I stood there watching as she found him, changing the countertop and door of the kitchen in my mind to accommodate this find, and praying for a favorable response. A few minutes later she came back.

"He will take $2,000 and you can have the one that you don't need—maybe you can find a use for it somewhere," she said.

"I really don't need it but thank you." I thought a few minutes, looking them over again. "I would prefer $1,800 and maybe you can sell the other one." She went back and talked to the boss again, this time I followed her out of the storage area and waited by her desk. After a minute, she returned.

"Do we have to deliver?" she queried. I realized Carol had made her truck available to me since she had been helping at the building during the winter months when she had no other work.

"No need," I told her. "I can make arrangements to pick them up."

"Okay, if you can pay us today, you can have all of them for $1,800."

With the leftover two hundred dollars, I ordered my window decals from Tom, and stopped by the Village Offices to inquire whether I needed a special permit to use a lift truck to paint the exterior of the building. The time was closing in, and spring was on the way. I needed to get pictures on the internet and generate some business for June. While I was in the Village Offices, Phil O'Connor, the codes officer, asked me if I might rent the apartment to a friend of his who was going through a divorce. He said he'd vouch for him, and that he was a part time court bailiff in the Village Court.

"You're a young woman alone, taking on an awful lot. It might be nice to have a man around to help out now and then," he said, patting me on the shoulder. "I know Buck wouldn't mind shoveling in winter, taking the trash out, minor repairs . . . and you'd have a solid, trustworthy tenant."

"Send him over to talk with me," I told him. "The apartment is just about ready to rent. I want $400 a month for it, plus security. Now, do I need a special permit to use a lift truck? I have made arrangements to rent one to deal with outside façade and window trim." The building itself was brick, about the size of half the block, with stately Italianate details, decorative arches, and pillaring. I had chosen to cover the gaudy gold auto paint Don had painted the front of the 1709 entrance with, as well, but that only went up to the second floor, and could be done with a ladder or scaffolding.

"Why not just use scaffolding?" Phil wondered aloud. "It's a lot less expensive."

"Because it will also take longer and be a nuisance to other businesses on Front Street. The Lorrys have already complained about it, and I only mentioned the idea."

"Well, as far as I am concerned, you don't need a special permit. I wish you luck, though. The Lorrys are a real pain in my ass," he confided. "If I were you, I'd get rid of 'em first chance I had. They're sleazy slumlords."

"They haven't paid a dime of rent yet, so I am probably going to evict them," I told him. "Can you imagine running a business, making money, and never paying rent?"

"They're playing you for a fool. Don't put up with it," he clucked. "I don't like them at all."

TWELVE

Courage is not the absence of fear; rather, it is action in defiance of fear.

MAY CAME IN ALL its glory, and Buck, the bailiff, moved into my apartment. I wasn't a hundred percent sure I wanted him for a tenant, but then I got a reference from the local village Justice George Head. Between him and Phil O'Connor, his references were good. He was a strapping, but tall and thin guy, maybe thirty-six or thirty-seven years old. He was simple, but friendly, and knowledgeable about repairs, having a love of carpentry. He didn't mind the idea of traipsing through the inn hallway to get to his apartment on the far end of the second level, and the studio was all he needed. Eventually I thought I would turn it into a part of the B&B, but for now, funds limited that option.

David offered to go with me to pick up the lift truck. It was about a forty-five-minute drive away heading toward Malone. I was renting it from a friendly local business man, Art, who also had an old farmhouse out that way. He saw what I was doing with the building and encouraged me a great deal. Though he seemed to be of the era of Bud Bezio and Don Lorry, Art was married to a younger, very savvy Russian woman, and together they ran a business out of their other home, just about a half a mile from mine. I had been chatting with them one day about the expense of a lift truck, over $750 per day, when he offered me the use of his old one for $175. He was so eager to help, he even changed his plans for it. Jon went to a friend's after school, so Dave and I set out. Along the way, we enjoyed the same meaningful conversation we had become accustomed to in the previous months and the time flew by, even though we stopped a couple of times to take pictures of the scenery. Pulling in the long driveway to the old farmhouse, I saw instantly why Art and his wife bought it. It was large, in great shape, on a beautiful lot with terrific shade trees, and just enough sun. Art was nowhere in sight, so we made our way to the old covered porch, calling out to him through the screen door.

"Hello!" Art called back from inside. "Come on in." As we entered we noticed boxes of old dishes, piles of linens and newspapers, stacks of books, and various old kitchen paraphernalia. "As you can see, we're just beginning to go through everything that came with the house—it was an estate sale. Then, we'll start the restoration process," he smiled, winking at me. "You know a thing or two about that now, don't you?"

"Just a little," I grinned, as he motioned us into the living room area.

"I'd say a lot," David chimed in. "What's all this?" He pointed to papers strewn on the table next to an ornate box.

"Treasure!" Art declared. "It's what it's all about . . . a love story."

"A love story?" I inquired, accepting a dainty, yellowing piece of paper from his hand.

> My Dearest Love, It has been too long since the ravages of war have torn you out of my arms, but I carry you always in my heart. My mind dwells on you and my heart yearns for you in the depths of night.

"Wow. This is beautiful." I felt overcome at such sincerity of expression, at the same time embarrassed at my reaction in front of Dave and Art. Dave continued reading.

> My Love and My Life, you are the apparition that awaits me in slumber, the very beat of my heart in the long days. Your love is what keeps me alive. You are my hope and desire. Though I miss you desperately, I shall return to your arms, your lips, and sweep you up in eternal embrace though hell tries to keep me away.

Dave paused a few seconds. "Is this from the man who owned the house?"

"I think so," Art answered, smirking. "He has the same name that was on the deed. The house was passed down the through the family a couple of times or so. Care to read some more?" He handed another letter to Dave.

> My Darling, I live for every word you pen, hearing your voice say the words in my heart, my body longing for your presence with passion.

"Woah! This is old-fashion' steamy!" Dave exclaimed to our giggles. "How long ago?"

"This one says August 5, 1918," I told him. "And here we are in 2003. This must have been during World War I."

"Yep. It's what life is all about. Love," Art stated, looking back and forth between us. "If you don't have love, nothing else matters."

I squirmed uncomfortably. Even though I had been seeing more of Brian lately, I thoroughly enjoyed the time David and I spent together every day. I kept pushing it out of my mind, telling myself he was not available, but at times, I caught myself anticipating his arrival. Others had noticed it, too; like my helper, Julie. She and her husband Gary watched Dave and I interact every day and kept asking why we were not dating. I looked at David, whose face was flushing a bit. *Is he as uncomfortable with this as I am?*

"Art, thanks for showing these to us. It's very moving," I told him. "But, we have a long way to go back, so perhaps we should get the truck now?"

"Yeah, we still need to get some dinner somewhere on the way home," David piped in.

We headed out behind the house and Art gave Dave and me a quick lesson on how to operate the old cherry picker, as he called it. It was *very* old but seemed safe enough. He cautioned that sometimes there might be a small leak from the hydraulic line, which could be caught using a simple coffee can. After a few other niceties, we said our goodbyes and Dave got in the truck. I followed him as he drove slowly all the way home, forgetting to stop for dinner like we had planned. By the time we got to Keeseville and parked it, he jumped out of the cab, wiping his brow.

"I'll tell ya somethin', Karen," he said, his voice agitated. "I'm glad you don't have to drive this thing but across the street! It's rickety. You should have Art come pick it up himself when you're done with it."

"Is that why you didn't stop for dinner?" I queried, searching his face. "I am sorry for the trouble—"

"I was so anxious to park this piece of junk that I plum forgot about dinner! I'm sorry. You want to go get something now?" he asked.

"No, it's getting late and I want to pick up Jonathan. Plus, I don't want Katlyn to be home alone too long, and I'm sure she's been home an hour already. I am really sorry about you having to drive that . . . I didn't realize."

"Aww, it's all right. I just hope you have the guys deal with it. Get Gary or Charlie to handle it for you. I'll be sick with worry at work thinking of you dealing with this old clunker." He was adamant, and I was a bit surprised. "I bet it doesn't have much life left in it, the old thing. If the lift works properly, that's all you need though, right?"

"Yes, and I can ask Art if we can just leave it at his house here when we're done," I replied. Dave reached for me, giving me his now customary hug as we parted ways for the night.

"See ya tomorrow," he whispered gently. "I'll run the phone lines for your back office after work, if you like."

"No, it's okay. I've taken enough of your time already this week." I felt that I had and wondered if I was getting too attached. I had mused over those love letters and Art's comment the entire trip back.

"Well, I'll come by and you can decide then, okay?" He observed my eyes keenly, still standing very close. "Besides, I have Guard duty this weekend, so if I don't see ya tomorrow, I won't see ya 'til Monday."

"Okay then, I'll see you tomorrow."

Getting the cherry picker on the sidewalk the next day was easy because Charlie, one of the crew, did it for me. Getting someone to go up in it, was not so easy. None of the guys would do it. I was shocked. No one had a viable explanation, but all had an excuse. Gary was afraid of heights, something having to do with his Vietnam days. Charlie just said I couldn't pay him enough to get up in the air, and he had plenty of carpentry work to do. Jeff, well I paid him too much as the crew manager to have him up in a lift with a paint brush.

"Okay then, drive back over to the parking lot and give me a lesson," I told Charlie.

"What the hell?" Gary blurted out. "You ain't goin' up in that thing! I won't let you!"

"Are you fuckin' crazy?" Charlie wondered aloud.

"Well, if none of you are willing, who is going to paint? I'm paying for this thing by the day!" I was dead serious. They knew it. After a pregnant pause, Charlie climbed in the truck and pulled it over to the lot. I walked across the street to meet him at the rear, followed by Gary. "Okay, give me a quick lesson." As I got in the lift bucket, Gary grabbed my arm.

"That building is at least eighty feet tall. Who's goin' to go get you when you're frozen with fear in mid-air?"

"I am not going to freeze with fear, Gary," I reassured him. I couldn't let on how anxious I was.

"I'm just lookin' out for you," his somber face, surrounded by his grey mane and beard, verified he was plenty concerned.

"I know, Gary, and I appreciate it," I smiled at him. "But unless you can convince someone else to do this, I'm going up there in ten minutes."

Charlie had by now put down the stabilizing arms and the lift was operational. He gave me a quick bit of instruction and I went up and down a few times, then side to side. It was a bit jerky, but the guys claimed if they added hydraulic fluid it would be fine. Sufficiently convinced I could operate it, I set the bucket down on the ground again and got out.

"You're one hell of a woman," Gary remarked, thrusting his arm over my shoulder.

"Just say a prayer for me, Gar," I told him.

"You just might make me start praying," he laughed. "You just might!"

I painted at the very top first. I had chosen multiple historic colors to play up the buildings significant features, but I hadn't thought I'd be the one struggling with multiple cans and brushes up that high. In fact, I had developed a fear of heights when I was pregnant with Katlyn, at Red Rocks Park in South Burlington. I had been walking along with Bob and the twins when we came to one of the high ledges used by so many to jump into the lake far below. I had the strange sensation that I was being pulled over the cliff by my huge belly, and a dizziness came over me. A few years before, I had fallen off a ladder cleaning a window, and was knocked unconscious. Those two things combined made it difficult for me in high places, so I had just stayed away. Today, however, it was do or die. I had to face my fear and do the job. Gary nervously checked on me out the upper windows every fifteen minutes. After about his ninth or tenth time asking, "You doin' okay?" I finally asked him to go next door and order us some pizzas for lunch.

By the time Jonathan got out of school for the day, I had accomplished a lot. He loved to come to the building and help and I paid him for his efforts. Julie met the bus as I was high in the air. When she pointed up so he could see me waving at him, he ran up the tall stairs, burst into the kitchen and right up to the window.

"Mom, you are doing a great job!" he exclaimed with glee. "Can I get in there and help?"

"No, buddy," I said laughing out loud. "It's too crowded in this thing. How about a snack?"

"Can I get a slice of pizza?" he wondered aloud.

"Sure, tell Miss Laurie that I can pay her when I get down," I replied.

"But can you give me some money now? I want to go the store," he said with excitement.

"Well, I think my purse is in my office. What do you need? Something for school?"

"I wanna buy one of those little cameras, so I can take a picture of you in the air!" His enthusiasm was entertaining and contagious.

"But you have to be so careful crossing the street, buddy," I sighed, realizing he was growing up fast. "Promise me? You'll look both ways, two times. Actually, if Miss Ericka is free, ask her to tell you when it's safe to cross. I'll be watching you."

"Thanks, Mom!" He dashed away and the next thing I knew his little voice was yelling up to me from the sidewalk. I watched him go into Little Italy next door to order his slice, then out again and down the street to Ericka's wine shop. She stepped out onto the sidewalk, waving at me and giving me the thumbs up. He crossed at her approval and went into the pharmacy. A few minutes later, he was back out, looking to cross the street, and there was David. He had just been dropped off by his carpool. I watched them high five each other, and then cross the street. Realizing Jon was safe, I turned back to painting. A few minutes later, Jon yelled up to me again.

"Mom! Mom! Look at me and smile!" He held the little disposable camera to his eye and snapped away. Dave stood there with his mouth open and eyes wide, shaking his head from side to side in amazement. Gary rushed out to greet him—and probably defend himself. I felt like I conquered a giant, though I was weak in the knees and felt queasy every time I looked down. I did it anyway, and I set an example for my son.

THIRTEEN

*There is much satisfaction when one's vision takes shape
and presents even better than hoped for.*

APPARENTLY, PEOPLE IN THE village have an extremely up-to-date grapevine or are abundantly curious. By the time I had been in the lift the next morning for only an hour, a crowd gathered below me. Cars and trucks went by literally honking, with arms stretched out of windows giving me a thumb's up multiple times. The mayor, one of the trustees, the owner of the hardware store, and the grocery store manager were but a few of the onlookers. I noted Stephen yelling from down the block as he approached, "The place is looking great!" Ericka came by as usual with a morning coffee, which I enjoyed from the bucket, while she stood on the inside chatting with me. She was a remarkable friend. Eventually, I noted Gary across the street talking with a man I had not seen before, pointing to the building, emphatic in his movements. About ten minutes later, they were below me, and Gary was motioning for me to bring the bucket down to the ground.

"This is Mark," he said, opening the bucket and offering me his hand to get out. "He's gonna take over for you."

"Hello Mark. Are you a painter?" I asked, noting his scruffy appearance.

"I used to paint, ma'am, before I went to jail," he said sheepishly, grinning big enough for me to notice he was missing two front teeth.

"So, you've been in jail? How recently?" I wondered.

"Well, ma'am, I been out 'bout two months, but ain't nobody givin' me a chance to work. I got some—whatch you call it—disability, but I'm a damn good painter, ma'am."

"I've worked with Mark on a few jobs," Gary piped. "I'll vouch for him. He'll have this façade done in three more days, tops. He'll do a good job, too."

"Well, okay then. How about a trial run?" I replied. "Have you operated a lift before?"

"Yes, ma'am, I have. I'd be so happy if you give me a chance," he remarked. "I'll do a good job. You'll see."

He worked an hour as I watched every few minutes. He didn't slack, and he appeared to be doing well. Gary confided in me that he was a little slow mentally, and trying to fit in with the wrong crowd, ended up stealing some things and getting caught.

"He's a good guy, really," he told me. "He just needs some guidance, and when I saw him, I knew it would get you out of that lift!"

"Gary, I appreciate you always looking out for me," I smiled. "Thank you. By the way, I see there's a little oil spot or something below the lift today. Did we forget to put the can under the drip?"

"Shoot! Yeah, we did," he replied. "I'll go get it now."

"Well, while you're at it, why not go across to the hardware store and get some kitty litter to soak it up. I have some TSP and I'll wash the sidewalk down at the end of the day."

"You're the boss," he put his hand up to high-five me.

Now that I could get out of painting outside, I went back to my planning and color choosing inside. I was beginning to get email inquiries and take reservations by phone since Dave and I had taken just enough pictures to get the website up and running, but I needed to complete more rooms. I had a theme for each room, and each had a private bath. Liberty's Suite was historic red, white and blue, with a framed antique flag from 1776 hanging on one wall, painted plank floors, and an optional second bedroom, which I dubbed the Underground Railroad Room. Ericka and I met one night after we had our kids settled for the night and textured the walls with beautiful shades of green and pearl, and slight marbling of a rose quartz color for a beautiful faux finish. My friend Kathleen made me a freedom quilt wall-hanging for that room to match my color scheme, and I outfitted the room with white wicker furniture. It could be added to Liberty's Suite, or to the room on the other side of it, The Chasm Room.

The Chasm was outfitted with memorabilia from AuSable Chasm, a centuries old popular tourist attraction less than a mile away on the river. It had a cozy feel since there were no windows, it felt like a chasm. I utilized soft yellows and blues, wainscoting, and even the walk-through closet. Pedestal sinks and walk in showers were purchased for most rooms, but in The Valcour Room across the hall, on the river side of the building, I salvaged and re-enameled an antique, cast iron, soaking tub, too. Apparently the Lorrys, or even a previous owner, found it too heavy to remove from the building, so in an attempt to modernize they built a frame around it. It took a lot of effort to get it up on a flat dolly, but once we did, I took great pleasure in doing the work myself. Then, I utilized the windows I discovered when I took down the drop ceiling, at the very top of the wall separating what was once a galley kitchen and the bedroom. Idealizing the Valcour Island lighthouse (on Lake Champlain, just a few miles away), I painted the outside of the tub to look as though it was a boat in the water, positioning it in front of the eight-foot window, with a canvas sail as a curtain set on a mast. I also installed a single shower in the corner, and hung netting around filled with sea shells and star fish. Accessories with anchors, and rope completed the beach feel, and the windows allowed light from the bathroom—where the only window to outside was in that suite—into the bedroom, giving an impression of a lighthouse.

The main hallways were wide, about seven feet across, leaving ample room for pine cabinets I had discovered in the basement to be used to store fresh linens and supplies, with decorative items on top. The best room of all was what I called my Adirondack Suite. The Lorrys had boarded up and enclosed the former fire escape to the building to squeeze another apartment in, even removing the old stairs outside. I discovered that I could meet code with a drop ladder and an emergency exit in the same location and felt horrible at the realization their greed ended up costing lives. I enlarged the suite to the new hallway I created for a fire escape and supply closet, rather than taking the space for another room. This meant that the Adirondack Suite also backed up to the river below and had a living room as well as large bath and bedroom. To make good use of the scenery I had a small deck, about eight by ten feet or so, built off the room, overlooking the river and the old historic mill. I ordered custom Pella insulated French doors with a transom and trim, matching the other windows I had to replace, in historic colors. The partial wall between the bedroom and bathroom boasted his and hers large pedestal sinks in front of a huge mirror, and I ran a glass shelf the length of the wall and mirror above them, supported by antique cast iron brackets. Plants adorned the top of the wall, cascading down both sides. Nearby was a toilet, then a double shower with seats, and across from that, in front of a window overlooking the river below was a two-person jacuzzi tub I managed to buy at a bargain price because someone had custom ordered it and it was the wrong shape for their space. I had Jeff enclose it with wainscoting in pine, then I found spectacular, hand painted tile at a renovator's supply outside of Montreal, which I painstakingly laid myself. I painted the bath and bedroom in soothing pine green, since there was so much natural light from the doors, transom and window, it would not be overpowering. I used rustic Adirondack furniture for the bed, side tables, and an Adirondack style quilt. Accent colors throughout the suite were shades of terracotta, beiges, and greens for an earthy feel.

In the living room, I utilized the brick removed when I enlarged window space in the bedroom to accommodate the French doors, to install a gas fireplace, with post mantle and chimney. The living room ran the length of both the bedroom and bathroom, so I placed a small dining table and chairs on one end, with a medium sized, vintage looking cabinet and countertop for a coffeemaker, water, and various items. The other side had an Adirondack style couch and oversized chair, with a rustic coffee table made by Gary, in front of the fireplace. Outside the entrance to that suite, across the wide hallway, was the parlor with a powder room, and beyond it a dining area, as well as the entrance to the kitchen. I opted to keep the kitchen entry open except for saloon style doors. It was very large, and beyond it, a separate eating area faced the front, adjoining the small dining area beyond the parlor.

At first, I attempted to knock down the wall there and join both dining areas into a larger one, but we had some trouble. Jonathan and Katlyn had been helping that day and were having fun taking turns swinging the sledge hammer, but it just wouldn't budge. I got involved, peeling off layers of plaster, and discovered old tongue and groove, in an interesting narrow pattern. As we worked our way down the wall, we discovered original milk paint stenciling on the wall, in a border along the top and midway down. It was beautiful, with flourishes of terracotta, blue, and a faint brown and green. Once we removed old boards, then plaster and lathe, from the entire section, there was some mildew, but I felt it was salvageable. I called Stephen over to look at it and did some research on the best way to clean it without damaging the milk paint. There was a chiseled-out area in the center where someone in the past had installed the old knob and tube electrical lines, then put plaster over the wall, so we knew the wall was placed before electricity. My research suggested it was original to the 1840 construction date of the building.

The same type of thing happened in the kitchen. As we demolished the plaster and lathe, to run new electrical lines and drywall, we discovered a tiny door which had been buried by layers of wood and plaster. It was barely tall enough for me to walk through without bending over. Once inside, I discovered a pantry like area, lined with shelves positioned above the long stairway, inside the main entrance. This was a find that improved my kitchen, giving me more options. Wherever possible, I utilized the old brick, treating it with a sealant to strengthen it, then finishing it with a patina from a stain mixed with an acrylic. (The older brick is, the more it tends to soften from the inside out.) I utilized the types of detail work around doors and trim as would have been original to a fine home of the era and worked diligently to restore the old plank floors wherever possible.

I usually knocked off work when the kids were out of school, going with them to soccer games or school activities. I began the day early, as soon as they were headed out the door. As my deadline approached, and the bulk of the work left was my decorating and finishing touches, I frequently went back to work late into the night. I would wait until Katlyn was ready to read in bed, and Jon was tucked in soundly, leaving a phone with each of them, then go back down the street to work some more. I reminded them I was only two minutes away if needed; the first few times, they called to be sure. I was always happy to prove my devotion to them, even if it meant going back and forth a couple of times. I was grateful this project was so close to home and that we had our wonderful golden retriever, Luke, to stay with them.

FOURTEEN

Appearances are not facts, and reports may be exaggerated, but motivation is eventually recognizable.

"WHAT'S THIS I HEAR about you in a lift truck?" Brian's voice gave away his amusement. "You won't have dinner with me because you're spending all your time working and now you're even operating heavy equipment? What's next?"

"How are you?" I wondered, not having spoken to him in a week or so. "My, news travels far, all the way to Plattsburgh."

"I'm okay. Wondering about you. I drove by yesterday on my way to open my camp on Butternut Pond. Stopped in to see you and heard the tale of how you've got grown men scared to say 'no' to you for fear you'll show them up!" He snickered.

"Well, it has to be done, but I'm at a standstill for the moment. I found a note on my door this morning from the mayor, claiming I damaged a tree with the lift."

"Seriously? Those half dead things he has enclosed in those lame boxes on the sidewalk? No doubt if you took off a branch or two it was dead already and needed pruning!" he retorted.

"I know. In fact, one of our projects with REST is to replace them with flowers and nicer dwarf trees, more appropriate for the block. All the business owners are upset with how the current trees block their signage, and the Village won't let us hang signs off the building into the sidewalk area." I told him. "Anyway, for today, I'm dead in the water since he says I can't use the lift truck anymore. I have to wait for my oversight committee to stop by this afternoon."

"This guy's a jerk—isn't he the same one who called you 'nothing but a stupid woman'?" Brian sounded exasperated.

"The very same. Mayor Bezio, who has also interfered with my drawdowns, showed up and told the crew he wasn't going to give me any more money, so they may as well go home and not come back because he was putting an end to my project," I sighed with exhaustion. "Yeah, he's a real humdinger."

"Did they finally all come back, though? I thought you got back on track after that."

"All but two, but they are nervous. I can do without the others at this point, and I think Charlie was offered another job. Anyway, how are you doing?" I could just see his handsome face in my mind and wondered why he hadn't been in touch.

"I've been busy, had a few projects going on with my son, but am happy to say it's getting to be camp weather," he sounded upbeat. "I was wondering if I could convince you to come have dinner with me this week? You need to take a break now and then. You know what they say about all work and no play."

"Can I let you know, Brian? I don't mean to put you off, but I need to put my kids first, and I've been working so hard. . . " I thought about Jon and Katlyn's schedules and what had to be done over the weekend. "I asked Katlyn to squeeze in some Mom and horse time this weekend and promised Jon he could have a friend sleepover."

"Okay. Are you just playing hard to get?" he asked wryly. "Or not interested?"

"No, no. I'm being honest, and I'm tired," I told him, realizing that tears were welling up in my eyes.

"Okay then. Call me anytime," he said sweetly. "I'll be thinking of you. Keep kicking ass down there. You're doing a fantastic job."

Brad and Doug showed up to look at the "damage" Mayor Bezio was complaining of and laughed out loud. They told me not to worry, that they would call a meeting of the board and once again prevent Bud's interference from being an issue. I reminded them I was paying for that lift by the day and if I couldn't use it, the costs went up considerably, not to mention that it was preventing me from getting all the pictures I needed online and may prevent me from opening on my projected date of Memorial Day weekend. Meanwhile, I issued a notice and invoice to the Village, formally charging them with cost overruns due to his constant interference. I sent a copy to John Clute and the Village Offices, as well as showing it to Brad and Doug. They no sooner left when a truck pulled up from the NY Environmental Protection Agency. I was still standing on the sidewalk, getting ready to lock up for the day.

"Where's the oil spill?" the first of two uniformed men approached me.

"Pardon me?" I thought maybe I heard him wrong.

"The oil spill. We got a complaint from a Don Lorry that there's an environmental hazard here . . . some sort of an oil leak on the sidewalk," he spoke urgently, impatiently.

"I'm not sure what you mean," I replied. "I'm not aware of any oil leak."

"Have you been operating a lift truck here on the sidewalk?" The second man asked, flashing some sort of badge, looking up from the report in his hand. "It says the oil leak is the result of the operation of a lift truck used to paint the building."

"Seriously?" I could scarcely believe my ears. "Um, there is a tiny leak in the hydraulic line. We usually put a coffee can under it . . ."

"So there *is* a leak," the first man pounced.

"Well, I noticed yesterday that my helper forgot to put the can under it, so I had him get some kitty litter to soak it up." I felt my body tremble and my blood pressure rise. "Then, at the end of the day, I swept up the kitty litter and put it in the trash, and scrubbed down the sidewalk with TSP, before rinsing it off."

"Well, ma'am, that was the right thing to do," the second man answered calmly. "Can you show us where the leak was, please?"

"Sure," I pointed to the spot just three feet away, where there was no indication it had even happened since I cleaned it up. "Right there."

"Right where?" the first one asked. "I don't see anything."

"Exactly. That's why I am so surprised you're here. It was only about eight or ten inches wide to begin with, and I cleaned it up."

"Ma'am," the second gentleman looked at me intently. "Do you know who Don Lorry is?"

"Yes. He's my tenant, right there in the laundromat," I nodded toward the entrance.

"If I were you, I'd get rid of that tenant," he stated firmly, reaching out to shake my hand. "I wish everyone took care of things as well as you did yesterday. I'm really sorry we bothered you." I shook his hand weakly.

"I think we should pursue a false claim against Mr. Lorry," the first man spoke again, offering to shake my hand as well. "What kind of mean-spirited man gets us all the way up here from Albany for nothing but to harass his landlord?"

"Umm, I'm sorry for the trouble," I replied worriedly. *What is Don up to?*

Dave had stopped by while I was in the meeting with Brad and Doug. He hung around for a while, waiting to talk, but I told him I would call later. We talked on the phone and I filled him in, then asked about his day.

"Well, I just found out I gotta go for my two weeks drill duty next month," he informed me. "Gotta say, I'm kinda looking forward to it. Since I switched to the Vermont National Guard, I'm liking it a whole lot more. I even love the drive over there. It's beautiful."

"Yes, I was just talking with Nana today about how much I love it over there," I told him. "Less drama and more like home. But, you might miss our first concert on the river. What are the dates?"

"I leave on Friday the 13th, and I'll get back on Sunday the 29th," his drawl more evident than normal.

"Oh, no you won't miss it, then, unless you go to Montreal," I hadn't talked to him about his girlfriend in a couple of weeks. He had avoided the subject, so I did too.

"No, I don't think I will. I think if she wants to see me, she'll have to come down here, but" he paused and let out a deep breath. "I'm about over this relationship. It's always her way, her family, her plans, and I just see how much a taker she is. Always asking for money—don't get me wrong, I give it to her if she needs it, but I think she's takin' advantage of me."

"I've been wondering that for a while now, based on everything you've told me." I hoped he was receiving that statement the way it was intended.

"Yeah, well," he paused. "I guess sometimes I'm just too willing to let stuff go, and I need to learn the lesson . . . she's a lot like my first wife, and you know how that went. Anyways, when's the concert?"

"Memorial Day weekend, at the gazebo on the river, behind my building."

"I'll put it on my calendar, but I'll see ya plenty before then. You doing okay? You sound kind of tired," his voice softened.

"I am beat. Not even going to try and deny it," I replied. "In fact, I need to get off the phone and clean up the kitchen. I want to relax a bit tonight."

"Get some rest, Karen. You need to give yourself a break," he cautioned. "Good night."

The complexity of the situation I faced plagued me that night. I just couldn't comprehend what Don might be up to, and the Mayor's actions were distressing as well. I had stayed at the building until 1:00 A.M. and 3:00 A.M. refinishing floors two nights that week, and I was bushed. With the children reading, I sat down to read myself, and decided to have a glass of wine while unwinding. I must have only read about five paragraphs and had one or two sips of wine, when I fell asleep in my chair. The book in my lap slid off and knocked the wine glass over, but I was oblivious. At some point in the next half hour or so, Katlyn came in the living room to talk with me. Seeing me asleep in a chair, with spilled wine next to me, she thought maybe I was drunk. Well, I was woozy with fatigue and overwrought with stress, which I had tried desperately not to let them see. I tried so hard to be positive and to have enough energy for them and their needs, but I was burning out. I thought about all those years ago, when, as a child, I had seen both of my parents inebriated numerous times. I knew it didn't matter if I was or was not, in a child's limited perspective, things can be easily skewed. I vowed to try and get more sleep, and not upset my kids.

FIFTEEN

*Without risk, there is no reward, but sometimes
even with risk, there is no reward.*

"HELLO? HELLO?"

"Haha! We did it again!" Nana laughed into the phone. "Were you just calling me?"

"Yes! Were you calling me?" I giggled.

"We are so connected, you and I," she said. "My sweet Karen. We're always thinking alike."

"We are! How are you today? I was going to ask if you and Papa want to come for dinner and our concert on the river." I never tired of seeing them.

"I was calling to say it's supposed to be a beautiful weekend, why not pick us up at the ferry dock?" She laughed heartily again. "So, we *are* thinking alike!" We set our plans and caught up on what was going on with the Lorrys and the mayor. "Did they at least pay you rent?"

"Finally, yes, but not for the whole time they've been there. They claimed I had promised them the first month free in exchange for letting me into the building before closing. And they didn't pay the whole security deposit yet, but at least Carolyn finally signed the lease." I wasn't sure what to do about them, but since they ended up not selling the business, and the mayor had given me such troubles, I needed the money and knew that legally, finally having a lease was better than what I had been experiencing since February.

"That's too bad. I don't trust them," Nana replied soberly. "I wish you had a better tenant."

"So do I, but the fact is, a lease is enforceable—which is better than what I've had so far," I was confident that at least I was covered if they continued to play games. "I'm anxious for you to see all I've accomplished in the last couple of weeks since you've been here."

The night of the concert, Nana and Papa were obliged to go see my Aunt Shirley. She had been complaining that they were spending time with me, but not her, and she was only ten minutes away. I had invited her numerous times to join us for dinner, but she would rather be the hostess, and it seemed, she never included me. We had an enjoyable afternoon together, with Papa and Jonathan putting on the lawn, Katlyn, Nana, and I walked the horses, then we all enjoyed a barbeque, chatting, and even some game and snuggle time. Brian called to say he was coming to the concert and ask me to have a drink with him after or before. Jonathan made sleepover plans with a friend, and Katlyn went to a youth group activity. It seemed I was free to spend an evening with Brian after all. I had no excuses, but I was nervous.

I introduced him to Ericka and her husband, Ben, and we had a glass of wine at the bed and breakfast—with Ericka and I excitedly showing Brian and Ben all the changes of the past two weeks. As we sat on the balcony of the Adirondack Suite, the band assembled their gear below at the gazebo and a small crowd began to gather. I saw David walking toward the gazebo, realizing he must have gotten back together again with his girlfriend. They walked hand in hand, her daughter trailing a few steps behind.

"I am really impressed, Karen Marie," Brian smiled, sliding his arm around my waist, his eyes fixed on mine. "It looks like you could open tomorrow."

"Thank you. I am hoping to get my certificate of occupancy by mid-week," I replied, quivering under his gaze. "It'll be a couple weeks late, but that's not too bad, I guess. The rest of the work can be done as I am operating."

"I am so proud of her," Ericka chimed in, with her inimitable grin and encouraging tone. "If it wasn't for the mayor and the Lorrys, she'd have been open early!" Ben nodded, having been keenly aware.

"I couldn't have made such progress without great friends like Ericka, and a good crew," I replied.

"I told Karen Marie she needs a little fun—a night off from stress," Brian commented, sliding his hand up and down my back in a soothing manner. "So, let's leave the mayor and the Lorrys out of our conversation tonight." He winked at them, then looked back at me, dark eyes probing my face. I could just melt.

"Good idea," Ben replied, looking at his watch. "What do ya say we head down to the concert?"

I had folding chairs, but Brian brought a blanket. He spread it out, sat down, and patted the ground for me to sit next to him. I worried that I might be too vulnerable to be objective but relished his comfort. As he embraced me, I allowed myself to lean in and relax a bit. The sky was clear and getting dark, the stars appearing one by one, and music filled the air, accompanied by the rush of the river below. When the concert was over, Brian suggested we get a snack and talk for a while, so we headed back upstairs to the bed and breakfast inn. He poured us wine while I made us a plate of bruschetta and cheese, then we sat and talked about life. I knew a lot about him already, but I had the sense there was something I didn't know. I just couldn't put my finger on it. When he left that evening, he walked me to my car.

"Can I see you again?" he asked, pulling me to him with both of his muscle-bound arms.

"Yes," I answered. I blushed a little, then thought, *What's wrong with me? I'm a grown woman!*

"How about, I make you a nice dinner at my camp?" He looked down at me, then leaned forward, kissing my forehead and cheeks ever so gently, his strong hands caressing the small of my back. "Say, Friday night?" he whispered.

"I'm not sure about Friday," I said, enjoying his caresses, moving my arms up over his shoulders. "I will see what the kids' plans are . . . I didn't know you could cook." He laughed softly, pulling away just enough to look me long in the eyes.

"You're so adorable," he sighed. "I am full of surprises, my dear."

Wednesday came, and Phil O'Conner showed up to do the final inspection for my certificate of occupancy about two hours late. I couldn't understand why because I had seen him go into the laundromat an hour earlier. I was confident we were ready. Jeff showed up to go over any questions he might have. Gary and Julie hovered close by, nervous for me, but proud of their part, too. We all knew it should go well, but we had experienced so much dysfunction at the hands of the mayor, the Lorrys, and even Phil, anxiety was fitting. I walked him around as he went over his checklist. It seemed he was determined to find something to demerit me for.

"I may have changed my mind about the drop ladder..." he said as we got to the newly reinstalled fire escape hallway, emergency door, and ladder.

"What? You approved this already! I submitted plans, and I checked the codes for historic places." I tried not to be too incendiary, but my nerves were making that difficult.

"Well, I am goin' to have to check them again, just to be sure," he replied. I went to the cabinet in the kitchen where I kept a copy, retrieved the pertinent pages, and handed them to him. "I highlighted the pertinent part." He read for a minute.

"Okay, well . . ." he reached up, removing his ball cap long enough to scratch his head, then put it back in place, still looking at the copy. "But the door goes nowhere. It just drops."

"Yes, it's an emergency exit, with a ladder. You said it would be fine," I reminded him.

"I think you have to put a gate across the outside, something someone could unhinge and swing open in an emergency, but you don't want the liability of someone just stepping out into the air," he said.

I looked at Jeff, who had been listening in at the end of the hallway. "Can you do it this week?"

He came closer, looked at the codes, then engaged Phil in a little theoretical discussion. When they were finished, he looked at me again, and nodded. "So, Phil, I want your word that you will accept what he is proposing."

"I will make a note of it," Phil commented, looking down on me from his lofty stature. "As long as he does it the way we just discussed."

"Okay then, let's see if there's anything else you might want done so we don't have to go through this again. Bathrooms?" I began listing off the rooms and items on his checklist.

"Check, uh huh, yep," he grunted along.

"Okay, so the only thing you need to open the bed and breakfast portion is the gate at the emergency exit, right?" I queried, my paralegal brain kicking back into gear.

"It would seem that's it. Call me when it's done and I'll come right over." Phil smiled, then patted me on the head as if I was a little kid. "Good job."

Later, I ran into Renee Guyette at the Village Offices when I went to pay the water bill. The Village had participated in the closing in February, everyone was aware of the change in ownership, but for some reason, they never changed the water and sewer bills. All of a sudden, I was faced with a shut-off notice, and whopping invoice. It had been in Carolyn Lorry's name, and then crossed out in red ink, with my name written in. It was quite a tussle to get the clerk to separate the Lorry's hefty bill—due to the excessive usage at the laundromat—and mine. The inn wasn't even operational yet, so there was very little on mine. As the clerk rewrote the bills and entered information into the computer program, I sat next to Renee, eager to ask him why he changed his mind about my project.

"Because it's a set up," he replied somberly; so quietly I had to ask him to repeat himself. "You were set up," he said, looking at me as if to see if I believed him.

"What do you mean? How?" I asked, unable to grasp how that could be so. I had a legal closing, all but finished the project, and was set to open for business in just days.

"Bezio turned on ya, didn't he? And you still gotta deal with that snake, Lorry." His shoulders slumped forward, his head barely raised as he spoke. I watched as he clasped his gnarled hands, then just looked at me, appearing conscience stricken.

"Yes, but, all the paper work is legal, and the work's been done." I wondered if he was just a paranoid old man, or if there was something I didn't know. The clerk called me back to the counter to go over her changes. When I turned to leave, he was gone.

SIXTEEN

If you listen well enough, even people trying to deceive you will tell you the truth.

I TRIED NOT TO be impressed by the ominous status of Friday the thirteenth. I thought about how Phil O'Conner promised there was nothing more to be done, and the potential of a sweet relationship with Brian, who called me a couple of times a day since the previous weekend. We finalized our plans for dinner, citing my certificate of occupancy would be cause for celebration. Nana and Papa made plans to come over for brunch at the inn on Sunday, seeing as how it would be officially open, and some other friends had agreed to join us. David had stopped in every day, as per usual, and said his goodbyes for two weeks of drill. The phone was ringing and emails coming in; I even received my first deposit and reservation by mail with a check made payable to The Kingsland Inn Bed & Breakfast. I wanted to frame it rather than cash it. As I added finishing touches to each room or suite, I updated the pictures on the website, rewriting the room descriptions, too.

Julie expressed an interest in helping me with upkeep of the inn and working in the shop downstairs, which was now free of construction debris. It was looking more and more like an antique shop, with a cozy sitting area toward the back, in front of my new fireplace on a partition wall. I had reinstalled a window which the Lorrys previously had boarded up—it was a natural, see through barrier into my office, just beyond the partition. It swung open or closed on a hinge on the office side, for privacy. David had long ago run my phone lines and he and Gary moved the antique safe to an appropriate place, where I opened it, lined it with black velvet, and draped antique jewelry inside. Don Lorry hounded me about using his kiosk leftover from the emporium, but he never came and moved it when requested in previous months. Once I started using it, he sent me a bill for $2,000. I told him he had until the end of the week to get it out of my way.

Tom came and personally put up my window decals; since he had not paid me yet for the website work, we called it even. We owed each other about the same amount. Once I saw how small the sign was, I knew I had better come up with more for those enormous old storefront windows. I had set up a spot to sell Lake Champlain Chocolates and fresh flowers from an old Pepsi cooler Aunt Shirley had given me from her abortive restaurant and had been given a truck load of antiques on consignment from a dear old friend in Pennsylvania to help me kick things off. The downstairs was really taking shape, and Julie had been with me from the start. Her love of antiques and knowledge of the building, along with her understanding of how I wanted things run—first class—made her the perfect assistant for me. I was grateful for all she and Gary did and treated them like family.

Jeff finished the hinged gate on Thursday afternoon, but it was too late to reach Phil O'Conner. I left him a message, then called again first thing Friday morning.

"I can't get there until 3:00," he said on the phone. "I have other commitments today."

"Are you sure you can't squeeze me in any earlier? Will you be in town?" I wondered.

"Sorry, no. I'll be there at 3:00, sharp," he promised.

I knew I would have to run to school and pick Jonathan up before then, and that my first mortgage payment would be due in just a couple of days. I hoped he would just give me the certificate easily enough. I saw him go into the laundromat around 1:00, while I was on the phone in my shop. He was in there about ten minutes, then out again. I tried to get to him before he got in his vehicle but missed him. Three o'clock came, and I heard him trudging up the long stairs to the inn, as I stood in the kitchen waiting. Julie, Gary, Jon and I were washing dishes and putting them in cupboards.

"Hi Phil," I said as I went through the saloon doors to greet him in the hallway. "How are you?"

"Phew, I'm still not used to those stairs," he sighed. "Good. How are you?"

"Fine, thanks. I tried to catch you when you left the Lorrys earlier today. Is there an issue with the laundromat?" I asked, realizing if there was I should be made aware.

"No, it's one of their damn properties," he pulled his clipboard out and began filling in a form. "They're such slumlords, it's no wonder this place burned. Did you get the gate in?" We walked down the hallway, toward the emergency exit.

"Yes. We put it right here; now no one can access the emergency door without utilizing it."

"I thought it would be on the outside of the emergency door," he exclaimed.

"But Phil, that's impossible. The emergency door opens out. If someone wanted to open the emergency door, the gate would preclude them from doing so; the gate has to be on the inside," I told him emphatically. "I even put up a little sign."

He read it aloud. "'In event of emergency, open gate, grab drop ladder, use emergency door and ladder.' Well. I suppose that makes sense," he didn't seem too convinced. He tried the gate a few times, opened the door, noted the position of the emergency ladder, and repeated that scenario. Finally, he picked up his clipboard and started back toward the main hallway. "And you got your exit signs?"

"Exit signs? I have a diagram of exits in each hallway, but technically, I'm zoned residential," I told him with trepidation. "I don't need exit signs."

"Oh yes you do," his face got red. "Even if you're residential."

"Phil, I read the codes." I didn't want to upset him, but I felt he was just looking for something to be wrong or making stuff up.

"I am calling this mixed use, and I say there must be exit signs," he retorted gruffly.

"Okay then, I will run across the street and buy them right now. Anything else?" Gary and Julie stood nearby. When Gary heard my comment, he came into the hallway.

"How many?" he asked me. "Do they have to have arrows?"

"Phil? Gary is going to run and get them now. How many do you want me to have?" He mumbled and looked around, while I tried to be calm.

"Four. But they need to have the right colors, bright colors," he glared at Gary, who didn't notice since he was already grabbing Jon by the hand and heading down the stairs.

"Is everything else okay?" I asked.

"Well, if you put those up, then all I need is your electrician's certification and you're good to go." He began filling out the form again.

"Great. I gave you those a couple of weeks ago," I told him.

"No you didn't. I don't have 'em," he said, looking through the file.

"I did," I said, trying to curtail my frustration. I paused a minute, then continued. "I brought them by your office."

"Well, I don't have 'em," he repeated. "And I need originals."

"Yes, that's what I gave you—the originals." By now I was ready to burst into tears. By the time Gary and Jon came back with signs, I was digging through my drawer looking for a marker to put arrows on them.

"Well, you got your signs; let me see you put them up," Phil remarked. "I'll go double-check my office for those electrician's certificates and come right back."

But he still couldn't find them and would not accept my copies. I tried to call the electrician but had to leave a message. I didn't get my certificate to open, but I made an appointment for Monday to try again.

Brian picked me up at the inn, and we headed straight to his camp. It was my first time visiting that side of Butternut Pond, and there was still enough daylight to appreciate the quiet surroundings. Evergreens lined part of his lot and his camp neighbors were far enough away for some privacy. It was a tiny little thing but more than adequate, with an old kitchen, living area, two bedrooms and a bath. The best part was the huge outdoor patio with fire pit, from which you could see the pond clearly. We sat outside for a bit, while the sun still shone, and then he handed me a glass of wine and told me to relax, while he began dinner preparations. The way he talked about his cooking I was expecting something special so when I eventually meandered into the kitchen from the patio, I was entertained to see him furiously stirring a small pot of white rice and opening a bag of frozen mixed veggies.

"Can I help with anything?" I grinned.

"No, I've got this," he remarked. "Can I get you more wine? Do you like salad?"

"Love salad." I admired him as he grabbed a beer from the refrigerator, realizing he must work out a lot more than I thought. "I still have some wine, thanks."

We went back out to the patio where he grilled us a steak, chatting about his cooking skills, which he largely developed working as a fireman and being a single dad. Eventually, he declared it was time to eat. I assumed we'd eat outside, but he had set the little 60's style café table in the kitchen. I sat down as he held a chair out for me, then refilled my wine glass and grabbed himself another beer. We didn't talk much as we ate, which felt a bit awkward to me. Finally, as he pushed the last few bites around on his plate, he apologized for his silence and quick eating.

"I was starving," he remarked dramatically. "I didn't eat a whole lot for lunch and had a long workout today."

"How often do you work out?" I wondered aloud, picking at my iceberg lettuce topped with a tomato slice.

"Every day. What do you think? Does it show?" he winked and smiled broadly.

"Yes, it does," I told him honestly. "Does your son work out with you?"

"Most days, but now that he's eighteen, you know, there's sometimes better things to do . . . like chase girls." He laughed. "Seriously though, I'm on a campaign to stay healthy, but I also feel like there's just no way I can be forty-two years old. I want to stay young."

"I understand. I am approaching my fortieth birthday, and it seems like a milestone or something, one that seemed impossibly distant just a few years ago."

"You don't look like you're approaching forty," he exclaimed. "I guessed you were about thirty-four—was trying to figure out how old your kids were and do some math!"

"Thank you. That's kind of you to say," I wasn't sure if he was telling me the truth. "You don't look your age either."

"I mean it. I am really surprised," he said. "Do you think you might have more children in the future?"

"I doubt it. Why?" I thought his question strange.

"I want to have more kids eventually," he told me somberly. "I just feel like—I don't know. I know I'm getting older, but I always wanted to have more children." I studied his expression, wondering what deep thoughts lie beneath. "Enough of that for now. . . . Finished?" He pointed toward my plate.

"Yes, thank you. It was delicious," I said politely. "Let me help you clean up."

Clean up was quick and easy. Brian grabbed a box of matches and some candles, then motioned me to follow him back out to the patio. I admired the glow of sunset as he lit citronella candles and set them around, before I knew it he was standing by my side, arm around my waist.

"You are so beautiful," he whispered. "Are you enjoying the sunset?"

"Yes, I am, very much." I wrestled with my feelings about him, knowing how vulnerable I was. "Thanks again for dinner."

"My pleasure—and still my pleasure watching you enjoy my favorite place. It's great, isn't it?" Before I could answer, he sat himself on the patio wall in front of me and began kissing me. It had been so long. I felt wonderful. We kissed each other passionately until darkness embraced the earth. Then he led me by the hand inside. Grabbing a large candle with his other hand, he brought me to his bedroom, setting the candle on a bureau, he removed his polo shirt, and reached for me.

"I am falling in love with you, Karen Marie," he whispered, kissing my neck, caressing me. I thrilled at his touch. As I embraced him he scooped me up off the ground in a tight squeeze, head buried in my neck, pressing my waist so firmly against his body I felt his erection. He put me down again, pulling the clip out of my hair, burying his face in it as it fell to my shoulders, breathing deeply. "Mmm . . . you intoxicate me," he whispered again, stroking me, getting more intimate. I knew this was too soon, not right, but it had been years . . . and I was weak. He swept me up in both arms and sat me on his bed, placing his hands on the sides of my breasts. His eyes penetrating me with desire, he slowly lifted my shirt over my head, before removing his shorts. He looked like Adonis standing before me in the candlelight. I was overcome with longing.

Brian knelt in front of me, reaching around to unhook my bra, he nestled his face in between my breasts, kissing me gently, softly. Exploring me as if I were a hidden treasure.

"I have tried to imagine you, many times . . . your breasts are perfect," he panted, sliding onto the bed and pulling me to lay next to him. He ran his fingers, then his lips around my nipples so gently it made me quiver, catching my breath, which delighted him even more. Just as he moved to remove my shorts, I had the sudden realization I was making a huge mistake.

"Wait," I moaned as he kissed my neck some more. I felt his thick hair on my cheek. "Brian . . ."

"Is everything okay?" he asked in between kisses.

"Yes, but . . . no," I told him, so confused. I knew something was horribly wrong, but I didn't want to stop.

"Are you all right?" he looked me in the eyes, inches above my face.

"I don't want to mislead you. This could be wonderful, but—" I fumbled for strength and words. "I am not sure about us . . . and I don't want to hurt you."

"Sweetheart," he sighed. "If you don't want to hurt me, then let's continue."

"Brian, I like you a lot, but I am not sure I love you, and I don't want to use you." I thought about how we met at church and wondered about the depth of his convictions.

"If I'm consenting, you're not using me," he whispered with a slight laugh, kissing my forehead and cheek. "I'm willing to let you use me; it will be worth it."

SEVENTEEN

*When you have a close friend, you have a gift from God
that speaks into your life in loving, affirming ways.*

"WHAT WAS GOING ON with you last night?" Linda's voice had an unmistakable urgent, earnest tone. "You were on my mind all night, I was really praying hard for you."

"Well, thank you." I sighed. "I needed the prayers."

"Did you have dinner with Brian? How did it go? Honestly! I had some intense feelings that you needed support!" Though there were at least four hundred miles between my besties and me, I was so grateful for the ongoing connection.

"Yes, I had dinner with him, and yes," I exhaled deeply. "I had an intense decision to make. I mean—"

"Are you okay? Was he forceful, or—?"

"No, nothing like that, Lin. It's just, it's been so long and, well I'm vulnerable," I wasn't sure how much to tell her, only because I was still trying to sort it out myself. "But it was wonderful, and then, suddenly, I started to realize what it is I couldn't figure out about him."

"Was he pressuring you to have sex? What is it?" she wondered aloud.

"Well, a little but it is definitely a mutual attraction. Um, the thing is, I see . . . I guess I can see in him the unhealthy reasoning of lust—like I have seen before due to everything I went through with Bob."

"Ahhh," she sighed. "You are wiser."

"I hope so. I think he's wonderful in a lot of ways. And, he's certainly good looking," I shivered as his Adonis like image flashed in my mind's eye. "I could have easily given in, but I knew it would be wrong, on a couple of levels."

"I mean, it must be hard," Linda empathized. "No one would blame you, but you love so wholeheartedly, and we'd hate to see you—"

"Yeah. I know. I'm loyal to a fault."

"Yes!" she exclaimed. "It's a good thing sometimes, but—"

"Yeah, I know. But last night, well, I saw a glimpse of his reasoning and—it was more like lust than love. I can't go there, it's not the right reason to be with someone."

"I'm so proud of you, for what it's worth," Linda said. "I know you get lonely, I know you were lonely even when you were married, but like you said, if you're seeing that now, there's probably more to it. Trust your gut."

"I know, that's what I'm thinking, too," I was sorry I had to agree.

"Are you going to see him again? I mean, was he totally upset? How did—"

"He said he'd call me later. I guess the only way I will know if my instincts are right or if I'm just gun-shy is if I get to know him more. I just have to trust God to guide me." I gave myself to the idea as I spoke it.

"Well, was he a good cook at least?" she joked, trying to lighten the discussion.

"No!" I laughed.

Sunday came, and I went to the inn to prepare brunch, leaving Jon and Katlyn to do the morning horse chores until it was time to pick Nana and Papa up from the Port Kent ferry dock. I no sooner got there and began cracking eggs for my stuffed French toast batter when I heard the inn door open, and someone climbing the steps. Sticking my head out the saloon doors just as he reached the top, I was greeted by David.

"This is a surprise. Is everything okay?"

"Yeah, it's kinda embarrassing really," he shrugged and smiled. "I didn't pass the neck test, so they sent me home."

"The neck test?" I had never heard of such a thing, not that I was very familiar with the military.

"Yeah, they have you do all this physical fitness stuff, run two miles or more, so many push-ups, and they take your measurements—my neck is too fat!" He laughed. "Between that and the fact that I hurt my foot so I couldn't do the run—"

"You hurt your foot?" I interrupted.

"Yeah, nothin' serious, but I couldn't run, and the drill sergeant wasn't happy with me walking it." He sighed. "Well anyway, I guess my response was too civilian for him, and he offered me the chance to do a different two-week training. It's such nice weather, I took him up on it. Thought I'd come by and surprise you."

"Well, I am surprised." I wondered why he didn't go to Montreal and see his girlfriend.

"Are you open? Do you have guests?" Eagerness marked his brow. "I see you're getting ready to make breakfast, so—"

"Long story. Hopefully I can officially open tomorrow. Today I'm making brunch for Nana and Papa, the kids, and a couple of friends, care to join us?"

"I would love that! Can I help ya?" he smiled, looking about the kitchen. "Put me to work."

David got a lesson in grinding coffee beans and frying slab cut bacon, which he happily enjoyed. I appreciated his efforts and the conversation. Brunch lasted for two hours as we all sat around and talked. The kids got tired of the adult conversation after a while, so my friends and their kids left. Nana and Papa wanted to see David's Navy photography, so he dropped Jon and Katlyn off at home, picked up his album, then returned.

"I didn't realize you were an actual photographer," I told David as he went through an album seated between Nana and Papa. "I thought you meant it was a hobby."

"No, I was part of the official Naval photography pool. I covered all kinds of events, like for instance Nancy Reagan's visit to an aircraft carrier, which these pictures here are from." He flipped a few pages and held up the album for me to see over Nana's shoulder.

"That must have been exciting work," Nana commented. "Do you miss traveling? I bet you got to see the world."

"I do miss traveling a bit, but I don't miss Navy life. There are lots of places I'd like to go back to as a civilian," he replied thoughtfully. "I used to dream of taking my wife back with me to Spain, or even Madagascar, but you know, life gets complicated when you're not living on a sailing city at sea."

"Yes. Life doesn't always go the way we expect. Right, my Karen?" She winked at me, her beautiful face softly smiling, her perfectly styled, fading ginger hair matching her many freckles.

"What did you say?" Papa asked, trying to follow the conversation.

"She said 'life doesn't always go the way we expect,'" I said, facing him so he could watch my lips, enunciating clearly, and using a louder tone.

"That's true," he said. "But if it did, we might get bored!" We laughed, and he smiled, pleased to be a contributor to the conversation. I knew it must be hard for him to understand David's drawl, but Papa was genuinely interested in what he was saying, and in his pictures. After cleaning up, we went back to the house for a while to hang out with the kids, and David said his goodbyes.

"He's a nice guy," Nana told me, relaxing on the porch. "He's not the guy you had dinner with?"

"No. That was Brian. David is just a good friend." I thought about how well he got along with everyone earlier and smiled.

"Well, how did your dinner go? Do you like Brian?" she probed.

"Yes," I said with a sigh. "I do, but I am not sure about him. I am not in any hurry to jump into something I might regret."

"Good for you. It seems that you and David get along so well, maybe you should be dating him," Nana pointed out in the way only she could.

"Well, I thought we might date, when we first met, but then his old girlfriend came back into the picture, and we have just developed a really great friendship. We see each other just about every day, except some weekends." I thought about his contributions to my project, our good conversations and his encouragement. "I guess, if I could meet somebody more like him, I would be more willing to get involved in a dating relationship."

"I get the sense he's more interested in you than you think," she said quietly. "Where does his girlfriend live? Does he see her a lot?"

"In Montreal. He sees her a couple of times a month or so, but she calls him nonstop. It's like she hounds him, or something." Nana's comments brought to my mind the numerous times David had complained about her. "Maybe you're right, Nana. I don't know."

On Monday I got hold of the electrician, and he provided me with another certificate of electrical service. Phil O'Conner showed up, duly noted them, reviewed the signage, and once more going over the emergency exit, had no choice but to give me my certificate of occupancy. It was about a month later than I should have opened, but at least I was open. My mortgage payment for the building was due the same day. I paid it, barely, using rent proceeds. My first guests were due on Thursday, for the Adirondack Suite, so I was open just in time.

I furiously worked to promote my opening. We had another riverside concert planned, so I decided to advertise an open house the same day. As part of our ad campaign, we promoted a sidewalk sale of sorts for other local businesses. Ericka and I had put forth a request for businesses involved in REST to buy matching hanging baskets, which we coordinated pick up for, as well as to donate flowers to put in the always empty boxes on Front Street, the ones that held the trees. I sent out a notice to the Press Republican about my grand opening and the coordination of REST events. This proved fruitful since they sent a reporter to do a story on what I had begun in Keeseville. It ran on the front page of the business section and beyond, complete with pictures.

As business picked up, Don Lorry continued his antics. For example, he sat outside my entrance on the decorative benches, flanked by five-foot hibiscus trees, and told would-be guests that he heard my inn was dirty and full of cockroaches, as if he was doing them a friendly service. More than one guest informed me of this upon being pleasantly surprised and very satisfied with their stay. I had retained Al Burczak, a wonderful man and attorney who was also a friend of Ericka's to help me sort through the situation with the Village. He felt the Village should reimburse me for the cost overruns and intentional delays caused by the mayor, and Phil O'Conner as well. He set a meeting with the trustees, suggesting they issue a moratorium on my payments until that could all be evaluated and made right.

ABN AMRO continued to add interest to the late fees they charged on my home mortgage, racking up a delinquency, despite what Ms. Lester had assured me. Thus, though I was making payments, they were showing me as delinquent. I tried calling again, and this time was told that I had no authority to speak with them, and that the mortgage would go into foreclosure status unless I paid them an additional $6,000, some of which was for insurance escrow. I already had insurance and certainly didn't need more. I was incredulous, citing the documentation I had sent in repeatedly, and Bob's statement authorizing me to handle the account, let alone the divorce order. After many calls, I finally heard from Ms. Lester that Bob himself had withdrawn his statement, but if I could come up with $20,000 she could make the mortgage assumption happen right away. To say I was stressed out would be a huge understatement. Bob was behind in his alimony and support, by this time, roughly $10,000. I contacted the Department of Child Support Services and launched a case. I also contacted Bob again and told him he had better stop playing games and reauthorize me to speak with ABN. I shouldn't have needed to do that given the court documentation, and thankfully Ms. Lester worked with me, but the customer care department was clueless about the court order, preferring their own interpretation of their own rules, over what the justice system had provided for me.

EIGHTEEN

If you don't like being in the dark, you must welcome the light without dictating where it may cast shadows.

THE MONTHS PASSED QUICKLY for me. I saw Brian casually a few times; for example, dinner at Little Italy one night. He came to see me at the antique shop for lunch another day; he called me frequently, always asking if I needed his help with anything. Summer was in full swing, so I was busy with the bed and breakfast, and my children. I had decided to just get to know him and take things very slow.

August came and with the excessive heat that year, came the now infamous collapse of the power grid in the Northeast. Ontario, New York, parts of New England and parts of the Midwest were in the black. It happened in the afternoon, just after I checked a couple of guests in early and went home. I wasn't sure how long the outage would last, but I knew I didn't have many provisions at the inn for guests to be in the dark. As I wondered about the wide-ranging theories and news reports, I remembered Brian had mentioned a generator at camp if needed. I knew I had a generator for at least my refrigerator and a few appliances at home, but it was an old salvaged one from the former air force base that Bob had left in the basement. I had no idea how to work it. I tried to reach Brian for help, and to see if he could loan me his generator for the inn but had to leave a voicemail.

As it approached mid-afternoon, I got concerned at more reports the outage would not be restored for at least a day or two. Jon came with me to buy more candles and flashlights for the inn and discuss the situation with our guests. Katlyn had just begun working part time at Little Italy, right next door. Realizing food would spoil, yet I had people to feed, I put in another call to Brian, leaving a second message. We touched base with

Katlyn and our guests, who requested ice and a cooler. Promising to return with it, Jon and I headed home again.

"Mom, I think maybe I can help you with that generator," Jon said with authority beyond his years. "Let's see if we can get it outside and get it started."

"Jon, that's heavy, and I am not really sure it works, buddy," I told him. "Maybe I can borrow one from my friend."

"C'mon mom. We can figure it out," he told me earnestly.

We went to the basement, opening the door to let light in, we saw the old generator was still on a flat dolly. Wheeling it over to the doorway, we managed to get it over the frame and then outside in the daylight. I couldn't find directions anywhere, and I was pretty sure Bob had rigged the plug on his own, so I was afraid to use it. As we stood there, looking it over, Jon occasionally pulling on the start cord, David's car pulled into the driveway.

"You all right?" he asked, anxiously jumping out of the car.

"Yes? Why?" I asked curiously.

"I've been trying to reach you for hours—since the outage began," he walked up and high-fived Jon. "I tried calling both the house and the inn, no answer, but couldn't even get ya on your cell phone, either. So, I got worried."

"Oh, it must be because of the outage." I still didn't understand his anxiety. "What's wrong? Are you okay?"

"I'm fine. I've just been worried about you. I finally told my boss you might need my help and I left early. Figured with the inn being so new, and you having guests, plus the house and the horses," he let out a deep breath. "Well, Karen, I was worried about you."

"Oh, well, I'm sorry. Thank you." I saw the same gaze that appeared from time to time as we talked, like the first night we met, when he said goodbye.

"No need to be sorry, it's just," he blushed a little. "Just that I wanted to be sure you and Jon and Katlyn are okay. I was worried, so . . . what're you doing with this old thing?"

"I told Mom we could probably get this going for the refrigerator and stuff," Jon boasted. At that, David squatted and undertook thorough study of it, explaining to Jon how it's supposed to work, and why it might not, given the way it had been altered and unused for years. Jon was fascinated, hanging on his every word.

"I used to repair generators in my first station with the Army National Guard," he grinned, standing up again. "They were old things, but this here is ancient! So, what's Plan B?"

"Coolers and ice packs, I guess—for my guests anyway." I remembered I needed to get back to them. "Plenty of candles, too. We should be fine here if we don't open and close the refrigerator or freezer too much. I left a couple of messages for Brian about borrowing his generator for the inn."

"He hasn't called you yet?" Dave seemed shocked. "You'd think he'd be worried. Well, anyway, I'll help ya, and you got this great helper here," he winked, patting Jon on the shoulder.

"Yeah, Mom," Jon remarked proudly. "We got this!"

We set about collecting candles, flashlights, lanterns, buying lantern oil, more matches, and bags of ice. My guests were very understanding and commented at how romantic the evening would be. We brought Katlyn home with us, and David and Jon looked over the generator one more time, before deciding to help by grilling burgers for dinner. Katlyn got the horses in and I made us old fashioned potato packets and salad. After dinner, all were thrilled that the ice cream had to be eaten before it melted. Satisfied that he had done all he could for us, and instructing us to call him if needed, David gave me his usual goodbye hug with an unusual extra squeeze before leaving around 8:00 p.m. The kids and I hung out by candlelight in the living room, reading, and then decided to go to bed. Just as I was snuffing out candles, my phone rang.

"Hey! Are you in the dark? You should be seeing me more; I'll enlighten you." Brian sounded like he was only half- joking, but I wasn't up for it.

"Yes, like you, I assume." David's comment haunted me.

"Sorry I have been tied up all day. I could probably get you the generator tomorrow night if you still need it." He sounded sheepish.

"I hope this will be over by tomorrow night," I replied earnestly. "Or I stand to lose a lot. What's kept you so busy all day?"

He launched into a diatribe about some project he and his son took on as a side job, north of Beekmantown, but it didn't make a lot of sense to me, because the power was out there, too. As I listened, I caught myself thinking about how pleasant it was to have David around, and about the contrast between the two of them.

When we hung up, I went to bed, and wondered if things would be different had I let things continue that night at his camp. If that were so,

I didn't want to date him anymore. I hoped it wasn't true, but I prepared myself if it was.

The power outage lasted for us only another day, so we were much more fortunate than other areas. I was able to welcome my weekend guests and go forward.

I made my August mortgage payment to the village but received a citation from the code officer, Phil. He claimed I had too many things in the hallways, "impeding traffic flow." I didn't even know he had been in the building, but apparently Buck, my apartment tenant, had let him in. Now the hallways were at least six feet wide probably closer to seven, so they were not just for traffic flow. I had an antique Sheridan style cupboard on one end with souvenirs for guests, and on another wall, a narrow, high dry sink, of sorts, which contained leaflets of activities and local attractions for guests to take. Other than that, I had an umbrella stand, in the other hallway an antique spinning wheel given to me by Nana, and a couple of plants. There were pictures on the walls, but the walkway was still unobstructed by easily four and a half feet. When I notified Al, my attorney at the time, he told me to put a stop payment on my mortgage payment, notify my oversight committee and he would be setting up an emergency meeting with the board of trustees, so I did. I sent a letter to the village explaining and reminding them that they still had not paid my invoiced overruns.

Business picked up with each week I was open, and I was pleasantly surprised to find that my most expensive suite, The Adirondack, was also my most requested suite. David had been long scheduled to go on a two-week vacation with his girlfriend beginning Labor Day weekend, and my family of besties was due up for a visit then. To say I was looking forward to spending time with all of them would be a gross miscalculation. Indeed, when the time came, I was so happy to welcome them to the inn, and the kids took over the house, even setting up tents on the lawn. We had a fantastic weekend catching up, as usual. Their encouragement and pleasure at what I had accomplished since February buoyed me up, letting my hair down with safe people refreshed me. After several good chats about my not-so-existent love life, yet newfound contentment, I realized I was ready to permanently say goodbye to Brian. I also knew that if I was ever going to date seriously again, it would be because

I enjoyed someone's company as much as I enjoyed David's. The kids went back to school, and I turned my focus toward foliage tourism, and winter planning.

Just a couple of days after everyone went back to Pennsylvania, I was working in my shop office, and Julie was getting ready to leave for the day when David appeared at my window.

"Hi," he drawled, pushing the window open a bit.

"What are you doing here? Is everything all right?" He had only left a few days before, so I was sure something didn't go well.

"Yes, everything's fine." He looked very sober to me. "But, not really, I mean . . . I need to talk to you."

"What's up?" I presumed he had a fight with his girlfriend and readied myself to be a sounding board again.

"Actually," David looked around, seeing Gary come into the shop and Julie watching us curiously, tilting her head to listen in nonchalantly. "I need to talk to you in private."

My gut tightened. Instantaneously I felt my breathing become stifled. "Sure," I tried to let out a sigh, putting my paperwork down, I shut the window and went out around the doorway into the shop.

"Um, Julie is just about to leave—"

"I can stay a while longer if you two want to go up to the parlor," Julie smiled.

"I'll sit here an' keep her company," Gary chimed in, with a smirk on his face. "Go on up."

"Are you sure you don't mind?" I quizzed them, still wondering why I was suddenly nervous. I looked over at David who seemed more serious than I had ever seen him.

"We're fine; just go ahead," Julie reassured me. "You won't be interrupted up there."

"Thank ya'll," David said, as he ushered me toward the door. We silently went out, crossed to the inn entrance, then up the long stairs. As we reached the kitchen door, I turned toward him.

"Do you want some iced tea or something?" Instead of answering, he just looked in my eyes for several seconds, then reached out and hugged me, only this was not his usual hug. He didn't let go. After a minute, I pulled away, searching his face for some hint of what was going on in his mind. "What's wrong?"

"Nothing's wrong," he said. "I just, well . . . something has been wrong; I realized it when I went away."

"Did you and Sylvia quarrel?" I wondered aloud.

"No, not really. But . . ." He let out a deep sigh, still looking at me intently. "It was beautiful, and everywhere we went I kept thinking, *Karen Marie would love this*."

"Aw, that's so sweet of you," I told him, still uncertain of his message.

"And I would order stuff at a restaurant because you told me how much I would like it, then I would think, *Karen would love this*," he cleared his throat, and then reached for my hand, holding it lightly. "I found myself thinking of you when I was supposed to be trying to spend time with Sylvia. And I just realized, I don't love her. I enjoy being with you, talking with you, hanging out with your kids even. Life is short; I want to spend time with you."

The weight of his words hung in the air like a storm cloud on a humid day. I felt my heart pound as I thought about how I had recently decided I would much prefer a relationship with him, but he was unavailable to me, or so I thought. I could hardly speak in that moment.

"Imagine," he continued, filling the silence. "We have such good times together even doing stupid stuff like phone lines and dealing with power outages—we do all that without planning on being together and enjoy it. What about if we start plannin' on being together? Seeing each other intentionally?"

"I have to admit, I've wondered that myself lately," I confided. "I broke things off with Brian permanently because I realized I am getting more emotional fulfillment in our daily talks and time together. My relationship with him was not reciprocal, among other things."

"You did? You broke it off?" He was pleased. "He wasn't right for you. Just like Sylvia isn't right for me."

"Yeah, I did, just a few days ago, not that I've seen him much lately anyway." I finally let out a deep breath, relieved that the truth was out in the open. "You broke up with Sylvia for good?"

"Yes, an' she is blaming you, but I told her you're innocent—you don't even know how I feel about you." He grinned, "Until now, anyway. I want us to spend more time together, to be intentional about it. Do you want to?"

"Yes, David, I do," I smiled. He wrapped me in a big hug and kissed me on the cheek.

NINETEEN

Reason is not always accurate; it is frequently clouded by past negative experiences. To reason well, it is necessary to reconcile the past well.

DAVID AND I SAW each other every day, as usual, only more. He had already terminated his lease in Keeseville, in preparation for colder months soon approaching. Before he went on his curtailed vacation, he signed a lease on a cute little house near Saranac; it began October first. So, I helped him packing up his apartment a little here and there, and he spent most of his free time with me, or me and the kids. On one of his packing days, I approached his back door, just in time to see him throw out a box of videos.

"What's all this?" I queried. "Why are you throwing these out?"

"They're old, an' not good for me to have around," he nodded. "Remember I told you that when I was in the Navy I had a problem with porn? That was a long time ago, and I'm over it, but I found I had some old videos in with a box of movies I taped off HBO." His admission to previous use of porn, more than twenty years ago, was something he had told me one day during one of our earlier long talks. I was still determining how I felt about it; still watching him for other signs of addictive behavior, or lust, which I had become adept at recognizing. I hadn't seen any.

"Oh, well—" I wasn't sure what to say.

"Look, Karen," he said, taking my hand and leading me inside. "I know what you went through in the past, an' I'm tellin' you right now, I don't want to give you any reason to worry about that. I'm free of it, and I don't want to have anything around that might tempt me to get back into it."

"I appreciate that," I smiled weakly. "Honesty is important; you didn't have to tell me what they were, but you did. Thank you."

"I did have to tell you. It's only right," he said adamantly. "But, I worked too hard to be free of it. Remember I told you? When I was still in Tennessee, how I used to go walking every night with my Bible, and just talk to God?" I nodded, recalling how many times he told me since I'd known him. "Then I'd find a spot in the park to sit and read and pray; I learned so much. God really helped me, I didn't even have a desire for it anymore. I just kept gettin' closer to God in my heart and walking away from that life. It means a lot to me now to be free, besides having this relationship with you. I wanna do this the right way. I wanna be honorable toward you. You deserve that."

"Thank you, David," I watched him intently, knowing him well enough to know he was sincere.

Al and I met with the Village Board where Doug and Brad, my oversight committee, agreed with us insisting on a moratorium on my payments due to the delays and other problems the village caused. The resolution was passed and we all left the meeting, eager to put it behind us. I continued to send invoices monthly, adding interest as appropriate, so by now the total they owed was more than $28,000. My meager payment of about $1,000 per month seemed like nothing in comparison.

Phil O'Conner had set an appearance date for me to appear in the village court over his citation, but Al and I cited the codes and finally got him to see how ridiculous he was being; he withdrew the citation with no appearance. We also admonished him to stay out of my building without an invitation from me. "She passed inspection and is free to operate without you hounding her at every turn," Al told him. "Your job is not to go looking to make trouble for people."

ABN AMRO sent me a notice of foreclosure, even though I was still paying the mortgage on my home. I contacted my divorce lawyer and brought him up to date on what had transpired since Bob withdrew large sums of money from my account, which prompted him to respond to the letter, as well as write a letter to Evan Tracy regarding Bob's inappropriate and harmful conduct. He demanded that Bob finally provide me with the warranty deed he was required to pursuant to the divorce so that I could get on with refinancing.

Throughout this time, my kids were keeping me busy with soccer games and plays, and work activities. Katlyn wanted her learner's permit, and of course, she wanted to start dating. She was at an age where everything is an emotional drama or shrouded in secrecy. Life was busy, let alone the business. I purposely am leaving out the personal details of my children's struggles out of respect for their privacy, but being a single parent, with a not only non-existent, but harmful ex parent, is wearisome and sometimes feels like a losing battle.

One Friday afternoon David came by the shop looking sheepish and agitated. When I asked him what was wrong, he replied that he had heard from his former girlfriend, Sylvia. Her daughter had also written him an email, telling him how upset and sad she was that he had broken up with her mom.

"I feel bad," he said. "I mean, I've been there for her daughter for years now, and they both depend on me."

"Are you serious? If you want to get back together with her, then go. I'm not interested in fighting over this," I surprised myself at how calm I was, yet something in me knew where his heart really was. Instinctively I thought he was being played, once again, and that he still wasn't used to being free of codependency. It was easier to spot now, because I had come out of that trap, but I remembered how foreign it felt to walk away and how easily manipulated I had been for so long, too.

"But I thought you cared about our relationship?" he queried, shocked at my answer.

"I do. I care enough to know that I am not going to get into manipulative games with you, or Sylvia, for that matter. That's not good for either of us." I sighed. "I am interested in a healthy relationship, not another disaster."

"She wants me to go see her this weekend and talk about it," he said meekly. "She says it's the least I can do. Maybe she's right; I'm not sure."

"If you want to go, go. I am not standing in your way," I told him sincerely.

"I'm so confused," he sighed. "I'm not sure that's what I want. I'd rather stay here and spend time with you."

"Then why are you letting her manipulate you again?"

"Is that what she's doing?"

"I think so, yes." I watched him closely, confusion evident on his face. "Do you love her? Do you want to be with her? Then go."

"I don't think I love her. I just feel guilty for ditching our relationship on vacation and for leaving her daughter so sad." He folded his arms across his chest, squarely facing me. "Will you be upset if I go? Can we talk about it Sunday, when I come back?"

"No," I said emphatically, to the surprise of both of us. "I have never been the other woman, and I am not going to be her now."

"But . . . you are so supportive of me figuring out the truth, and I want to be with you, but I feel like I owe her something." Frustration evidenced in his tone.

"David, search your heart and see if that is just a guilt trip. Meanwhile, remember, I have been supportive as your friend, but this is different. It's not my fault you pursued two women at the same time; you can't have us both."

He was upset at my accusation that he pursued us at the same time—so upset that he said he would talk to me Sunday, he was going to Montreal, and left. However, an hour later, he called me and apologized. We spent some time hiking on Saturday, after getting guests checked into the inn. Sunday morning, he went to church with the kids and me.

The fall season went well at the inn, and come November, I had a letter from John Clute, on behalf of the Village, giving me some terms for the moratorium.

"Brad? This is KarenMarie," I spoke into the phone, trying not to sound too anxious or upset. "How are you? . . . Uh huh. Good. Well, the reason I'm calling is, did you know that John Clute is changing the terms of your resolution on my moratorium?"

"He can't do that," Brad said confidently. "We took a vote and it passed, with no special terms or conditions. It goes until next September, I think."

"Well, I know that when I was there with you and Al, and the rest of the board, there were no conditions, but now he is insisting that I pay what amounts to one and a half times what the payments would be, lump sum, for the moratorium to be official!" I exclaimed, still shaking since opening the letter.

"Get out! That's absurd," Brad remarked. "We didn't put any conditions on it. What does he want all that for, anyway?"

"Let's see, a year ahead in property taxes, escrow for insurance—which I've already paid separately—interest," I sighed. "Is Bud up to his old tricks again?"

"If he is, John shouldn't be helping him! We hauled him into the office in front of John months ago. John told him he'd better leave you alone because he was endangering the village of a lawsuit," he sighed. "Let me look into this and get back to you. Have you called Al yet?"

"He's my next call," I replied. "I'm getting ready to sue, even just for the invoice that hasn't been paid."

"I don't blame you, but, let me look into this some more. Relax," he said reassuringly. "We took a vote. Bud can't change it."

While I was dealing with unpleasant legalities, I also contacted Ms. Lester at ABN AMRO, and she ultimately put me in touch with a Linda Maas there. Ms. Maas had already initiated the foreclosure proceedings on my home, citing the back fees and interests constituted a valid default, despite the fact I was paying the mortgage. I explained how I had sent the payments in, Bob withdrew money unbeknownst to me, the checks bounced, so I sent in cashier's checks which kept being returned to me with the notation "You are not the mortgagor."

"That's absurd," she told me on the phone. "We don't care where the money comes from, as long as the mortgage gets paid."

"I tried to tell your customer service reps that repeatedly," I sighed heavily with exasperation. "They wouldn't listen. I even sent in the divorce documentation and a statement from my ex granting me permission—which I shouldn't need—to deal with the account. Now you're holding me responsible for ABN's mistakes!"

"I have a hard time believing this is so, I mean, we should've just accepted the payment," she replied.

"Forgive me, it's not personal, but your institution is too big; one hand doesn't know what the other is doing. I have personally handled foreclosures as a paralegal in Philadelphia and I have never seen anything so ridiculous as what I am experiencing with ABN right now."

"I'm sorry," she said tersely. "I will look at the history and notes and see what I can do."

"Please don't get off the phone without giving me your direct extension and assuring me that you are withdrawing the foreclosure action," I practically begged. The frustration and anxiety I was experiencing over ABN AMRO's abuses was a huge issue for me personally. She gave me her contact info, then told me she would not withdraw it, but put it on hold until she could determine the best thing to do after some research. I hung up and wrote a letter to the judge of record, Judge Dawson, who also happened to be the judge that finalized the divorce, just to cover myself. My divorce lawyer, Livingston Hatch, wanted another two thousand dollars to handle it for me, and since Bob owed me so much, I didn't have it. I copied him on the correspondence and believed reason should prevail. I knew if it had been me handling the case in my former capacity, it would have been a successful resolution, which lawyers and judges and mortgage departments are required to abide.

When David moved into his new place, he never even hooked up his large screen TV or his desktop computer. He literally went home after work, took a shower, then headed to my house or the inn. He helped Jon with homework, or projects, helped me cook dinner, do dishes, whatever needed to be done. He frequently stayed late as we discussed every issue imaginable after the kids went to bed and fell deeply in love. We had more than attraction; we had common interests, common goals, but also enough diversity to make each of us curious and interested in growing. It seemed reciprocal to me, what I always wanted. It was mutually satisfying. His biggest struggle seemed to be that he had always been in relationships with unhealthy, manipulative women. This translated into him expecting me to tell him what to do, when to do it, and being afraid he would do or say the wrong thing.

"Dave, I am not going to be like every other woman you've had a relationship with. I enjoy our relationship. I don't want to kill it by insisting on my way," I explained to him one night.

"I guess I need to get used to what it's like to have a healthy girlfriend," he replied. "It just seems too good to be true sometimes . . . like, I worry that one day I'm gonna wake up and discover you aren't happy with me 'cause I don't agree with you on something." He was dead serious.

"Well, then, that would not be love! Besides, if we agreed all the time our relationship would be boring. I respect your opinions, it doesn't mean I agree with all of them, but we seem to agree on the major things." I was sincere. He had recently awakened in me something I hadn't realized was dead: the ability to freely be myself and appreciate his delight at who that is.

"It sounds stupid, but—" he fumbled for the right words. "It's like, I've allowed myself to be manipulated for so long, it's a little intimidatin' to be free to choose—to be myself."

"I understand. I was so used to dysfunction, I married it," I laughed. "I had to learn to be free, even when there was no more cage around me."

TWENTY

*Don't give your problems permission
to keep you from enjoying love.*

IT TURNED OUT THAT after Doug and Brad, Al and I had left the village board meeting, Bud Bezio, the lone dissenter in the vote for a moratorium, beseeched the remaining Podunk trustees to change the moratorium to include the terms written about in Mr. Clute's letter. They took another vote, and it passed given there was only a quorum left, and they all as backwards as the mayor. Therefore, there were two votes on the moratorium; the choice was theirs which one they wanted to enforce. Brad and Doug were quite upset at the deceit and promised to work on their end. While Al and John Clute duked it out over that issue alone, he asked me to gather documentation, revenue and lost revenue data due to the village's tactics. I was beside myself with anxiety and wonder over whether this was some elaborate scheme, like Mr. Guyette had eluded to, or if these people were just that ignorant. Either way, the malfeasance was deeply disturbing, and calling them to account was not so easy.

Linda Maas got back to me and offered me a forbearance agreement on my home foreclosure action, provided I pay one and a half mortgage payments monthly, to "catch up." ABN AMRO was not budging on the fees they themselves racked up, let alone the interest. My only hope was to make the payments and speed up the process of collecting what Bob owed me. I had no choice but to agree. When the paperwork finally arrived about a month later, it was all wrong. It read as if Bob would be making the payments, had no mention of my name, let alone the facts being askew. I called the lawyers office from which it was sent—Fein, Such & Crane in Rochester. They insisted it was correct, take it or leave it. Frustrated beyond comprehension, I called Ms. Maas again. She told me to mark it up appropriately, send it to her and to the law firm. I did, then waited.

Meanwhile, I finally received the warranty deed from Evan Tracy, for Bob. The only problem was, it contained a lien covenant. The divorce decree and terms of our settlement agreement clearly stated Bob had to give me a clear title to our home; Evan Tracy thought it amusing when I called him, upset about the deed.

"Evan, you know as well as I do this is wrong," I told him calmly. "You can't pass a lien to me that is a debt rightfully belonging to Bob—which he agreed to accept in court, and the Judge affirmed."

"I can do whatever I want," he laughed snidely. "If you don't like it, take us to court."

"So, this is how it's going to be? What about the agreement of sale and warranty documents you owe me from my closing with the Lorrys? It's going on a year since closing."

"Sucks to be you!" He laughed and hung up the phone. That had me fuming; remembering painfully how Bob used to say the same thing, in the same way, whenever he had been abusive and unrepentant. *What is going on with these people?*

I was coming into the winter months and unsure how much business I would have since I was not as close to Whiteface Mountain as other area bed and breakfasts. As the large heating bills rolled in, I wondered if it was wise to even stay open. I knew it was not worth keeping the antique and gift shop open beyond Christmas, Keeseville didn't have enough traffic for it. I did host tea parties and other events, including private dinner and wine tastings, working with Ericka and Ben. Those generated some revenue and helped get the word out that the inn was beautiful, available for events, or friends and family of locals coming to visit the area.

"My Karen, I worry about you," Nana said sweetly. "You're under so much stress right now. It's just not right."

"I admit, it's stressful. I was thinking of just putting my house on the market, but the kids love it so much, and—I want that stability for them. I had an appraisal done. I only owe about $95,000 and it's worth at least $195,000. To me, if I can just hold the bank to account and get my money out of Bob, I will be fine." I sighed.

"It seems so wrong. To think of all you put up with for him, and now he does this nasty stuff," she paused and let out a sigh of disgust. "How are things going with David? Papa and I really like him." She looked at me soberly, and I knew she knew what I was thinking.

"Well, Nana, I am not telling a lot of people this, but," I said with a smile. "I am in love with him; I can't lie to you."

"I could tell," she winked at me. "And I'm happy about it. He's a really nice guy—it's obvious he loves you, and the kids, too. Do you think you'll get married? Is it hard dating him with the kids around?"

"Don't you think it might be a little too soon to get married?" I asked her, surprised that she was so open to the idea.

"No. You're forty years old, you've been around, been through a lot. You know what you want, I'm sure he does, too." She watched me intently, pushing her teacup aside. "Have you discussed it?"

"Actually, he brought it up a while ago. He was leaving one night and instead of saying goodbye, he told me he wanted to marry me. I was surprised, since he used to be against it, due to his first marriage more than ten years ago. Plus, we have only been seeing each other a few months or so." I searched her for wisdom.

"When you're older, that doesn't matter," she said matter-of-factly. "But you two have been good friends longer than that, and you spend a lot of time together. I think it's been quality time, right?"

"Yes, that's true."

"It must be hard to be dating with young kids at home, so much responsibility. If he wants to get married, do you?"

"I have to admit, I do." I paused before reaching for more tea. "I am just concerned about when, and the kids. More tea?" She nodded.

"Thanks, that's enough," she pulled her cup back and took a sip. "Mmm. That's good. Well, Babes, you've got a good head on your shoulders and I see how good you and David are together. I think at your age, you can do what you want, don't worry about the kids. They'll probably be happy about it. Papa and I will be."

"I know Jon would be thrilled and, I think Katlyn is warming up to the idea. But I don't want to saddle him with my problems, either," I confessed.

"Have you talked about that? Does he know all the details?" she inquired.

"Every little thing," I told her. "He's keenly aware. He goes through it with me day to day."

"Well, then he knows what he's getting into then and evidently, he loves you more."

"Yeah, I guess you're right. It's just—" I hadn't articulated it before, so finding the words was difficult. "I don't want him to think I am marrying him to have help dealing with my problems, either. He's always been in relationships with such needy, manipulative women, I want our relationship to be better than that."

"Babes, that's no reason *not* to marry him either. Marriage means you're accepting the difficulties together, and besides, I am sure he knows you aren't like that."

We eloped the night before Thanksgiving. It was a meaningful, sincere little formality of vows before our pastor and his wife, in the parlor of the inn. We stayed in the Adirondack Suite, and David insisted on preparing me a wonderful meal of pecan crusted salmon. It was delicious; the evening was romantic in every way. Nana and Papa took the kids to Burlington for the night, then onto New Hampshire to visit all the cousins and my parents; we joined them there two days later.

"Hello, Dad. Happy Belated Thanksgiving," I said, entering the family room where he sat watching the propane stove flicker. Papa sat nearby watching football, the grandchildren were rambunctiously playing in the snow visible out the bay window behind them. David followed me into the room.

"Hi," he said in his unmistakable drawl, a big grin on his face.

"Dad, I'd like you to meet my husband, David." The shock on his face was priceless. He stood to his feet, stretching out his hand to meet David's already outstretched arm.

"Did you just say 'husband'?"

"Yes, sir." David smiled, moving over to greet Papa, who by now was pushing himself out of the barker lounger. "Hi Papa."

"Well, David, hello!" Papa smiled as they hugged each other.

"Did you know about this, Dad?" Dick, my dad, asked Papa, still trying to comprehend the news.

"Know about what?" Papa asked, looking back and forth between David and me. I approached, hugging him and giving him a kiss on the cheek.

"David and I got married," I said looking him in the eyes and enunciating clearly so he was sure to understand. He grabbed my hand to see the wedding band, as a smile of recognition spread across his face.

"I had a hunch," he said to Dick. "I am very happy about it." He patted Dave on the shoulders and shook his hand again. "Welcome to the family."

"Thanks, Papa," Dave replied.

"So, I'm the last to know?" Dad asked, a little annoyed.

"Not really, you're one of the first to know," I told him. "We got married two nights ago. Nana kept our little secret, but she and Papa have gotten to know David a lot in the past year." As if on cue, Nana entered the room, followed by my mother.

"There they are!" Nana squealed with delight. "Kathy said you were here!" She hugged and kissed us both, then laughingly grabbed David's arm, still hanging on to me. "I already gave you my blessing and considered you part of the family, but now it's official!" She winked at him.

"Kathy, did you know about this?" Dad asked.

"I found out when they came in the door! Isn't it great?" Mom replied. "Why don't you open some champagne. I think there's some in the garage refrigerator." They both left the room.

"I would've loved to see Dick's face!" Nana said under her breath with an impish giggle.

"He certainly was shocked," I told her. "I hadn't anticipated the shock value, I was just happy to be free of the drama over our decision." I laughed.

"This was the best way," she said, patting my knee as she sat down next to me on the sofa. "We will all be ready when you have your public ceremony next year, and he won't be able to pull any last-minute stunts!"

"We just felt it would give us and the kids time to get used to being a family, without a lot of hype and scrutiny, but—you're right! That's a side benefit I hadn't thought of." David winked at me, then sat down next to Papa.

"C'mon, Papa," he said teasingly. "You weren't just a little surprised?"

"No, not really," Papa shook his head. "Just happy."

Dad returned holding a champagne bottle followed by Mom who had a tray of flutes and shrimp cocktail.

"Congratulations to the newlyweds!" Dad announced as the cork shot into the air.

TWENTY-ONE

Prayer can shake the heavens; mere men may move the earth.

THE FIRST EIGHT WEEKS of our marriage were blissful. When night fell, and the children were settled, David and I enjoyed romance like I had never experienced before. Because of the abuses I had suffered, and even the environment I was raised in at my parents' home, I had learned to accept as normal the transactional type of intimacy that was offered randomly, if ever, by Bob. I learned a lot through the process of his issues coming to the forefront; indeed, if I had not, I would never have come to understand that the very things I longed for were healthy and normal in a reciprocal relationship. David made regular eye contact; meaningful conversation was a part of our daily routine. We discussed and shared responsibility for everything from dishes to laundry to bills and family time. The seemingly simple things that take place outside the bedroom are an important aspect of what make a couples' time in their bedroom more intimate and mutually satisfying. The circumstances of our lives were far from perfect, but we strove to prefer one another when issues arose, and we took the time to explore each other's needs and desires. I felt myself healing gradually, pleasantly, like a tiny compact fiddlehead unfurls into a gracious and stately fern, pushing up from darkness into light. Our nights together were an oasis of inspiration and refreshment.

When we made our decision to elope, David wanted to put it off long enough to buy me a diamond ring first, but I assured him I didn't need him to spend the money on it. I felt that with all the money woes I had, there was no reason for him to spend money on a luxury item for me. Christmas Day, as we enjoyed our first holiday as a family, I was treated to a beautiful diamond ring, among other gifts under the tree.

"Karen," he said in front of the children. "I want you to know, and I want Katlyn and Jonathan to know, I am committed to you, and to our little family. This is the happiest, I've ever been in my life. I love you," he said, handing me a tiny box. Tears filled my eyes as I opened it, Katlyn and Jonathan looking on with smiles and giggles. "You deserve more than this, and I wish I could give it to you," David continued, tears welling up in his own eyes. "But I wanted you to have a symbol of my commitment to you, and Jon, and Katlyn. You are precious to me."

The ring was a diamond solitaire, like the diamond I had sold to obtain enough money to hire my divorce lawyer. It seemed to me that I had come full circle. I only looked forward to things improving, and other conflicts being resolved. Finding love at that stage of my life was awe inspiring, infusing more joy into everything I undertook.

In January, I turned the heat down to fifty degrees Fahrenheit at the inn, except of course for Buck's apartment, which was on a separate control. I also kept the heat at fifty degrees in the shop and office, bringing much of my work to the house for the winter. I had only a few reservations here and there, primarily for my two larger suites, Adirondack and Liberty. The Lorrys continued to operate, their space heated by a separate boiler. Buck had already fallen behind in his rent, and bounced a rent check on me, too. When asked about it, he claimed that the Village had messed up his paychecks. I had a car payment due, and the lack of funds scared David a little.

"David, all I can tell you is, it's owed to me, I've asked for it, and I have prayed for it." I watched his face as he listened to me. "I believe I will have that money in my hands by the end of the day."

"Karen, I have faith an' all, but how can you say you'll have it in your hands by the end of the day?" he stated with some exasperation. "I mean, I know Buck said he'd catch up, but what if he doesn't?"

"Then it will come from somewhere else," I told him, totally at peace. "Please don't worry. I know it will be fine."

"Well, I don't get paid until Friday and that would make your payment late," David replied, getting ready to leave for work.

"Don't worry." I set my coffee cup down, got up, and walked toward him. "It will all work out. I will have it by the end of the day."

"I wish I had that kind of peace," he said, buckling his belt and reaching out to embrace me. "You really aren't worried, are you?"

"I was worried a few days ago, then I began praying about it until I had peace." We kissed each other goodbye and he went to work.

Later on, as I went to the inn to prepare for incoming guests, turning up the heat, and filling the refrigerator, Buck approached me.

"Hey, Buck, how are you? I thought you'd be at work?"

"I'm on a lunch break," he said. "I will have your money for you at the end of the day. But I sure could use a few projects to offset rent next month."

"Well, you still owe for this month, as well as last month. I can't really afford to do anything in light of all that," I told him honestly. "In fact, I have a car payment due, but—if it snows, you can take on the job of shoveling, just keep in touch about it."

"Okay, then you can take it off the rent?" He looked pleased.

"Yes, but you say I'll have your back rent today?" I asked.

"Yeah, I should be back here around 5:00. Will you be around?" He looked about, realizing there were no guests.

"I will be here. We have guests checking in. I appreciate it, Buck. I really need that money today." I went back to the inn about 4:30, based on the estimated arrival time of my guests. David saw my Jeep out front and stopped on his way home from work.

"Anything new?" He asked, as he rounded the corner into the kitchen, reaching out to hug me.

"Well," I said and squeezed him tightly, smiling. "Our guests called; they will be here in about forty-five minutes, and Buck will be here with his back rent in about a half hour."

"Seriously? I'll believe it when I see him put it in your hand," he said somewhat sarcastically. "Don't get me wrong, I hope he keeps his word, but . . ." as he was speaking we heard the door open at the bottom of the staircase, so I pushed my finger to his lips, winking at him.

"Are you in here?" Buck pushed the saloon door open. "I knew you were here 'cause I saw your Jeep outside. Here's your rent—well, most of it." Buck produced a small wad of cash from his coat pocket.

"Hi, Buck, thank you," I said, as he counted out 450 dollars into my hand. "I will get you a receipt."

"Hi, Buck," David offered quietly. "How are ya doing?"

"Okay, just had some problems with my checks being wrong," he responded. I handed him a receipt.

"I noted the balance due, $350 for this month, and the late charge. If you pay by the 20th, I will eat the bounced check charge myself," I told him.

"Okay, I'll see what I can do," he said. He and David engaged in small talk about the village as my guests arrived a little early.

A couple of days later, I was bundled up working in the shop, when I heard and simultaneously felt a loud explosion which shook the entire building. Instinctively thinking it was an earthquake, I ran out in to the street. The Lorrys' employee, Nancy, also ran out into the street, yelling. As we walked toward each other, we looked about and realized no one else was alarmed.

"I thought it was another earthquake," Nancy exclaimed, referring to the one that rattled the region just a year or so before.

"Me, too! But, it seems we're the only ones who noticed." I walked toward Little Italy, Nancy following. They didn't feel anything, but said they heard a loud rumble. "Well, something happened, right, Nancy?"

"Two of us can't be crazy!" She laughed nervously.

Going back over to my own building, I decided to have a look around the basement. After checking everything below my portion, I grabbed a flashlight and went over to the 1707 side. As I rounded the further corner, there, to my amazement, the old boiler had exploded, exposing flames, white-hot brick, and bursting a water pipe. I grabbed my cell phone and called a plumber friend, Bruce, trying to find the kill switch as I spoke with him. I used a bucket to trap some of the water and douse it on the hot bricks, as I waited for him to arrive.

"Holy shit!" Bruce exclaimed, when he surveyed the debris. "You're damn lucky this is all that happened."

"Really? It scared me to death! I thought there had been an earthquake. It could've been worse?" I wondered.

"Yeah, I red-tagged this boiler a couple of years ago," Bruce told me as he surveyed the back side of what had been a boiler. "Told the Lorrys it had to be replaced or it would do some serious damage, plus, it's full of old asbestos. You should cover your nose and mouth. Here." He reached in his tool bag and pulled out a couple of masks, handing me one.

"Red-tagged?" I asked, putting the mask on.

"Yes. That means it's not fit for use. Once a boiler is red-tagged, it's a violation to try to fix it or use it."

"Seriously? What a sleaze—"

"You're just figuring out that Lorry is a sleaze bag? Someone should have warned you!" He laughed a little, then soberly turned from looking at the boiler pieces to face me. "What's the game plan?"

"Well, I am going to have to add the 1707 storefront to my main boiler, I guess." Still grappling with the red-tag topic, I tried to shift into the emergency at hand. This would mean there was no heat in the laundromat, and in January, when temps could easily fall below zero for several days or even weeks at a time, I had to act fast.

"That's a nice new boiler you got there. I bet you paid a pretty penny to have that installed, and all the new copper pipes you ran . . . nice work whoever did it for you," Bruce commented. He had worked on my home but was away during the time the boiler needed to be installed at the building.

"Yes, it cost me over twenty-two thousand all together, but it's a commercial boiler, and it can handle the load of the whole building. I knew it would eventually come to that," I told him. "Can you give me an estimate? How soon can you begin working on it?"

"Given how high the ceilings are in this place, and all the new plumbing you ran, I'd say that was probably a fair price. It's a top-notch job," Bruce took off his ball cap and scratched his head. "It's none of my business Karen Marie, but do you have it in writing that the Lorrys have to pay you for heat? 'Cause if you don't, it might be worthwhile to just put in another small boiler here."

"Yes, I have it in the lease. Thanks for your concern, but I actually also have it in the lease that they have to pay for the cost of hooking them up to my boiler, in addition to heat." I knew getting them to actually do so might be an issue, but the lease was drafted by their own lawyer, Evan Tracy, so they shouldn't complain. "That's why I want the estimate ASAP. Would it cost a lot more to add a new boiler? I don't think it's worth it if so."

"Yes, you're looking at thousands more if you put in another boiler, but," he paused for a second, looking at the distance from the main boiler through the doorways. "Yeah, lots more. You're going to have some long runs here, but everything else is new, and why pay for another boiler when you have that big commercial one?"

"Okay then, I will notify them of the cost as soon as I have your estimate, and then let me know how soon you can get it started. Meanwhile, I'll have to get some electric heaters in there fast."

TWENTY-TWO

Being wronged does not relieve me of the obligation to do right.

THE LORRYS WERE NOT happy about the boiler. Don insisted he had a plumber that would fix it. "You cannot fix what has been blown to smithereens," I told him. I also rebuked him for removing the red tag and using it, then lying to me about it before our closing. Of course, I put all of this in writing, and sent copies to Evan Tracy, along with the estimate for adding them to my main boiler, requesting payment and giving them an amount payable for heat beginning immediately upon completion. Bruce began the work the next day, and the Lorrys balked at the expense of electrical heat in the meantime.

When I first took electrical heaters into the laundromat, I made sure to position them close to the pipes going up to the inn, and any water pipes. While Nancy was there, this was not a problem. She was happy to have the heat as the temperature had been dropping steadily. In the process, I noticed the back window open about six inches, despite the subzero temperatures outside. I also noted a hole in the brick wall, perfectly rounded, and only stuffed with a tiny piece of insulation, just six inches from my copper pipes heading into the Adirondack Suite above. I stuffed in more insulation, then covered it with plastic and duct tape for the time being, making a note to get it repaired. Going in and out of there so often during the lack of heat, I kept noticing things the Lorrys had promised to take care of in exchange for a lower rent payment which had not been even begun. I also placed a couple of thermometers around to keep track of the temperature.

We got a lot of snow that day, and the next, followed by screaming sunshine and cold. It was beautiful out. Bruce continued the work on the heat; the Lorrys had not paid me a dime yet. I went into the laundromat daily to check on things, making note of the temps, but each time, the heaters had been moved. I went back to the rear of the place again, behind the dryers, and each time the window was open, and my plastic and duct tape had been removed. I finally left Don a note about it, asking him to leave the heaters in place, and keep the window closed. Nancy claimed that he told her to open the window so the dryers would work more efficiently. When I asked about the hole in the wall, she had no idea. I decided I had better bundle up and work in the shop for a few days, so I could let Bruce in and out, and keep an eye on what the Lorrys were up to. It turned out, that was a good decision, since the next day Nancy came to see me about water coming down from the ceiling.

"It's coming from the back, over the dryers," she blurted out. "What's up there?"

"My Adirondack Suite," I told her, grabbing my keys and heading out the door. As I went into the suite everything looked normal, until I got into the bedroom. Water was pouring into the room from the ceiling, running down the walls, which were blistered with giant water bubbles. A pool of water lay on the floor, and beyond, I noticed a mound of ice outside the French doors. "Oh, my God!" I wailed, reaching for my cellphone. "Can things get any worse?"

The Lorrys had moved their commercial dryer vent to a downward position with an elbow-type cap, facing the metal roof they put on. It had been piled with snow over night, but when they started up the dryers in the morning, it melted the snow. When it cooled again, when the dryers were not running, it created ice jams in places. The whole process repeated itself daily. Later, I would discover that the roof had not been properly put down either. There was not enough overlap, and frequent gaps, let alone a lack of base, or proper screw technique used. It was an amateur job.

I began the process of cleaning up and drying, setting a couple of fans in the room, and turning up the heat. I also notified the Lorrys they had to reposition their dryer vent, with very explicit direction to vent away from the building, and away from the roof. They claimed to have done so, and night fell before I could verify, but I thanked them anyway. I had Buck chip away at the ice and asked him to try and keep the roof free of snow there.

The next morning, I went upstairs to check on the progress of drying, only to discover the same problem, only this time, whole sections of the ceiling had fallen, saturated, and the size of the blisters in the walls were two or three feet across. I cried. The new floor also blistered and peeled in places, and there was water everywhere. My best suite, the one everyone wanted to stay in, the one that was helping me pay the winter bills, was destroyed.

I wrote to Evan Tracy and the Lorrys once again. A reputable local contractor had given me his report of damages, saying the sole cause was the faulty roof combined with the improper use of the commercial dryer vents. I demanded the agreement of sale which contained the warranty document, yet again, and noted that regardless, the village attorney, Mr. Clute, only authorized the closing given their promise to execute it. I reiterated my demand for the costs of plumbing and heating, cited that the boiler had been red-tagged, and therefore the Lorrys were in violation of several provisions of our contracts.

Once again, I had to ask them to move their dryer vent, since they had positioned it higher up on the roof, but still facing downward creating ice and water damage. Having done all of that, I went to drop off a copy and check on the heat and status of things in the laundromat. I tried to access it from inside the building, where I had installed French doors between 1707 and 1709 (my shop), I couldn't. The doors wouldn't budge. Checking the lock, I tried again. Finally peering through one of the panes of glass I noted a bicycle chain wrapped around the handles with a padlock. *What are they up to now?*

I went outside to access through the front, where I was met by Nancy. "Don doesn't want you in here," she stated in a hushed tone.

"What are you talking about? I'm the landlord! I am paying to provide heat here, and need to inspect the damages they're causing," I retorted. "Where are they?"

"They're getting ready to go to Florida," she replied. "I think they leave tomorrow."

"Well they better not leave without paying me," I said, pushing past her to inspect the rear of the premises again. "Did you have more water in here this morning?"

"Yeah, about an hour after I got started for the day, it started coming down," she said. "What happened?"

"The dryer vents are creating ice flows and the roof is not sound," I noticed the back window open again, and a hand-written sign taped to the window saying, "Do not close window." Then I felt the pipes near the round hole in the wall, since now even the insulation had been removed. They were very cold. "Nancy, did Don put this sign up?"

"Yeah, he was pretty mad when he did, too."

"Why did you move the heaters? Why is this one unplugged?" I asked, seeing the one by the back pipes wasn't even being used. I looked for the thermometer but couldn't find it.

"Don said he ain't paying for too much electricity. He said if the dryers are working, there's plenty of heat, excepting the front," she told me in confidence, nervously.

"Did he tell you to close the window when the dryers aren't running?"

"Nope. But this dryer stopped workin' this morning after the water started comin' down," she said.

"Did he tell you to put the heaters back on when the dryers are not running, or at the end of the day?" I queried, making mental notes of her responses.

"No. He told me not to touch them," she responded sheepishly, obviously aware that Don would be unhappy if he knew she was discussing the issues with me. "When will we be hooked up to your boiler?"

"By the end of tomorrow, I think." I wondered about their impending departure, knowing well that they take two to three months in Florida every winter. I took some pictures and wrote another letter about what they owed me, as well as the fact that they could not lock me out while I was trying to provide them with permanent heat. Obviously, Don had been slipping in and out unnoticed, so I knew he would get it if I left it for him. I went next door to work on it, and after a couple of hours of phone calls, documentation, and referring to the lease, I went back outside to approach 1707 from the street. This time, I was met with a locked door, and another hand-written sign. "Closed due to lack of heat. Temperature inside only 42 degrees."

They had never given me a key to 1707. I owned it, but try as I might, they always had a reason. One time, they had left the extras at home, another, when I said I would take it across the street and make a copy, they were just about to lock up for the day—late for a doctor's appointment. There was always some excuse. At first, it seemed harmless, and eventually I had forgotten about it since I could access it from the inside. However now, I called Al. He wasn't so sure I could have the locks changed legally and wanted to review the lease first. I worried about the unplugged heaters and the outside temperatures, as well as that open window. I went around to the back of the building. Sure enough, the window was open, and the portico over the back door had all but fallen off due to a giant ice wedge that had formed from the dryer vent fiasco. There was a massive cascade of ice from the top of the building, all the way down. It strained electrical wires and threatened more damage.

TWENTY-THREE

It is helpful not to make the same mistake twice, but it is far more important not to make a loved one pay for the mistakes of a past lover.

WE GOT THE CALL on a Tuesday night. When I answered the phone, I knew it had to be serious; the man on the other end identified himself as Staff Sargent Miller. I anxiously watched Dave's expressions as he listened.

"Mmhmm . . . I see." His expression was not one I had seen before. "Yes, sir. So, you say . . . mmhmm. Yeah. When? Yes, sir. Okay. Thank you. Goodbye." He hung up the phone and let out a huge breath.

"What's going on, honey?" I continued to watch him, noticing a sadness take over his features.

"We're going to be put on alert for active duty," he said soberly, pulling me toward him. "He wants to give everyone as early notice as possible, but it's not official yet."

"Where? Iraq?" Numerous thoughts bombarded my mind, my nerves trembled, and my heart ached.

"Yes, Iraq. The 42nd Infantry is being called up," he gazed at me, solemnly, lovingly. "Sometime in the next thirty days, we'll know more."

"So, it's official? I mean, you are definitely going?" I was still learning the way things got done in the military and secretly wished Dave would give up the Guard when we began talking of marriage.

"No, it's not official," he touched my face, then squeezed me tightly. "It might not happen, but it looks like it will. Don't worry about it, okay? We'll take it as it comes."

But I did worry. It seemed we finally had what we both wanted, the kids were settling into our new family routines and enjoying David, too, and now all of it was threatened. It hadn't even been three months yet.

I know it bothered him because he was a little edgier at times than he had ever been. He kept making comments about how the Lorrys were causing me so much trouble and how bad things were for me, so he needed to be home and help me. Bob had stopped paying alimony again when he found out David and I got married, although under the terms of our divorce, he was to pay for five years, regardless. I hadn't spoken to him or seen him in so long, I was shocked to discover that he had been telling mutual friends he was going to 'win' me 'back', and that he was 'working on' himself so he could get me 'back.' He was so humiliated and embarrassed that I got married while he persisted in his dramatic claims—claims I am sure were meant only to derive pity from others and cover up his alternate lifestyle—he also had stopped paying child support again. The money he owed me, including his portion of medical expenses for the kids, hurt as much as what the Lorrys were up to. These things ate away at David and were exacerbated by his impending active duty.

One evening when Katlyn was behaving like sixteen-year-olds sometimes do, he snapped at her not to speak to me so disrespectfully. She retorted, "You're not my father! Stay out of it!" He cracked, yelling at her, finger pointing, "In my day, kids didn't speak to their parents like that unless they wanted a whoopin'!" I nervously tried to calm them both down.

"Okay, Katlyn, he's right, you're being disrespectful, but Dave—" I turned toward him, pleading. "Let me handle it, okay?"

"No, Karen! I've had it with how she talks to you! It's not right!" He yelled. I moved toward him, attempting to calm him by stroking his arm. I could see his face getting red and an anger that was unequal to the violation.

"Dave, calm down, okay?" He reached out, grabbing me by the shoulders and neck, shaking me.

"No! Don't try to sweet talk me! You let her get away with too much!" he yelled. Katlyn started screaming at him.

"Let go of my mother!" Jon could hardly believe what he was seeing.

Suddenly Dave released his grip. "Oh, my God! What have I done? I cannot believe . . ." He shook his head, still angry, but now, more so at himself. "Look what you made me do; just look what you made me do." He said soberly. "I'm sorry. I'm so sorry."

The evening was heavy as we all digested what transpired. I am sure the kids and I were dealing with post-traumatic stress still. This episode was hard for us to process, but it was also hard for Dave. For the first time, the things he told me about his abusive step-father seemed to me to be causing him traumatic stress, too. I wasn't sure if it was just that episode that embarrassed him or what, but he stopped making eye contact and our evenings became dull. I spoke with him about it, also about owning his behavior without accusing one of us of "making" him act that way. He wasn't as receptive and open as he had always been; it troubled me.

A few days later, I was at the inn trying to make repairs, and David showed up. It was only 10:30 a.m., so I knew something must be very wrong.

"Hey. What's going on? Why are you not at work?" I asked him, washing my hands and putting some water on for hot tea.

"Honey, I—" he looked at me, then down at the floor, for a few seconds. Finally, he picked up his head and looked me square in the eyes. "I need to talk to you. I have a confession to make." My heart skipped a beat. "Let's sit down, okay?" He led me into the parlor, where I sat on the couch. He got down on one knee in front of me, making constant eye contact. "I screwed up. I need to apologize. I did something I should never had done, and I already took action to be sure I don't do it again, but I have to tell you about it."

"What does this have to do with why you're not at work?" I asked, bewildered.

"I looked at porn at work, twice in the past few days. All the stress, well—the stress has gotten to me, but I shouldn't have done it." My mouth went dry and my heart pounded as I thought about all that porn had cost my kids and me in the past. "I've been suspended for a week without pay. I found out this mornin' that someone saw me and told my boss. He went to bat for me, so instead of losing my job, I got a week's suspension." He watched me; I'm sure I looked like I had been dragged out in the street and run over by a truck. "I am so sorry. I sinned against you and against God. I knew it. I went to see Pastor first thing, right from work. I'm goin' to be meetin' with him once or twice a week for a while, to help me deal with stress better. Can you forgive me? Are you mad at me? Are ya hurt?"

The raging conflict in my heart and mind at that moment was so intense, I could scarcely remain seated. I wanted to call off the whole marriage and run away from him. I wanted to erase the stress and give our relationship the best chance possible for success. I wanted to hold it against him and stop planning the ceremony. I wanted to forgive him but didn't know if I had the strength to face this demon once again. The pain of his confession was palpable in my very being. Voices of past trauma and regret, sorrow and loss shouted in my head, urging me to leave him. *I have been deceived again. It will never get better. Get out now.* But I loved him dearly. He loved me at least enough to own it, to go for help, and to ask for my forgiveness.

"Karen?" He looked at me with fear in his eyes. "Can you forgive me? I was so wrong. I love you, and . . . I am so sorry."

"I forgive you." I mouthed the words but didn't feel them in my heart. They were propelled by my will, that part of me that knew how dangerous unforgiveness is to me, to us. "I am not sure how I will get over this, honestly. You just set my trust in you back a very long way."

"I know, I know," he whispered, sliding up next to me on the couch. "I deserve that. I will work to overcome it, I promise."

"I—" I felt tears welling up in my eyes and a lump rise in my throat. "I want to say that I forgive you, but, this is a struggle for me. I will have to keep on forgiving, I think. I am very angry."

"I understand. I appreciate you. I know this is hard for you," he said, wrapping his arm around my shoulder. "I expected you would handle it much worse. Thank you for trying so hard."

"David, I love you. But I hate porn, and I hate lies. I hate it when we don't communicate." I thought about what brought this on and wondered how long he had really been free of porn. I knew that for some, it is a lifelong struggle, while others seem to overcome it and live above the temptation easily. Knowing how emotionally driven he could be at times, I worried that he would always be tempted; that it would always be a battle. "Promise me you'll find better ways to cope with stress? That we'll communicate through all this?"

"I promise. I wouldn't blame you if you wanted to throw me out. I love you, and I will fight to do this right."

He met with our pastor several times that week and began reading books that were geared toward helping him crawl out from under the hideous shadow of porn and all its entanglements. He also helped me repair the Adirondack Suite so that it could be used again. The lack of his week's salary hurt even more, but we managed to make the one and a half payment to ABN AMRO and squeak by. I was just getting by emotionally also. I found myself holding back from him, leery of his intentions, and easily offended. I knew I had to shake it, that part of it was my own post-traumatic stress. I didn't want him to pay for the pain Bob had put me through, but I also knew I had to be wiser and inspect what I was expecting from him in terms of progress.

TWENTY-FOUR

*Justice should never be wrought through illicit means,
for then it would cease to be justice.*

I MET KAT SMITH in December, before the whole debacle of ruin and being locked out of the laundromat. She approached me early in the month because she had been in negotiations with the Lorrys to buy the laundromat. Based on my experiences with them, she opted not to go forward with the deal right away. She was shocked to learn of the way they conducted themselves and decided to do more research on what their business was worth. She also began stopping by frequently and engaging with the agenda Ericka and I set for REST. We quickly became friends as she helped with various REST community projects. In March, when it became apparent I would have to evict the Lorrys, she reignited her hopes of starting a business in the 1707 space. It was extremely encouraging to me to have another tenant lined up, as I dealt with evicting them.

 I filed the paperwork in the Village court after consulting with Al. He insisted it should be a slam dunk eviction, saying once I had a profitable tenant in the space, then I could pursue the Lorrys for the excessive damages—now more than $36,000 in back rents, heating expenses, and physical damages—in the Essex County Supreme Court. He told me that with my paralegal background it should be a piece of cake for me to handle that part myself, then he would get involved at the Supreme Court level of activity. I paid the twenty-dollar fee to the court clerk and filled out the paperwork.

 A few days later, I got a call from the clerk, Kay Rock, asking me to come down to the court and see one of the village justices, George Head. I asked if she was also contacting the Lorrys or their attorney, to which she replied that the justice wanted to see me alone. I explained that was a violation and declined to go. A couple of days later, I got a call from Justice Head himself, insisting that I go see him in chambers. Confused, and aware that this was very unorthodox, I agreed to go because I didn't think I had a choice.

"Hello, Judge Head. You asked to see me," I said entering his chambers as I had been directed. I wasn't even sure I should call him "judge" since technically, the small town and village justices in New York are elected officials; barely any of the 1,970 of them statewide are even legally trained. At best, they receive a few days of training at the Office of Court Administration and a handbook. He rose from his chair slightly, reaching over his desk to shake my hand.

"Have a seat," he said, pointing to the chair opposite him. "I understand you're having difficulties with the Lorrys. I see your paperwork."

"Yes, but I'm not sure why I'm here," I stated honestly. "When I had issues with Mayor Bezio last year and filed a claim against him and the Village, you forwarded that to the Village Attorney rather than transfer it to a better jurisdiction. I still haven't got a resolution on that issue, although I confess my legal experience is not in New York state."

"Yes, well, he hasn't bothered you since, right? I mean, Mr. Clute and I made it perfectly clear he was to leave you alone, what else is there?" He asked pointedly, his eyes narrowing as he put his elbows on the desk and folded his hands in front of him.

"There's the matter of damages," I stated politely. "Which, at the time were only $5,000—enough to be heard in a village court, whereas now, the damages are in excess of $30,000."

"But he's left you alone, right?" He asked again.

"In a manner of speaking, yes."

"Good. The reason I asked you here today is to discuss the Lorrys." He leaned back in his chair, moving his elbows to the arm rests as the chair squeaked under his weight. "I know about the Lorrys; they are your commercial tenants, right?"

"Yes, sir, they are," I answered, still not sure how this could be a legal discussion without them or their lawyer present.

"Well, when you have a commercial tenant, you have bigger issues," he announced like a sports commentator. "And when you're dealing with the Lorrys you're dealing with bigger pains in the ass."

Before I could stop myself, I laughed out loud. "With all due respect, you're not telling me anything I don't know!"

"Well, in this case, I think there's a better way to deal with this pain in the ass than most," he said with a chuckle. "I put in a call to Judge Dawson, down at Essex County Supreme Court, I want you to follow up with him personally. It would be best if you ask him what he would like to do about this situation."

"Judge, I'm not sure that it would be appropriate—"

"Just trust me on this one," he said, leaning forward again, looking me straight in the eyes. "I think the case should be transferred to his court and, well sometimes you have to help the system along a little." He paused and winked, but it didn't seem to me a friendly wink. "Tell Jim Dawson I told you to call. Tell him what I said."

"What about my court date?" I queried.

"I can move it back a week," he said quickly. "That'll give us some time to deal with the ass pains you're having."

I was more than confused at his recommendation. Something like this would never happen in my past legal experience. I was not sure the current situation rose to the level of such *ex parte* communications, but, I also knew I was desperate to get relief. I put my request in writing to Judge James Dawson, outlining the advice of Justice Head and seeking his recommendation to transfer the case to his own court. When I had heard nothing from him a week later, I contacted his office. Upon hearing that Justice Head had urged me to contact him, his secretary immediately put me through.

"Good afternoon, Judge Dawson. Thank you for taking my call," I stated professionally. "I am contacting you based upon the request of Judge Head that I do so."

"Oh? Okay, well what is this about?" he asked brusquely.

"Well, sir, I wrote you a letter about a week ago regarding a case I filed in the Village of Keeseville Court against Donald and Carolyn Lorry. Judge Head suggested that you may want to handle the case personally given the amount in controversy is already in excess of the village court threshold, even though I am seeking an immediate eviction."

"The Lorrys? They're your tenants?" he asked.

"Commercial tenants, sir. Yes. They've caused severe damages and are not paying rents and charges under the lease. Judge Head felt the case should be transferred to your court *sua sponte*."

"George Head said that, did he? The damn fool!" With that he hung up the phone.

I sat stunned for a moment, trying to grasp what might be happening behind the scenes. Why would he be upset with Judge Head over a request like that? I had no idea. After a few minutes, I contacted Kay, Judge Head's clerk, to inform her that the hearing would go on. It was scheduled for Thursday, just two days away. I also contacted Al, who thought the whole episode was bizarre. A few minutes later Kay called me back.

"Judge Head wants to know if you did what he told you? Did you contact Judge Dawson?" she seemed flustered.

"Yes, I did," I replied. She got off the phone for a second, I heard muffled conversation.

"And he's not going to handle it?"

"No, apparently not," I replied, then listened as she relayed the information.

"Okay then, I guess we'll see you Thursday," she confirmed. "Goodbye."

When Thursday morning came, Ericka offered to go with me to court. We sat there waiting, and waiting, until about forty minutes late, Judge Head entered the courtroom. During our wait, Phil O'Conner and Evan Tracy kept going in and out of Judge Head's chambers. I questioned Evan about approaching the judge without me present.

"I am seeing him on another matter. This is not Pennsylvania," he retorted.

When we sat down in our respective places to begin the proceeding, Evan asked if he could approach the judge about the paperwork. Judge Head consented, as Don and Carolyn looked on with ease. I heard them mumble for a second, then realized that I should be allowed to be included.

"Your honor, if I may approach," I stood and spoke clearly. He motioned me forward.

"Mr. Tracy says your papers are not in order. The affidavit of service is not proper for an eviction proceeding." He held the papers up and waved them as he spoke, reading glasses perched half way down his beak-like nose.

"They were served by Buck, your own court bailiff," I replied. "He does this all the time for proceedings here. This is a form used by the court for all service affidavits, as I understand it."

"But Buck didn't fill it out properly," Evan smirked coyly. My stomach did a flip and grimaced at his demeanor. "It's defective on its face."

"An error of the court is not attributable to the Petitioner," I summoned my wits and ignored my tummy. "And, it is not a blatant error that would prejudice the Defendants or affect the outcome of the proceeding. I'm not even sure I see what the problem is here." Evan glared at me, then looked up at Judge Head, who looked somewhat stunned at my legal argument.

"You see it is not properly noted that he served Don Lorry by serving upon his wife, Carolyn, and, it is not properly notarized with a seal." Evan countered, face turning red.

"Are you saying that Judge Head shouldn't trust his own bailiff not to lie about legal service of process? Or that service upon a spouse is not proper service? What rules are you reading?" I asked, shaking a little, but also happy with my retort. He whipped out a legal book, flipped open to a citation, and pointed it out to Judge Head. Judge Head read for a moment, then looking from one of us to the other, then over at the Lorrys, he finally shifted in his seat and cleared his throat.

"I have no choice but to dismiss this case on the basis of faulty service. Court is adjourned." He picked up his gavel and slammed it down abruptly, getting up from his seat and quickly heading into chambers.

"Show me what citation you showed him," I demanded of Evan. He just laughed and rolled his eyes at me, tossing the book onto the desk.

TWENTY-FIVE

Woe to those who make unjust laws, to those who issue oppressive decrees.
ISAIAH, THE PROPHET

"MAYBE YOU SHOULD HIRE a lawyer to do this for you, Babes," Nana said, anxiety in her voice. "I think they must have different ways in New York."

"I tried, but my lawyer says this is supposed to be very easy, then when I get the simple eviction, he will take over going after all the money they owe me." I felt badly that my exasperation was upsetting her. "Anyway, when I told him how it went down, he decided to put me in touch with a friend of his, another former Assistant Attorney General, who specializes in these types of things. When I called him, Stephen Johnston is his name, he said the same thing Al said! Plus, he wants a bigger retainer."

"And they're still not paying you?" she inquired. "The Lorrys?"

"They are only paying partial payments, claiming that I caused them damages and lost business when they exploded the boiler! Can you believe it? So now, they deduct some arbitrary amount from their rent every month, they've never paid for heat—but by law I have to heat their premises—and they haven't paid charges due under the lease or damages they caused."

"So, what are you gonna do?" She worried.

"I filed the paperwork again and I triple checked it. I coached Buck on how to fill out the affidavit properly, and I am going to try again. The next hearing date is set for a week from Thursday. But, in the meantime, there is now a new mayor; he asked to meet with me to reestablish better relations with the Village. I am supposed to meet with him next week."

"Let's hope this gets over with soon," Nana sighed. "It would be good to let that friend of yours run her business in there. How are the wedding plans coming along?"

"Pretty well, I think. One thing we hadn't counted on was the town code officer came by and told us we have to put a deck on the front of our house. Otherwise, we face a fine and code violations. So, we have to get that done soon."

"The same code officer?"

"No, the Chesterfield code officer—for our home," I replied, realizing how confusing these issues were even to me.

"Like you need one more thing!" Nana moaned.

"Well, it's something I've been wanting to get to since we moved in. It seemed crazy to me to have to block the front door, with such a beautiful view out there, just because the former owner decided to leave it without ever putting a balcony or stairs. It's an eyesore, having the deck will up the market value of the house." I didn't like the thought of another expense, but it was cheaper than being fined and our insurance company was already charging us at a higher rate because they considered it a hazard. "This way our insurance rates will go down, too. At least the wedding will be cheap, since we're having it here on the lawn."

"I think it will be wonderful to finally have it done, but can you get it done cheap enough?"

"Yes. Buck is doing it for us in his spare time," I told her. "And David is helping him, to keep the costs down."

"Oh, that's good. How are things with you and David?" she wondered. "Is everything okay?"

"Yes," I reassured her. "Things are going very well. We haven't heard another word about active duty, so . . . "

"Phew! I hope you don't!" she exclaimed. "I would hate to see him go to Iraq. That's a bad spot right now."

I awoke to someone ringing the doorbell at about 4:45 a.m. Stunned awake, I threw on a robe and ran down the hall. Peering out the side window I noticed it was Julie and her son.

"Is everything okay? Are you all right?" I asked opening the door.

"I didn't know where to go," Julie whined. "I need a hug. I need a friend." She was crying as I wrapped my arms around her.

"What's happened?"

"Gary's dead!" she sobbed. Her son Paul stood behind her, alternately patting her back and wiping tears from his eyes.

"What? Gary? What happened? Oh my God!" I suddenly recalled a conversation I had with him just a month or so ago. He came in the shop and told me that if anything happened to him, he wanted me to watch out for Julie and keep the Lorrys from taking advantage of her. (Before I came along, she had worked for them, but couldn't stand it, so she had quit.) I thought it was odd and asked if he was having health issues. He adamantly denied it but told me all our conversations and the way things happened on my project had caused him think about God again. He wanted me to know he was finally "right with the man upstairs."

"He had a heart attack, about 10:30 last night. He was fine one minute, just watching TV, and the next thing I know he staggered out of the house, clutching his chest, and fell to his face on the lawn. I've been trying to call you, but your phone isn't working. I wanted you to meet me at the hospital."

"Oh my God! Julie, I'm so sorry!" I realized that as much as Gary hated going to the doctor, he must have known something was wrong. Regret mixed with sadness weighed heavy on my heart. I should have pushed him for more information, asked him if he'd go to a doctor. I wept for him, for Julie. What a sad loss.

It turned out my phone wasn't working because though I mailed the payment, it was received late. I had to jump through hoops to prove it was paid and get service restored the next day. Meanwhile, funeral arrangements were made and scheduled for Thursday. The Lorrys and I mutually agreed to postpone the court date for one week. Evan Tracy penned a letter confirming same, with Judge Head approving the rescheduling.

It seemed so strange to see Gary in that coffin, but at the same time, he looked more peaceful and at rest than I had ever seen him. As I knelt next to the casket, I was overwhelmed with good memories and gratitude for all he did for me, for his caring. It seemed we had known each other much longer than a couple of years or so. I looked at his hands folded neatly across his chest and thought, *Gary would never sit still like that!* I smiled, then remembered his urgent question, "Who's gonna go up there and rescue you when you're frozen with fear?" I thought about the many times we all had lunch together, him sitting across from me telling stories of Vietnam, a sprinkle of salt in his beer. He never would eat, unless I left some pizza crust on my plate, then he would claim it and happily munch away. "You left that for me, right?" he would wink.

"Thank you for everything, Gary." I whispered aloud, tears streaming down my face. "I will do my best to honor your wishes. Be at peace."

As I stood up, wiping my eyes, Don Lorry approached. I moved to another room, closer to the main entry, but he followed me.

"Karen Marie," he grabbed me by the elbow, motioning for me to turn aside. "I am just wondering about a way to resolve our issues. Maybe we don't have to go to court." I watched him warily, not expecting for one moment he was being truthful. "It occurred to me that you are in way over your head with the building, and just not up to the tasks of such a big undertaking. Why don't you just turn it back over to Carolyn and I and we'll work out something with the Village to take over your financing?" I could hardly believe my ears. Feigned concern on his brow, he watched me closely.

"Are you out of your mind?" I asked him quietly.

"No, I mean, I'm sure you are tired of all the stress," he stammered a little, then regrouped. "It's a lot for one person, especially a woman. You probably didn't expect to get into so much trouble. I could put apartments back in there and work with the HUD program again—it'd be better than what you're doing with a B&B."

"Don, let me just set the record straight right now." I squared myself to face him eye to eye, seriously. "First of all, I didn't start this project, or my business, to fail. I did this for my children's future. I have worked my butt off to establish it. Second, I am fine. If you would uphold your end of our agreements, I would be better. In addition, putting apartments back into the space is out of the question—not that it's any of your business." I paused, waiting for a reaction, but he just stared, probably a bit surprised at my confidence. "So, unless you have some solid idea of how you are going to pay for all your damages, and do it fast, let alone your back rents, I'll see you in court next week."

"Okay, well I tried," he sighed dramatically, throwing his hands up in the air. "You'll be sorry."

"I'm only sorry I ever let you stay on in the building as tenants, Don. If you had a real proposal—one that was not absolutely ludicrous, then we might have worked things out." His audacity angered me, let alone his chauvinism, but I tried to speak calmly. I wanted a resolution. All my training and expertise was geared to win-win resolutions, but I was beginning to see that you cannot reason with a terrorist and that's what

Don had become in his greed. I knew I had to firmly but coolly state the truth.

"Well, you've got David now," he said, dripping false sympathy. "Let him take care of you, you can be free of the stress of the building. We'll take it off your hands. I'm sure I can get the mayor to work something out with me for your financing."

"And what do you propose I would get out of the deal?" I queried more sarcastically than he realized.

"You get out scot-free," he said in all seriousness. "You're out from under it."

"No way." I saw Julie down the hall; brushing past Don I went to speak with her.

The following week when we appeared in court, I was ready. Though I was extremely confused about what Judge Dawson had said and done, and Judge Head's reluctance, I was sure I had filled out the paperwork properly and had thoroughly reviewed Buck's affidavit of service. I knew it should be a piece of cake. Ericka came with me again. We sat and watched as Don and Carolyn made small talk with Phil O'Conner, who was now also a part time bailiff in the court, as well as remaining the code officer. Then Evan Tracy arrived to represent them. He approached me quickly, a malicious smirk on his face.

"I hear that Don proposed a settlement offer to you," he stated, still smirking. "And you refused it?"

"That was not a settlement offer, Mr. Tracy," I replied with complete composure. "It was a hostile takeover offer."

"Ha! That's your opinion. I guess you're entitled," he sneered.

"Do you have an answer to the petition?" I asked, noting the papers in his hand.

"I'm not gonna need one," he said laughing out loud. "But, you can have this if you want it, for posterity." Just then Justice Head could be seen in the doorway. Phil O'Conner stopped chatting with the Lorrys and made his way to the front where he bellowed as if there were fifty people in the room instead of merely five, "All rise!"

"Judge, if I may approach?" Evan said immediately as Judge Head took his seat.

"Already?" Judge Head asked.

"I have here in my hand the rules of procedure, Judge, and the very reason why this proceeding must be dismissed again today," he smiled, putting his notepad on the table next to Carolyn, then approaching the judge's lofty perch.

"Judge Head, if I may—" I began, but he motioned me to come forward also. As I neared, he took the rules from Evan Tracy.

"What are you saying, Mr. Tracy?" he inquired.

"Well, Judge, in a contested eviction proceeding, the hearing must take place after seven days but within ten days of the service of papers upon the defendants. My clients were served over fourteen days ago, Your Honor. Therefore, this hearing cannot go forward. The case must be dismissed." He continued smirking as he spoke.

"Your Honor," I began, incredulous. "All parties agreed to the continuance due to the death of a mutual friend. You, sir, even signed off on the continuance, therefore, no matter what the rules may *appear* to say, these defendants have not been prejudiced against. In fact, they have had *more time* to prepare their response; they have not been harmed in anyway. This is an advantage to them. Furthermore, I have been harmed in the delay as the uncollected amounts due and owing, and their continued harmful presence in my building, is keeping me from receiving the benefits of my own property, and of justice."

"Your Honor, the rules are clear," Evan said adamantly, again opening his book to a page which had been marked by a torn piece of paper and handing it across the bench to Judge Head. Judge Head looked at it for a minute, then looked at me over his glasses, before looking at Evan Tracy.

"Case dismissed," he announced, striking his gavel then retreating to his chambers once again.

TWENTY-SIX

*Sometimes one's enemies are so brazen,
they boast about their deceptions by telling the truth.*

AFTER MY APRIL MEETING with the new mayor, Mark Whitey, I was slightly encouraged, but not enough to believe he didn't have an agenda, too. He claimed that he understood the Lorrys to be slumlords, a bit backwards. He asked me why I felt the code officer and former mayor had caused my delays and damages since he had to decide what to do about the charges I had invoiced the Village. He wanted more information, or so he claimed, to make an informed decision. In the process of meeting with him, I was so distraught I poured my heart out about the events, then played him a taped conversation I had with Phil O'Conner. It was not really a conversation, but one of a series of phone calls wherein Phil called me at home and berated me, yelling, shouting, swearing and calling me degrading names. When David found out about it, he installed his phone in our bedroom and told me the next time that happened to push record on his handset—a feature I didn't have on my phone. I tried to get Phil to explain exactly what he wanted from me, but all he would do is yell and scream, and make threats of shutting down my business. When I played the tape of his call for mayor Whitey, he sat back in his seat, thought for a moment, then made some notes on his yellow pad.

"I'm sorry about that," he said with a strange look on his face. "Can I have the tape? I want to play it for our lawyer."

"No," I replied. "I can transcribe it for you, if you want, but you cannot have the tape."

"Okay, well, I promise you that will stop. Phil won't bother you again," he said soberly. "I want you to gather some information about the business for me, revenue, gross receipts, liability, rental info, and forward it in the next week or so. I'm going to speak to the Village Attorney about restructuring your loan to offset what we owe you and get back to square one."

The day of our wedding ceremony arrived amid cooler than usual temperatures, a mixture of clouds and sun, and strong wind gusts. It was not a typical Memorial Day weekend forecast, but it was enjoyable enough, once we taped down the table cloths and put stones in the bottom of the flower vases. I believed the restructuring of my mortgage with the Village was in process, so that burden felt lighter. I enjoyed the wedding preparations and the wedding itself. Nana and I had shopped for a dress which she insisted on buying for me. We settled on a vintage-looking, ivory tea length sheath with a sheer duster, both detailed with sequins and embroidered detail as only April Cornell can. Dave wore a dark navy three-piece suit. By now he had been shaving his head, which only further set off his strong cheekbones and piercingly bright eyes. We enjoyed the ceremony, since there had not only been no more issues of porn, but he had made strides in how he dealt with stress. During the months leading up to the ceremony, the trust and intimacy between us had been reestablished; we were grateful for the opportunity to repeat our vows again, especially to each other, but also before our family and friends.

Despite the hopes of an imminent restructuring, I had plan B in place. The situation with the Lorrys had been dragging on so long, and the financial bind a source of angst, I felt it should be dealt with one way or the other, for good. I put the bed and breakfast on the market for $699,000 furnished, or $599,000 unfurnished. When I spoke to Uncle Frank about it, he was distressed.

"You're giving up on your dream?" he asked, shock and sadness on his face. "I hate to see that, kiddo."

"Well, Frank, I just don't know what else to do. I must be responsible about this, even if it's someone else's fault I'm in this predicament. It's not fair, but…." I wasn't sure myself, but I could see how difficult the Lorrys were and knew I had to keep my children's home, first and foremost. I watched him carefully, ready to hear any advice he had. My respect for him is immense, my appreciation just as vast. If he had some wisdom for me, I wanted to hear it.

"I just hate to see you give up on your dream," he said. "There's got to be a better way."

"If I could get some traction in court, get paid back for the excessive amounts they owe me—" I believed that's how it should work, but reality seemed to be at odds with justice. I sighed loudly. "Well, I need to be able to pay my debts and not go under in the process."

"Keep me posted," he said soberly.

In June, just a few days after the wedding, we got another phone call from Staff Sargent Miller. By now we were convinced the alert would be cancelled, but instead, it was made official. Unless things drastically deescalated in Iraq in the coming months, David would be on active duty by the end of December.

Business was picking up at the bed and breakfast and thankfully, with the warmer weather heating and electrical expenses were going down. I decided to pay Stephen Johnston his retainer and have him file the Lorry eviction case. By now they owed me more than $60,000. I needed another month or so before I could come up with the full retainer, but I felt it would be worth it, since obviously, the deck was stacked against me going it alone. Stephen was intrigued by the abrupt dismissal of my previous cases, but didn't look at the paperwork until July, when I went to pay his full retainer, drop off my documents, and go over the entire case with him. He still believed the best thing to do was get them out fast, so I could make the space profit me, then go after them in the Essex County Supreme Court for the damages, which were too high for the small village court jurisdiction.

I also began paying on the Front Street mortgage in July, the conclusion of the moratorium. John Clute never did get back to Al about the added lump sums. Al sent him a demand letter, along with documentation of items I had already paid and losses I had suffered due to the mayor's interference. It was sort of a stalemate, I guess; though I wanted to pursue it, there was only so much I could handle at once. When I made my payment, I issued a check, based on income generated from the bed and breakfast. Most guests paid by MasterCard and Visa, so I had to wait for those funds to be deposited to my account, which usually took about three days. My bank, Evergreen, was a local bank and had just begun offering online banking; something new at the time. I habitually logged in to verify that my deposits were in the account, balance my register, then pay bills. In the case of my payment to the Village, I did just that, but for some reason, the next day the bank returned the check for insufficient funds. I inquired as to why in person.

"Because the funds were not available, even though they were in your account," Ms. Bezio, the branch manager stated briskly.

"What do you mean? I verified that my deposits were added before I even wrote the check and dropped it off." I told her, somewhat irritated.

"Well, the deposits were there, but we had not cleared them yet," she said. "Basically, we have to be sure the deposits will clear before we release the money. It's kind of like a hold."

"Then how am I supposed to know that?" I asked in utter frustration. "I logged in to my online account and there is no indication the funds are not available. In fact, it said 'account balance $2,674.12.'"

"Well, online banking is a new feature, so I am not one hundred percent sure . . ." her voice trailed off as she sat at her desk and logged into her computer. "Well, here," she said, pointing at the screen. "You see? It's all available today. Account balance . . . but we charged you a twenty-five-dollar fee for insufficient funds, so that's coming out today."

"But, if you look at it, it said the same thing two days ago. And why did it bounce so quickly?"

"The Village does their banking at this branch, too," she said with an air of superiority. "But you need to be sure all the money is available."

"Okay, fine. How?" I asked again.

"Maybe call us?" she wondered aloud. "Or you could come into the branch."

"You mean there is no way for me to know that even though I have plenty of money in the account, I cannot access all of it, without coming into the branch or calling?" I felt like I was in an *I Love Lucy* episode.

"That's about right," she stated with a smile. "We may change things in online banking again soon, so maybe you'll see it more clearly in the future, but . . ."

"I confess, I'm a bit perplexed," I sat across from her. "Shouldn't a direct deposit from another bank be free and clear right away? These are MasterCard and Visa deposits. As it is, I wait about three days or more to even get them in the bank, now I am going to have to wait another three or more to use the funds? I need to know because my tenants owe me a small fortune, I account for every penny until I can collect from them."

"If I were you, I'd call your merchant account manager and ask about that. As for us, I think you should just call us or come in and see when things are available. I can waive this fee today, as a one-time courtesy," she said.

I wasn't satisfied, but I withdrew the cash and took it up to the Village Offices to give to the clerk. I explained what happened at the bank and asked them to return my check to me when they received it in the mail. For August, I triple checked funds available before paying my mortgage with the Village. Meanwhile, Dave and I continued to pay one and a half times the regular home mortgage payment. I looked forward to fall tourism and hoped to get the Lorrys out before winter. Kat Smith and I had become much closer friends; she was determined to begin her own business in their space.

Stephen filed the eviction pleadings in Judge Head's court in August. The initial hearing date was postponed several times by Evan Tracy, with Judge Head concurring, but when we finally did appear for it, Stephen got a good look at what I was up against. As we stood talking outside the courtroom, Don, Carolyn, Tom, Betty, Nancy and others filed in, joking and making light of the situation. Phil O'Conner and Buck stood by and the new mayor, Mark, hurriedly rushed in to speak with them, then went into Judge Head's chambers. From where I stood talking with Ericka, I saw Evan Tracy finally make his appearance and saunter toward Stephen Johnston, who was shuffling through papers.

"Ahh, Stephen! How are you?" Evan greeted him, sticking out his hand. Stephen put his papers on the bench next to him and reciprocated the hand shake. Nodding his head in my direction, Evan boasted, "We've been trying to starve her out so long, we're surprised she could afford you!"

"Ha, oh . . . " Stephen narrowed his eyes at me over Evan's shoulder, then smiled a professional sort of smile at Evan and turned away. Evan walked into the clerk's office, Judge Head's office was just beyond, door open. I was watching Evan so intently that I was surprised when Stephen pulled me quickly around the corner to the entrance of the men's room.

"Listen very carefully," he whispered seriously. "Did you hear what he said?"

"I could hardly believe it!" I whispered back. We heard footsteps passing by, he put one finger over his lips to be sure I stopped speaking. When he was sure it was safe, he began again.

"What do you think the Lorrys have on Judge Head?" he asked, still whispering.

"What do they . . . hmm. I have no idea."

"It's time for us to find out," he replied. "Be careful what you say. Pay attention to everything that happens; keep notes. We need to look into this more." Then, he glanced around the corner. Seeing no one nearby, he pushed me toward the hallway and followed me out quickly.

TWENTY-SEVEN

When you do right and are treated as if you've done wrong, don't look within, look about. Caveat emptor.

WITH SEPTEMBER CAME ANOTHER round of bills. I went to the Village to pay my mortgage directly, with cash. I waited at the clerk's counter until one of them could assist me, then counted out one thousand and one dollars, in front of Lynn. She snatched it up and recounted, then went to get the mortgage register and receipt book. After looking at it a moment, she remarked, "Well, okay. But this doesn't make you current."

"What?" I gasped. "Of course it does. That's my mortgage payment amount. I paid it last month in cash, too, remember?"

"No, Mayor Whitey instructed me to put last month's payment toward water and sewer," she replied with mindless equivocation.

"Lynn, why on earth would I pay ahead on water and sewer and not pay my mortgage?" I retorted. "You can't just arbitrarily decide where to apply my funds. When I pay my mortgage payment, with a coupon especially, it goes to my mortgage, period. Why would you think it should go to water and sewer? What is my balance on that?"

"Umm, let's see, you have a credit ahead of $920.65." She looked up from the register, tapping her pen on the calendar pad in front of her. I could not fathom the idiocrasy.

"Is that why I didn't get a water and sewer bill? Lynn, did it occur to you that maybe it's not right to move my money around randomly? Why would I want a credit it will take me a year to use rather than pay my mortgage?" I asked again.

"I just take orders from the mayor," she replied. "I don't make the decisions."

"Well, I demand that this be put back on my mortgage account immediately," I told her, as calmly as possible.

"I can't do that until Mayor Whitey authorizes it," she said, staring me down.

"Lynn, if you don't do it, I am not paying this payment today. How am I supposed to trust that you'll apply my payment where it belongs?"

"Sorry, Karen Marie," she replied. "I am not changing anything without Mark's permission, and he won't be in until tomorrow."

My mind raced in several directions, trying to comprehend the best legal thing to do. I pulled out my cell and dialed Stephen's office, walking out into the hallway so Lynn would not over hear the conversation. He took my call right away, dumbfounded, but still wondering if it was just more Podunk rationale. He advised me to go to the Village Attorney, John Clute's office to pay each payment directly from then on. "Get a receipt from him personally," he noted adamantly. I knew I had another couple of days before my payment would be considered late, and that there was no way I could make it there before closing, so I made plans to do so the next day.

Before going up to Mr. Clute's office the next day, however, I called Lynn and asked whether she had been given the go ahead to put the mortgage payment I had made the previous month back where it belonged. She indicated that she had spoken with Mark Whitey, but he had not given her the green light yet.

"Are you going to make your payment?" I couldn't decide if she was amused or curious as she asked.

"Yes, I am," I told her. "But not at your office. Please ask Mark to give me a call as soon as possible." I hung up and went to Plattsburgh to do errands and pay at John Clute's office.

Walking up to the entrance of the old train depot which was now beautifully restored, I recalled Mr. Clute's comments at closing about how much over budget he went in the renovations and wondering if I could succeed. I then thought again about how Evan Tracy had still not supplied me with the executed warranty document and agreement from that same day. *Can these lawyers really be that corrupt?*

Once inside, I told his secretary that I needed to see him personally, or at least, leave her a payment for which I wanted a receipt. Perplexed, she excused herself to go find him, asking me to have a seat and wait. About ten minutes later she came back, so I stood to my feet and pulled out my wallet.

"Um, Mr. Clute said to inform you that we will not take your payment here," she said quietly, putting out her hand as if to stop me from opening my wallet.

"Excuse me?" I thought I heard her wrong. "Mr. Johnston instructed me to come here, pay personally and get a receipt from your office."

"Well, Mr. Clute said that he just got off the phone with Mayor Whitey who has instructed him not to take your payment. He wants Mr. Clute to initiate foreclosure proceedings against you instead."

"Foreclosure proceedings? They cannot do that! My payment is not even late until after the tenth of the month and I have been paying them!" I tried to remain calm, but my nerves were quickly and easily frayed.

"I'm sorry. I don't know what else to tell you," she said, then returned to her desk. I sat down and tried to reach Stephen, but his assistant said he was in court. Devastated, I left.

Stephen had successfully demanded a trial on the day of the hearing. Judge Head uncomfortably promised to get in touch with both parties as to an actual date. In the coming weeks, there were several rounds of letters and phone calls—initiated by Stephen—before we finally had a trial date, December 14th. Meanwhile, the episode outside the courtroom and the incident in John Clute's office hounded me, even in my sleep. Stephen's question was a yoke on my shoulders; the message relayed by Mr. Clute's secretary, a constant ringing in my ears.

"Julie, what do you know about Judge Head?" I asked her as we cleaned up the kitchen after breakfast one day.

"What do you mean?" she answered warily, which told me I was onto something already.

"I mean, does he have a dark side? Is he shady?" I watched her for a minute, leaning against the counter rather than continue loading the dishwasher.

"Yeah, you might say that," she remarked. "He left his wife years ago, after five kids, to live with a young man who everyone knows is gay. Before that he had an ongoing thing with another married man, everyone knew it but their poor wives."

"But being gay isn't shady. I mean, hiding it from your spouse, is, but . . ."

I pondered this knowledge. "How old are his kids? Or the young man you're talking about?"

"His kids are all grown and moved away. The young man, I think his name is Brian, anyway, he was really young when they first got together, maybe 18? Even now he tries to make himself look like a little boy, so . . ." She stopped for a second, folding one arm across her chest, resting her other elbow on it, she put her hand on her chin thoughtfully. "There are always young men around Judge Head's place, drifters, no one knows where they come from. You see them at all hours of the day and night, standing outside smoking in their underwear before going back inside. And, he's known to buy alcohol for them, all of them are underage for sure."

"Seriously?" I could not even comprehend this to be true of a judge. "Do you think that's what the Lorrys have on him?"

"Maybe, but Don himself has a shady bunch of stuff going on, too, I think." She lowered her tone as if they could hear us from the laundromat.

"Such as?"

"Well, Gary told me once that Don was pimping one of his female tenants up here, and that he helps move stuff for the Akwesasne with the laundry."

"Stuff? Like drugs? Pot?" I wondered aloud, still having difficulty grasping this information.

"Yeah, that's what Gary said. I don't really know, but if you ask around, someone is bound to tell you more. It's a small town," she joked. "Not like he can keep secrets well either!"

"Do you think Don sells drugs?" I asked, recalling the stash I found in ceiling tiles on the north side of the building during renovation. One of the crew offered to take it off my hands, but I got rid of it in the used paint cans after we cleaned the brushes in them.

"I think Don does whatever he can to make money and lord it over people," she replied. "You should talk to that other woman he screwed out of a business here, about five years ago, Susan . . . Susan—I can't remember her last name, but she had a ceramic shop here. Don really screwed her out of a lot of money. She took him to court, got nothing out of it. Going to court in Keeseville is always a losing battle—unless you're friends with Judge Head."

"So, do you think I'm going to lose, too?" I asked earnestly.

"Well, I think you have the best lawyer to stand up to the Lorrys;

maybe Judge Head will pay attention now that you've got Mr. Johnston. Everyone knows Mr. Johnston doesn't mess around. He's good."

When I conveyed to Stephen what I had learned, his advice was to keep it on the down low and keep learning more. We prepared for trial, including gathering about thirteen witnesses to the damages and incidents that had transpired over the previous year or more. Things were rough, since the Lorrys still would not pay for heat or other expenses and did not pay full rents either. I had already given them a break, and now they were making up their own rules. Winter was fast approaching, I needed a good paying tenant in that space. Kat Smith approached me again more seriously than ever about turning the laundromat premises into an upscale laundry service with alterations and assorted hand made goods available for sale. She had done her research about buying her own machines, rather than Don and Carolyn's old, very worn ones. We continued meeting and planning through the fall; in early December, when it was time for me to get help serving the subpoenas on the witnesses, she offered to do so.

The two of us spent a lot of time in the car talking about the whole episode as we drove from house to house in various places to serve the subpoenas. She was very curious about George Head, and decided to ask some of the people she knew about him as well.

When the day of the trial came, the Lorrys packed the courtroom with friends, while all witnesses had to wait out in the hallway. That meant that Carolyn Lorry could be in the courtroom—because technically I had to sue her alone, Don had not allowed his name to be on the lease—but Don had to wait outside, since he was a witness. Nancy also had to wait outside, but after they testified, they were both allowed in the courtroom for the remainder of the proceedings. Some of my witnesses included the local clerk for my fuel company, Bezio's, who had confided in me that she had received a phone call telling her not to authorize any more fuel deliveries to my location because I would not be able to pay for them. It had resulted in me running out of fuel and having no heat, until we got to the bottom of it. Another was the man who helped repair the Adirondack Suite, and yet another was the plumber who had initially red-tagged the boiler they rigged which exploded.

Throughout the first day, the Lorrys paraded in an out of the courtroom, passing each other notes, in plain view of Judge Head, who did nothing about it. Stephen tried several times to point it out. Finally, by the end of the day, Judge Head finally made mention of the "distraction" asking them to be more considerate but refusing to impose any reprimand for what was clearly misconduct and sharing of information from Don to Carolyn and vice versa. This came as no surprise in the sense that Carolyn couldn't have an opinion or state a fact without Don interjecting, but it was a huge surprise in the obvious display of judicial impropriety. At times, even Phil O'Conner or Buck passed the notes back and forth.

Additionally, Mayor Whitey, who refused my mortgage payments beginning in September, as he instructed Mr. Clute to do, strutted in and out of the proceedings all day. He had a keen interest in what was transpiring, as the Lorrys were obviously outnumbered and out of facts while I still had plenty to go, he became edgy. After the third day of the trial, Judge Head pronounced that he was done.

"Your Honor," Stephen Johnston exclaimed. "We still have plenty more facts, and more importantly, seven more witnesses to present testimony."

"I don't care how many there are, I've heard enough," Judge Head retorted edgily.

"With all due respect, Your Honor," Stephen said authoritatively, "These seven witnesses have waited three days to testify. My client has paid to put her case on trial and deserves—"

"I said, I've heard enough!" Judge Head bellowed. He proceeded to call the trial over, even without closing arguments, declaring he would issue a written decision in the coming weeks. I went home and days later was served with notice of foreclosure action by the Village; it had been filed the day after the trial concluded.

TWENTY-EIGHT

Sometimes relying on an advocate is a false sense of security.

"STEPHEN, WHAT DO YOU make of this foreclosure complaint?" I asked him. "I still don't understand how they can return my payments when I was never late!"

"I think it's time for you to go the Attorney General about what's been going on here. You'll need to file a complaint—and feel free to tell them to contact me. I am going to hound Judge Head for that decision, and—how's the prospect of selling the inn going?" he thoughtfully asked.

"I've had about twenty inquiries, so far, but my listing is expiring soon. There are people coming to see it in February and March, but nothing sooner. I also have been trying to refinance." I really didn't want to sell but would if it meant saving my home and my credit.

"Keep working on the refinance end and let me know if you decide to relist it," he replied soberly. "I cannot emphasize enough that something's fishy. It's important you go to the AG. As far as the foreclosure action, you'll need to get another lawyer if Al can't handle it. My dance card is full, and that's not my area of expertise. How is Al feeling these days; do you know?"

"Not well from what I hear. I will call him, but . . ." I felt badly that Al had been so ill lately. He was in and out of doctor's offices and taking time off from his practice to rest more.

"Then you might just call Mark Rodgers. I'll give him a call and let him know what's been transpiring if you want. He will most likely want a retainer, but he knows his stuff." I appreciated Stephen so much, I just wished he could handle everything I faced.

"Thanks, Stephen," I told him earnestly. "I appreciate that."

On December 20, 2004, I went to the Attorney General's office in Plattsburgh and was given a form to fill out. When the Assistant Attorney

General came out to speak with me, he notated on the form that Mr. Johnston had called him, asking to hear me out.

"Hello, I am Assistant Attorney General Glen Michaels," he said, stretching out his hand to shake. "I understand you have quite a situation going on." He stood about six feet tall, wore a red sweater over top of a buttoned-down oxford and a pair of tan, wide-wale corduroys. After we shook hands, he crammed his lanky figure into a small chair with desk side arm and awkwardly crossed his legs.

"Yes. I feel like I'm living in a nightmare and I can't wake up," I told him earnestly.

"Tell me more about it," he said in a friendly, relaxed tone. "Mr. Johnston is a former Assistant Attorney General himself, he seems to think there's something foul going on."

For the next forty-five minutes or so we discussed the situation. I wish I could say that I believed I had been set up, and that I relayed that, but the fact is, all my previous negative conditioning still had me second guessing my own intuition. I was still learning to navigate the healing process, to trust myself, and to believe that—contrary to what I always thought—some people are bent on evil, even if you treat them the way you want to be treated. After a long bit of questions and answers, Mr. Michaels handed me another form and his business card.

"I've come to learn that the truth is stranger than fiction," he said convincingly. "I believe there's something going on, but obviously, we need to know more. I want you to fill this form out, include as much information as possible. Take it home, spend some time on it."

"Okay. I can do that. Should I drop it off when I am done?" I asked, watching him intently.

"Why don't you call me when you're going to do that. I will look it over and we'll chat more then," he replied thoughtfully. "Meanwhile, take Steve's advice. Keep your eyes open. See if you can learn more about what the Lorrys may have on the justice. Maybe it is bribery or extortion. . . . maybe it's less. And see if there's any way the mayor ties in. Why would the Village refuse your payments? Why would they want to foreclose rather than take the money? That's absurd on its face, right?"

"Yes! That's what I keep saying! It just doesn't add up," I bemoaned.

"It doesn't add up to an honest person," he said wisely. "It may make total sense to those with less than upright intentions."

I went from his office to Mark Rodger's office, Lewis Rodgers & Meconi, where I was ushered in for a quick debriefing. I explained what had transpired, including the refusal of payments even though I was not late, and the Lorry situation that Stephen was handling. Mark sat back in his swivel chair behind his desk, elbows balanced on the armrests, fingertips together in front of him.

"So, let's review what your prospects are and our plan of action," he said quietly. "You can refinance, possibly, you can sell, and you can fight this and win, possibly."

"Do you think I will win?" I asked, somewhat fearfully. "I mean, will I get a fair shake around here?"

"Listen, I don't know what the heck goes on in the Village of Keeseville court," he smirked as he looked over the desk at me, putting his hands down. "But there should be no impropriety in the Essex County court. You have a solid case. John Clute can be a hard ass, but I have a good working relationship with him. Why he would do something so foolish as to not accept your payments, I have no idea. If the village were my client, I would have advised against this action, given the facts I am aware of at present. But, he took orders from his client, it's their call, unless he doesn't know the facts and they are pursuing in bad faith. That's a notion I can discuss with him."

"I think there can be no other explanation than that they are pursuing it in bad faith. Stephen agrees," I told him.

"Stephen Johnston?" he asked, eyebrows raised.

"Yes, he said he would call you and fill you in."

"Oh, that would explain the message," he replied. "I haven't had a chance to call him back yet."

"You may also want to talk to Al Burczak, if you can reach him. He's been representing me against the Village, until now." Al's office was just a block away, but I wondered if he would be available.

"Al's another good guy," he smiled. "You've been dealing with the best, I see. Is he of the same opinion Steve is? Why isn't he handling this?"

"Yeah, pretty much. He's just not been in good health so—"

"Oh. That's too bad. I didn't realize," Mark replied genuinely. "He's a great guy."

"Yes. I am so fortunate to have had such great representation so far," I told him. "I am very grateful."

"Well, let's keep that track record, shall we?" He stood to his feet to grab a yellow pad off the nearby cabinet, then sat down again, pulling his chair into the desk, picking up a Waterman pen from its holder. "I'm going to make you a list of things I want to see right away, and then there's the matter of a retainer. I bet they've tapped you pretty dry, huh?"

"Yes," I silently prayed for favor, and a low retainer amount as I watched him.

"You've given me a copy of the complaint, now I want your responses to each item, just jot them down on a copy of it, or something. Tell me what proof you have of each of your responses, then I will need copies of that documentation as well. I have a week or so to pull this together, but with the Christmas holiday . . ." He looked at the calendar, counting off days with the pen. "Well, I will call John and see about moving the deadline. I might get a sense of what's going on when I talk to him."

As I drove home in the cold darkness, I tried to keep from sobbing. There were already heaps of snow everywhere and the icy roads glistened in the streetlights. Though I had some hope that justice would prevail, I was exhausted and weary of pressing on. On top of that, Dave's departure was imminent. The sorrow I felt over that was heftier than the other burdens combined, or maybe it was because of all of them. I really didn't know, but I tried not to be depressed during his final weeks at home.

> *God, please provide for this retainer. I don't have it, but I know you can bring it about, even in a day. I know this is not a surprise to you. Help me get through this. Thank you for representation. Thank you for good lawyers, who seem to see what's happening.*

The next day as I gathered documentation in my office in the Front Street building, Kat appeared in the doorway. She claimed she had just had another phone call from Don Lorry trying to sell her the laundromat again.

"What? He's in the process of being evicted and he's trying to sell you the business?" I laughed.

"I could hardly believe it!" she wailed in laughter. "He's got nerve! Like I don't know the trouble his business is in!"

"He's desperate, I guess."

"How did your meetings go yesterday? Did the AG think you have a legit complaint?" She sat down on a nearby loveseat and put her purse next to her. Through her coke-bottle-thick spectacles, I saw concern in her dark brown eyes.

"Yes," I sighed. "He wants me to write more facts out and go back to see him. The more urgent matter though is retaining Mark Rodgers to handle my foreclosure action."

"What? Foreclosure action?"

"I guess I didn't tell you . . . the other day, right after the trial, the village served me with an action in foreclosure for this building." I sighed again, coming out from behind the desk and sitting across from her in an oversized chair.

"Oh my God, Karen Marie! That's awful!" She was as shocked as I was just days before. "But they didn't take your payments, right? That's crooked!"

"Yeah, I think so. Stephen thinks so, but we have to prove it."

"Well, Stephen can't handle it?" she queried. "I mean, he knows all the ins and outs of your situation already, right?"

"Yeah, it would be nice if he could, but he can't. He sent me to Mr. Rodgers, now I have to come up with a retainer so he can represent me in this."

"Karen Marie, you really need a partner," Kat said solemnly. "I mean, I know I mentioned it before, but the more that happens—and David is leaving—oh my God! You must be overwhelmed."

"Yes, you could say that. I have a good cry, then I pray and trust and keep moving forward," I told her, trying not to become too emotional.

"Have you given any more thought to taking me on as a partner? I mean, my accountant says I have to invest some money somewhere. I could help you out and run the laundromat the way I want, plus we talked about the idea of a tea room in here, an event space. We could do it."

"I have thought about it a little, but I have to decide which direction to go in soon. My sales listing is expiring, and I haven't been able to refinance yet."

"I feel badly that you would sell your beautiful inn, after all your hard work, just because of the sleazy Lorrys and the village," she clucked in disgust. "Did you mention to your lawyer about a partnership?"

"Yeah, I did. He said it's a valid option, especially if it is proportional, and if I have the option of terminating it when the crisis is over—buying you, whomever it is, out." I pondered the idea some more. "I guess I have to decide whether I want to retain my business—the inn, the shop—at the expense of total ownership."

"But what happens if you don't take on a partner? Would you lose everything? Would you sell the inn?" she leaned forward, folding her arms in front of her and stretching out her legs.

"I would have to sell, I think. I am not sure I could hold on until the litigation is settled. It takes longer in the county court. Besides, even if I win the eviction case, I still need to file against the Lorrys in the county court to collect. They're not going to make it easy and just hand over the money."

"Well, I am prepared to put my money where my mouth is right now," Kat said purposefully. "If we can hammer out the details, I will put down some money to make it legit."

"How much are you talking? I mean, this place is worth a lot. Are you saying you want equal partnership?"

"No, I mean, maybe that proportional thing the lawyer talked about," she mused. "I have twenty-five-thousand dollars to invest in the next couple of months because of an inheritance I got. And, well I can't work because my husband makes too much money and it will just put us into an even higher tax bracket, so I would be working for nothing. That's why our accountant suggested I start a business and invest some money into it, so we can have a tax shelter and deductions, I still get to do something."

"Okay, then you would take over the laundromat space?" I asked her.

"Absolutely. I've already got my own source for machines and I can help you in the shop, we can do the tea room thing."

"How about we spend some time this afternoon hashing this out?" I asked. "I'm going to call my lawyer and talk to him about it again. I'll ask him what we need to do to put it together, but I can't afford to spend a fortune doing that. My retainer takes priority. I have to come up with that first."

"Your retainer should be a partnership expense, right? I mean, we have to be sure this gets fought," she remarked.

"No, it's not. For it to truly be a partnership, you would have to pay me something of value to buy into my 100 percent ownership. Whatever you put in, in relation to the 100 percent value, is your percentage of the partnership." I replied. "So, I have this place listed at $699,000 furnished,

$599,000 unfurnished. Less my personal items, just for example, let's say the total value is $500,000. If you put in only $50,000, your percentage of ownership is only ten percent. You wouldn't have as much ownership as I do, but you would be vested ownership of ten percent."

"Oh, I see." Kat thought for a minute. "Well, I talked to Kenny about this, and he doesn't care one way or the other. He doesn't want to be bothered, but he likes the idea of tax deductions and shelters. I would say that I would put in at least $25,000 in the next couple of months," she paused, reflecting on what she had just said. "Yeah, at a minimum. I could do more after that. Would that be enough to keep you from selling or going under?"

"I honestly don't have all the answers, but . . . " I did some calculations in my head: winter expenses, lawyer fees, insurance, fuel oil. "It would certainly mean I could get through until the next busy season. By then I could refinance because I will have three seasons in business—at least that's what they tell me."

"Okay. Think about it, Karen Marie," she told me. I need to go pick up my kids, but I will come back. We can put something in writing today if you want."

TWENTY-NINE

Deep sorrow makes a person blind and vulnerable.

WITH JANUARY 2005 CAME David's departure. The trek over to the armory in Vermont for family training and identification cards was cold. We didn't talk much as we contemplated what lie ahead. *This is for real. He's going to war, the worst part of the war, Ramadi.* Despite how hard I tried not to be emotional, I couldn't help it. We filled out paperwork, had our pictures taken, were coached on how to handle mail, internet, television news, media, and more. There were some things that had never crossed my mind until that day, like how I would be notified in the event Dave was injured or killed. They were very specific, and obviously, had done this many times, but they still showed heart, empathy, and genuinely took care to answer questions, even, give hugs.

It was only a week later that we were standing in the middle of uniformed dads and husbands, surrounded by clinging families and crying parents. The four of us huddled in that hangar at the Vermont Air National Guard base, holding each other, hugging, saying our goodbyes, trying to avoid the penetrating glare of television cameras and hoping for a safe return. I tried to hold it together, but I was failing. David and I stayed close while Katlyn kept her arm around me, and Jon hung on David. When it was time for him to finally go into lineup, I thought I would faint as I watched him. I saw his jaw tremble and tears fill his eyes as he looked at me. "You are my true love, Karen Marie. I don't want to leave you. I will be home again," he told me. Yet, he remained as professional and soldierly as possible.

"Jon, I love ya a whole lot, buddy," he said. "I'm counting on ya to help your Mom, okay?" He hugged him tightly, as Jon cried, nodding his head affirmatively.

"And Katlyn," he reached to hug her. "Be good to your mom. She loves you. This is rough for her, okay? I love ya, very much."

"I love you, too," Katlyn said, hugging him. "Good bye."

"Karen . . . I . . . " He turned to look me in the eyes and his tears fell. "I love you so much. Try to stay strong." We kissed passionately. "I love you."

"I love you so much," I told him, but the words hardly came out. "Come back to me safely."

When he hugged us for the last time, he wiped his eyes, then picked up his gear and went to line up. Watching him standing there, Jon was inspired and proud, especially. Katlyn was touched. I was a mess. I felt it cruel to have to say goodbye then go through the formalities, standing there, watching, trying not to dissolve in a pile of emotion. I finally had what I always longed for: a wonderful marriage and family life. But it had been such a short time and our country had asked us to give it up. I didn't want to give it up. It was too soon. We needed time to continue bonding as a family, the kids needed him home as much as I did. I had just begun to lean on someone, for real. I was going through so much, I needed to keep leaning. I needed the comfort of his arms around me, the reassurance we could get through it all together, no matter what. But he would be half the world away, facing the worst of enemies, on the front lines. Men came home every day with scars and missing limbs, to say nothing of the emotional trauma. Then there were those who came home in boxes, draped in flags. The reality of his departure was too much for me to bear in that moment.

The kids and I lingered at the airport, as they had an area for families to watch their soldiers board the planes and take off. I didn't want to stay, but I couldn't see well to drive. I needed some time. We went from there to Nana and Papa's house. It had been barely a year of marriage and suddenly I was doing life as a single mom again. I had let my guard down, let the healing and vulnerabilities come back into my life, my heart. Now, I had to give it up again. Somehow, I would have to retain the healing that had taken place because of our love for each other yet resume the life of invincibility that seems to be a criterion of single parenting.

THIRTY

Eventually truth rises to the surface much like cream separates from milk, and when it does, one must skim it off the top and use it richly.

KAT DID COME BACK that December afternoon, and after downloading a partnership form from a legal forms website, we went through each item, paragraph by paragraph. We settled on terms and signed it. I forwarded a copy to Mark Rodgers and asked about what other documents we might need to legitimize it. Within a few days, Kat paid me about five thousand dollars toward her initial twenty-five-thousand-dollar initial investment, and I had the retainer Mark needed. He filed an answer to the Village's complaint in foreclosure and put in a call to John Clute and Steve Johnston. John didn't budge, which, per Mark, was "surprising". They talked about scheduling depositions; Mark urged me to finalize the partnership. He thought that if Kat wanted to invest money, it should be enough to put me over the hurdle until the court could see what had taken place. Interestingly, the case had been assigned to Judge Dawson in Essex County.

Sometime after the holidays, my mother was hospitalized due to excessively high blood pressure. It was almost under control and she was scheduled to be released after a few days of tests and monitoring until an observant doctor and nurse noticed a pattern. Every time my father walked into the room her blood pressure went off the charts. She was in danger of stroking. Of course, Dad prided himself on his business and reputation with the doctors in that area of New Hampshire, he wouldn't let her admit to them that there was strife. However, this astute doctor made a point of seeing Mom after Dad left one day, asking if she was in any danger at home, or being abused.

"What do you consider abuse?" Mom told me she asked him coyly.

"It could be physical, or emotional," the doc replied. "Are you being harassed? Are you being manipulated and controlled?"

Mom said that at that point she burst into tears, explaining how difficult it is to live with Dad, that she feared being honest about it to anyone because of the business, and feared retaliation, even confessing that she had resorted to drinking too much again. She wanted help. I give her a lot of credit for that moment, but I feel so badly for her that it took that much physical distress before she got help. The next time Dad came into the hospital, later the same day, he was not permitted to see her. That did not sit well, but it was the beginning of the end. Within weeks, Mom left my father again. This time, she went to Pennsylvania to stay near my brother Ryan and his wife. She reached out often during this time, calling me frequently.

Judge Head still hadn't issued the order on the trial but wrote a letter to both attorneys suggesting that we go to arbitration. This was so insidious, and Stephen got so upset, I thought he might be the one having a stroke. He wrote to Judge Head again, explaining that we had paid for and put our case on trial, that we were entitled to a decision as a matter of law. He asked for an appointment to reargue the closing statements, which had only been submitted in writing after judge Head ordered his abrupt end to the trial. While we awaited Justice Head's response, Stephen also urged me to share this information with the AG. Glen Michaels was intrigued, but couldn't decide whether it was just ignorance, or if there was some other motivation behind it. As the situation stretched on, so did my other woes.

ABN AMRO had been taking the payments of one and a half times the mortgage payment amount for a year, but still pursued the foreclosure action. I had received a notice of motion for default judgement in the mail, but not until after the return date (the date which I was supposed to respond by) had passed. Distraught, I realized it was also assigned to Judge Dawson, so I called his chambers and asked to speak with the law clerk about it. I was told, "It's too late. There's nothing you can do. The Judge has already signed the order." I penned another letter to him, and to Ms. Lester and Ms. Maas at ABN. I also saved the envelope the notice and accompanying papers came in, showing the date stamp of mailing was beyond the return date.

By this time my office had stacks and stacks of paper piled around. I had documentation for everything, and every time an incident or strange event occurred, I had to write it down, along with date and time, persons present, and any other significant information, fax it to Mr. Rodgers, Mr. Johnston, and Mr. Michaels. I also continued to see what I could find out about Judge Head and Don Lorry. One day as Kat and I were applying a sealant to the brick walls in my shop area, talking and making plans, she told me about a social services counselor she had recently met.

"So, her name is Melanie," Kat said, standing on the old wooden shelving so she could reach higher up on the wall. "She told me that everyone knows that Judge Head is doing something strange with all these young boys."

"Yeah, everyone claims that, but . . ." I grimaced. "We need proof. And, we need people who will *actually come forward* and say something *factual* under oath. Everyone seems to be scared."

"Well, Melanie said that she often sees him bring young boys to court. He sits with them and then he gives them rides afterward. So, she asked her coworkers, 'Why is Judge Head always around these young boys in trouble?'" She climbed down off the shelving to refill her container with sealant. "And they told her that Judge Head is always finding these kids and buying them suits and letting them stay with him, he gets them out of trouble. He says it's his own 'judge's probation', but everybody knows he is taking advantage of their plight and using them for sex." She leaned against the shelves, shaking her head, eyes wide.

"Oh, my God! That's awful," I exclaimed. "What's worse? The judge using these poor kids or the social workers who know about it and look the other way?" Tears spilled out of my eyes as I thought about it.

"Isn't it awful," she replied. "It's amazing. Do you think knowing this will help your case?"

"It might, but what are we going to do about it? I mean," I thought for a minute, then sat down on a stool. "How can we discover if that's what's really happening? And then, how does it tie into the Lorrys? But, then what do we do about it? I don't want to be one of those people who looks the other way."

"I think you should tell Glen Michaels about it, at least," Kat commented. "Maybe he can tell you what to do. But, it wouldn't surprise me if Don already knows all this."

"And if he does . . ." I gasped. "If he does, he may be using it to blackmail Judge Head in my case!"

Kat looked at me with sudden shock. "I hadn't thought about that. But that would explain a lot, right?"

"Yes. It would explain Judge Head's dismissing the first few cases I filed, his reluctance to rule on the trial—even to hear the rest of my witnesses." I grabbed a phone to call Stephen but had to leave a message for him to call me back.

"I wonder if Buck knows about this? Is he still renting from you?"

"No, he left last month. A young couple moved in just a couple weeks ago. You haven't met them yet?" Kat had been hanging around so much, I thought sure she must have met them by now. "I'm glad Buck is gone because he let Don Lorry in to see the inn a few months back. It really made me angry."

"You're kidding? I thought he did that last year and you told him not to?" Kat wondered.

"Yes, I did. But, he claimed he forgot." I thought about all the links to what I was experiencing and the Village employees. "Something is very fishy. But, when I spoke with Mark Rodgers the other day, he told me that since my mortgage on the building is a HUD loan, I should be able to file a complaint with HUD itself as to the mishandling of my payments. So, that's next."

"HUD loans are good. You can usually refinance directly with them, too, right?" Kat queried. "That might help." By now she had gone back to applying sealer. I picked up a brush and began working on the lower wall, ten feet away.

"Kat, do you think you could get Melanie to sign an affidavit about what she has seen and been told?"

"I can ask her." She replied. "I know where her office is, I'll be going by tomorrow afternoon."

"Great. Thanks." I thought about the connection and recalled what one of my crew had said about Don moving drugs, then thought about Gary's comments. Bits of information floated around in my head like flying puzzle pieces. "Since Buck isn't here, I guess I had better go check on the Adirondack Suite again. I would hate to go through this year what I went through last year!"

"I'm ready for a break," Kat said, jumping down to the floor. "I'll come with you."

We went into the cold and entered the inn doorway, trudging up the steps. I rounded the corner ahead of Kat and let out a wail. There was water in the suite once again. Giant bubbles in the fresh paint, again. Ice mounded outside the door, again. I sat on the bed and wept for a minute.

"Oh, my God," Kat kept repeating. "Oh. My. God."

I pulled myself together a little and began the process of sopping things up. We moved the furnishings into the next room. Finding a razor blade, I slit the huge bubbles. Then began the process of trying to open the French doors and see outside. Kat gave me the name of a contractor she knew from her church; I called him. He came out later that day to verify that the dryer vent was creating the problem, then the next day, he got up on the roof to inspect it, since it was screaming sunshine and all snow had melted off. He had two other men with him and they proceeded to verify that the roof itself was faulty. There were entire sections that had not been nailed down properly and not overlapped. He fixed it the best he could temporarily but said it would take more work in better weather. When he left, he promised to give me a written estimate of repairs along with a professional, written opinion of the causes of damage and defective roof installed by the Lorrys to use in court.

THIRTY-ONE

Wait for the Lord. Be strong and take heart and wait for the Lord.
THE PSALMIST

THE VILLAGE HAD BEEN referring to and selling the revolving loan fund as a HUD loan for years. Through some research about how to file a HUD claim, I discovered that it had long before—in the 1980's—ceased to be HUD related. In fact, I discovered that the Village attorney and officers had been repeatedly warned to cease and desist making such exaggerated, blatantly false claims. It was precisely these types of gnarly facts which kept surfacing that were not only frustrating me, but now Kat, also. I similarly discovered from pouring through public records that previous recipients of the loan fund had suffered repeated discriminatory actions. Terri, another single mom, lost her building which housed the only local bakery, to the Village through the same types of fraudulent bookkeeping, and abusive actions by the mayor. Not so coincidentally, another friend of justice Head obtained the building for peanuts after that. While a close family friend of justice Head borrowed about $96,000 and never repaid a dime, without any enforcement procedures.

Kat and I, along with Mark Rogers hatched a plan to refinance the building and do away with the Village and the Lorrys in one fell swoop. She and her husband Kenny would "buy" the building for basically the value of the mortgage, so that I could pay it off and the Village would have no more strings to pull. Then, because I still had a court action against the Lorrys which justice Head had yet refused to issue a ruling in, they could begin a new action in their name—which would not be a conflict. Furthermore, as "new owners" in name only, they could simply terminate the lease, under the conditions of the lease already existing. Our partnership documents dictated that we would, in reality, *both* be owners, and a Memorandum of Understanding dictated further that I had the right to buy them out at any time, among other provisions. The extent of their financial input dictated the extent of ownership, since the building itself and my business and business assets were all housed there. We executed a sales agreement, had a commercial appraisal ordered, drafted leases for the laundromat, B&B, and the antique shop.

The process of getting this closing to go through so that we could get the Lorrys out and the Village out of our hair took a few months longer than expected. The commercial appraisal cost about $2,500 but was so worth it. The day the appraiser showed up, Don Lorry himself was in the laundromat. I showed Mr. Snowden the laundromat by accessing it through the main entrance since they still had the bicycle chain around the door knobs of the French doors.

"Excuse me!" Don bellowed. "What the hell do you think you're doing here?" He took a firm stance in the center of the hallway and folded his arms across his chest.

"We are appraising the building, Don. Get out of the way, please," I replied calmly, noting Mr. Snowden's surprise. I had warned him the best one can warn about the extreme actions of terrorists to those who've never experienced them.

"This is MY building!" Don shouted. "Get the hell out of here! *I OWN THIS BUILDING!*"

"Are you out of your mind, Don?" I asked. "I own this building." Exasperation and shock filled me.

"Excuse me, Mr. Lorry," Mr. Snowden spoke firmly, color rising in his face. "I disagree with you. I have verified the record owner is Karen Marie. I am here at her request and she is your landlord. She has every right to inspect the building." Don didn't know what to say, still fuming, he turned to Carolyn, pointing his finger nastily in the air as if brandishing a weapon.

"Carolyn! Get Evan on the phone! Now!" he snarled. She dutifully picked up the phone before he had even finished his demand.

We walked past him. I showed Mr. Snowden the multiple damages they had caused, including the hole in the wall near my new copper pipes, the now fallen portico at the back door which had come apart from the building due to the ice buildup, and explained about the never completed renovations which were supposed to be done in exchange for lower rent. Don kept trying to follow us or get in front of us to block our progress.

"Don, I'm asking you nicely, please back off!" I stated. He glared at me as if one look from his eyes had some sort of mystical power I should fall in obeisance to. I tried to remain calm and stare him down, but my knees were beginning to buckle.

"Don!" Carolyn called from the front. "Evan's on the phone!" He turned and walked away.

Once next door in my own shop again, Mr. Snowden remarked at what a detriment the Lorrys' presence is to the whole property.

"Yes, I know," I grimaced. "That is what I am up against and why this is the only way to get them out." Still smarting with exasperation, I continued. "Can you believe he has the audacity to stand there and claim he owns this building? Right to my face?"

"No, I really can't." he replied somberly. "I have encountered some strange situations with tension between landlords and tenants in my line of work, but never anything so brazen as this."

As the appraisal was finalized, the mortgage company began requesting various forms of verification, copies of our intended leases and verification of funds to complete the sale. I got a call one day from the mortgage broker stating that they had attempted to verify funds in the Smith's savings account and could not. When I approached Kat about it, she was shocked.

"I don't understand; the money is there," she insisted. "I'll ask Kenny if I gave them the wrong account number. But is the appraisal finished?" she tilted her head and shoved her hands into the front pockets of her tight, narrow wale corduroys, shrugging her shoulders as she did.

"Yes. And he even put in a section about the Lorrys being a detriment to the property value," I smiled.

"Well, what does it appraise for?" she wondered.

"Without the bed and breakfast, just the building itself, $260,000." I beamed. "Do you realize what that means? I am so pleased!"

"What?"

"That means what I bought for $55,000 I turned into more than $260,000 in a year, with an investment of $145,000, along with a lot of sweat equity. And that doesn't include the value of my B&B and assets in the antique shop! With the B&B the value is about what I had listed it when I had it on the market, well over $500,000." I felt so validated that I had made it to that point despite all the shenanigans of the Village, Phil

O'Conner, and the Lorrys. "There is more than enough equity here for me to move forward. Imagine how much easier it will be when the Lorrys and the Village are out of the picture!"

"Wow. That's awesome!" Kat exclaimed with a smile. "You should be very proud of yourself. You worked hard."

"Thank you," I replied. "Thank God."

"So, we have to discuss the actual sales price with the mortgage company next, huh? They gave us a few options, we have to see which one fits." Kat pondered the next steps.

"Yes, so let's get that funds verification taken care of." I went into my office and retrieved the fax from Navy Federal Credit Union which showed only a balance of $24.91 in the Smith's savings account. "Does this look like the right account information?" I asked, handing it to her.

Kat looked it over soberly, pursing her lips together and placing her hand below her chin.

"Yes, but . . . " She paused soberly. "There was over $25,000 in that account. I need to find out what Kenny did with it."

"Do you think you still want to move forward with our plans or should I do something else?" I asked calmly, realizing I had already been turned down for financing on my own and wondering what else I could possibly do. Still, I was at peace. I didn't want to proceed with anything that wasn't stable.

"I inherited $25,000 from my aunt a few months back," Kat said. "That should be in there. Plus, Kenny wants tax deductions and our accountant says we need to invest in something that will get us deductions. I just need to figure out what he did with my money. Don't worry. He probably put it into CDs or something. I'll get back to you, but we are definitely moving forward with this."

Later on Kat called me to explain that Kenny had used the cash to pay off his truck, and replenish the $7,000 she had invested so far into our partnership from their personal checking account. She explained that they had another savings account which she would alert the mortgage company to for verification purposes. We also decided that given the preapproval they had we would have to structure the sale in such a way that I took a second mortgage note of somewhere between $36,000 and $50,000 as the down payment, so they could get the best interest rate and still have all the funds needed for closing and partnership expenses. To save money, I drafted the note myself that night, and emailed Mark Rogers about the fine tuning of our Memorandum of Understanding, which Kat and I had drafted together a few weeks earlier. A few days later, she and Kenny signed it.

Even though Glen Michaels and others were pretty sure it was corruption, it didn't seem to matter. Things spiraled down quickly.

"I want you to compile a timeline of events, along with all your documentation, into a formal complaint for the Commission on Judicial Conduct," Glen said pointedly, glasses perched halfway down his nose. "I am sure that there is something we don't know yet about the connection between the Lorrys and Justice Head, but we have enough to move forward on this and hope they will investigate."

"Commission on Judicial Conduct?" I leaned forward to make eye contact. "You really think that will help? How long will it take them to look into this?"

"Unfortunately, it will take at least a few months, but don't rush this. You have a ton of documentation, and I am told this would not be the first complaint against justice Head…" He sat back and rested his elbows on the arms of his chair, concern evidenced by the scrunching of his brow. "How are you holding up? This is a lot of stress."

"Yes, it is," I sighed. "I feel like I'm living in a nightmare or horror movie that I just can't wake up from or leave. And, I guess the audacity of these characters just astounds me. It's like, they have no conscience…"

"I went through a very stressful time like that once. It was very painful and hard to come to terms with reality of betrayal and loss," Glen spoke softly. "Do you have a good support network?"

"Yes," I thought about it for a minute. "Yes, but no time to take much advantage of it. I miss my best friends, but they are always available by phone. I try not to discuss it too much with my grandmother because I don't want to stress her out. But, I will be fine. I guess I just need to realize there is more than the Golden Rule in play here."

"What do you mean?" Glen looked amused. "I have a background in theology. 'Do unto others . . . ' not good enough?"

"What I mean is, I have discovered that treating others the way you want to be treated isn't enough. There's a reason why Jesus also said, 'I am sending you out as sheep among wolves. Therefore, be innocent as doves but shrewd as serpents.' "

"Fantastic!" Glen clapped his hands together. "You're going to be just fine."

"I hope so. Maybe if I could get some sleep, that would help! But certainly, learning to be shrewd is something I never cared about until now." I was serious.

"You're going to make it," he reaffirmed. "Meanwhile, get crackin' on that judicial complaint. Check out the website I noted for you here, and feel free to run your first draft by me. I'm going to make a few phone calls and put out some feelers with the FBI, too."

"The *FBI*?" I sat up straight, leaning closer to study his face.

"Yes, I think there's a whole lot more we need to know about why justice Head is protecting the Lorrys and why the Village wasn't accepting your mortgage payments. It's all too cozy. This morning I went over all the paperwork in your foreclosure proceeding with the Village," he pointed to the short stack on the left side of his desk. "Doesn't it strike you as crazy that Mr. Clute would write to Judge Dawson and ask the court to appoint the Lorrys as receivers of the building while the foreclosure is litigated?"

"Oh! So, you did get my faxes!" He had asked me to keep him apprised by faxing events as often as possible, but I really didn't know how much attention he was paying until that moment. "Yes! I could not believe my eyes when I read that! They are not paying rent, causing damages, owe me a small fortune—which if I had I would be able to almost pay off my Village mortgage!"

"And yet we are supposed to believe that the interests of the Village and the building itself would somehow be better off if they were put in charge!" Glen finished my thought with enthusiastic sarcasm.

"I just haven't slept since I read that," I told him. "It's just too crazy. It makes me wonder about Judge Dawson, too. He's got his hands in too many of my affairs, and justice Head seems to think he has some inside scoop on the Lorrys."

"I think I've told you before, but it bears repeating," he sighed. "The truth is stranger than fiction. So, let's get at the truth, shall we?"

I left Glen's office that day feeling strangely elated at the thought that he was sure there was more going on than should be. Not because I wanted it to be true, but because it was the only possible explanation that made any sense and, because it seemed he would not let that alone. Even so, I had another sleepless night pondering it all.

THIRTY-TWO

*In life it is necessary to stress less, trust more,
and have faith in the right direction.*

BY NOW IT WAS April, and Dave had been gone since early January. I went for a routine OB/GYN appointment and was scheduled for a mammogram, due to my mother's family's history of breast cancer. The screening showed several lumps in my right breast which were speculative. I was very distraught about the finding, and worried about my kids, too. I didn't tell them about it, but I did borrow a natural health book from Aunt Shirley, who had decided to become more supportive in light of Dave's departure. I think the fact that he was on the front lines, serving our country while I seemed to be facing enemies on my own front lines weighed on both she and Tom. I am quite sure that Nana had something to do with it, too. Regardless, they became much more supportive and available to me during that time.

I quickly and drastically changed my diet. Aunt Shirley thought that maybe it was just fibrocystic breast tissue which she claimed could easily be dealt with. First, I had to address my stress response. I was not sleeping peacefully, heartsick, and overwhelmed, and I would hardly let a soul know it. My desire to remain strong took a toll on my body. I began spending more time in prayer and positively reflecting on all my blessings. I took gratitude breaks throughout the day and tried to release the negative situations I faced. I knew I could only do so much; being alive for my children had to be my highest priority. I cut out all caffeine except green tea, got regular exercise, and ate a mainly vegetarian diet. I also began supplementing with herbs. The biggest thing of all though was that in my daily reading I focused on the promises of Scripture. Verses like Jeremiah 29:11 were lifelines to me. "'For I know the plans I have for you,' declares the Lord, 'plans to prosper you and not to harm you, plans to give you hope and a future.'"

Psalm 27 also was something I meditated upon daily. But when I read 3 John 1:2: "Dear friend, I pray that you may enjoy good health, and that all may go well with you, even as your soul is getting along well," I realized that the connection between my fretting, my hurting, and the constant bitterness I had to swallow really was affecting my health. I set aside a week to fast, eating only vegetables, fruit, and drinking water, and to meditate on how to release the negative effects of what I faced without losing ground legally. I had some mental clarity to move forward with, but honestly, I don't think I mastered the skill for many years to come.

When the time came for my follow-up ultrasound and an additional mammogram with a specialist in Burlington, I was convinced that God had heard my prayers, and all would be well. It had been about seven weeks since the first one, and I had a new outlook on things. I was not fearful. I felt calm and at peace. I went through the mammogram and while I waited for it to be read, had the ultra sound, too.

Sitting in Dr. Harris' antiseptic patient room, scantily clad and shivering in the short covering I had been provided, it's opening in the front hardly addressed by the two snaps that managed to keep it on my body, I reflected on the mental transition I had made in the previous two months.

There was a brief knock on the door followed by the turn of the knob as Dr. Harris stuck his head in the room.

"I am going to be a few more minutes," he explained. "Are you in a rush?"

"No, just cold," I laughed.

"I'll see if we can get a warm blanket. Be back in a few." He closed the door again. I thumbed through a magazine I had brought in from the waiting room. A few minutes later a nurse came in with a blanket.

"Dr. Harris is just going over your results," she said as she unfolded it and draped it around my shoulders. "He'll be in shortly. Is there anything else I can get you?"

"This is perfect. Thank you."

"Okay then," she replied. "You're welcome."

About ten more minutes went by. I began to wonder if things were not as good as I had believed. Fear crept into my thoughts. Anxiety rose in my chest. I tried to recall my verses in my mind, breathing deeply. After a while, Dr. Harris reentered the room.

"Um," he looked agitated as he spoke. "I uh, think we have to do the test again."

"Huh? But why?"

"Well, you see," he fumbled as if he was embarrassed. "There's no way the results I have can be yours."

"What do you mean?" I asked. Then suddenly realized what he meant. "You mean, because there are no more lumps?" I asked excitedly.

"Yes, I mean, I think they must have mixed up your results with someone else's."

"Oh!" I laughed out loud. "No! I am sure they didn't. I am sure I am free of lumps!"

"You are?" He sat down in his swivel chair and folded his arms across his chest, his eyebrows arched incredulously. "Because they don't usually mix up results . . ."

"I am quite sure," I told him, smiling with relief. "I have been asking God to heal me, and I believe he has."

"I've never seen this before," he said soberly. "So, you don't want to do the tests again?"

"No. I don't need to. I know it deep down. I am well."

"Okay, well, I have no choice but to agree with you," he said, still incredulous.

The summer was busy. Just running the inn and keeping up with the kids took all my energy. John Clute, the Village attorney, scheduled depositions in their case against me. Mark told me it was simply the next step, and that we should spend some time preparing. He hoped that the truth would come out as a result and we could resolve our differences. Meanwhile, Ms. Mass of ABN AMRO finally accepted my revised version of our repayment agreement and so that was another load off my mind. I didn't have as much time to spend with Kat, but she and her kids helped me out from time to time, and she kept the pressure on the mortgage processor to move our closing along. We had hoped for a June 25th closing date, but the Village wouldn't agree to the payoff amount it had previously issued. That meant more restructuring and another flurry of paperwork.

"Good afternoon, The Kingsland Inn, may I help you?" I answered my office phone.

"Karen Marie?" Mark's familiar voice stated on the other end.

"Yes, how are you, Mark?"

"I'm well, but I have had some surprising news," he stated. "Pretty unusual, truthfully."

"Uh oh. Now what?" I asked, fully aware this couldn't be good.

"John Clute filed a motion for default judgment in your case," he stated soberly. "I need you to come in the office and spend some time going over it with me. We need to file our response."

"But, we just scheduled depositions," I wondered aloud. "Isn't that unusual?"

"Yes, it is," Mark agreed. "I have never seen anything like it. It's not professional courtesy, for sure. You'd think he would've at least told me his intentions when we set up the deposition."

As soon as I hung up with Mark, I phoned Kat and told her what happened.

"Those creeps!" her voice dripped with disgust. "They don't want you to win. They will do whatever it takes by hook or by crook!"

"It certainly seems that way," I answered. "But I really can't believe that people can get away with such dishonesty. They're public officials. There should be more scrutiny!"

"No one cares, Karen Marie," Kat said sadly. "No one gives a damn."

"Well, I have to send a fax to Glen now, so I had better go."

"The AG? Yes. For sure keep him posted. At least he seems to be interested in this," she replied.

"I hope so. Meanwhile, keep your ears open if you're out and about in town. The grapevine is loud and obnoxious around this village, but usually there's some truth to it. Haha!"

"That's very true!" She laughed.

THIRTY-THREE

If you don't think for yourself, you make everyone aware of that when you try to speak for yourself.

THE CLOSING DATE WAS set for August 29th. Finally, the Village would be paid off, and a new action to evict the Lorrys from the property would be filed. I was very pleased indeed.

Kat was happy, too, and was anxious to get the Lorrys out so she could begin her own business in the space. She drafted a letter she wanted me to deliver to them stating that they needed to be out of the premises within ten days of closing as the 'new owners' had other plans for the space. I had just recently been notified by my insurance company that the Lorrys were such a hazard they would no longer cover me, another loophole which allowed me to terminate their lease. I had notified them, but they didn't budge. By now they owed me in excess of $136,000. My mortgage on the building was less than $145,000, though Mark Whitey, the mayor, kept adding on fees and costs—which would not have been necessary had he just taken my money appropriately.

On the afternoon of August 27th, Kat and I went into the laundromat to hand-deliver the letter she had drafted, which I tweaked and signed. Carolyn was sitting by her little desk at the front in the sweltering humidity, a tiny fan blowing on her. Her spectacles were balanced halfway down her nose as she scowled at her paperwork, which kept lifting on the edges due to the fan. There were a couple of patrons in the back, folding clothes.

"What do *you* want?" she sneered, looking above her glasses at us.

"Hello, Carolyn. How are you?" I asked. "I need to deliver this." I handed her the folded letter, which she snatched and hastily glanced at.

"We're not leaving," she replied. "And George says we don't have to."

"The jig is up, Carolyn! You can't have it both ways!" Kat exclaimed.

"George?" I was incredulous. "You mean Justice Head?"

"Yes," she replied condescendingly. "He's a personal friend of ours."

"Carolyn, do you realize what you are saying?" I knew there was foul play, but I could hardly believe she was so brazen about it. "If he's a friend he should have recused himself from the case! Just how long do you think you can continue to operate your business here, causing me damages, making money for yourselves, and not paying a dime?"

"You had your chance to work things out with me," Kat pounced, pointing her finger, "and you refused to negotiate fairly. You could have sold me the business for a fair price and been done with this. Are you even happy here?"

"This is our bread and butter," Carolyn retorted. "It's worth something to us! This building was our retirement."

"*Was* being the operative word, Carolyn. You don't own it anymore." I sympathized with her but that was no reason to allow them to continue pushing me around. "You need to pay your rents and other charges due pursuant to the lease. You are causing me a ton of trouble."

"Well, Mark told us not to pay you any rents so he can take the building back and give it to us. He said he would work something out with us after he forecloses on you." Again, her honesty simply showed me what a mindless puppet she was.

"Mark Whitey? The mayor?" I was beside myself. I looked at Kat whose eyes were wide in disbelief also.

"That's fraud, Carolyn!" Kat howled.

"And what about the eviction proceeding? Even justice Head has finally admitted you owe me money and have caused damages—" I was hoping she would keep spilling her guts.

"Like I said, George says we don't have to leave unless he issues an official ruling that says we have to, *and he promised he won't do that!*"

"Carolyn! That is fraud! That is why Judicial Conduct is investigating! Don't you see? Why won't you do the right thing?" Exasperation is not a strong enough word for what I was feeling in that moment. Part of me was elated that the truth was out, another part of me was wondering how to proceed in the face of it.

"You need to get out. I'm calling Don!" she replied, picking up the phone.

"Carolyn, you can call Don all you want, but you still have to leave. You are not welcome here when the new owners take over," Kat raised her voice in anger. "You need to get out!"

"Okay, let's go. Bye Carolyn. Please take that notice seriously." I said, making my way to the door. Kat followed, muttering under her breath about how insane the whole thing was.

An hour later I went to the supermarket and was surprised to see a state trooper's patrol car parked in front of the laundromat. Kat called me a while later to report seeing the same thing.

"I have no idea," I told her in bewilderment.

"Did you call them? Send them to the building for some reason?" she asked.

"For what?" I wondered. "To arrest Carolyn for exposing the fraud? Not likely!"

A week later, some of my best friends—Linda and Sonny, Marie and Tim, and all their kids—came up for Labor Day weekend. The kids planned on camping in our yard, but the adults were going to stay at the inn. We had a barbecue at the house, with Kat and Kenny joining in. As I was prepping the food, I got a call from one of the local state troopers.

"Hey, Trooper Eric!" I had a lot of respect for Eric.

"Hey, Karen Marie. How are you?" he replied.

"Great! My best friends are here for a visit, and I am making them some dinner. What's up?"

"Oh! Nice! What time do we eat?" he laughed.

"You're welcome any time, Eric."

"I wish I could," he sobered a bit. "Listen, I am wondering when is the next time you'll be down at the inn? I have to go over something with you."

"I'll be bringing my friends down in a couple of hours. They're going to be staying there this weekend."

"So, can I just tell you? I am a little perplexed at this situation." He sighed into the phone loudly. "I can't do anything about it, but Judge Head issued a restraining order against you."

"What? How? For what?" I asked, my mind spinning.

"How else do you think?" he asked sarcastically. "It's the Lorrys again. They filed a complaint saying that you and Katherine Smith harassed Carolyn in the laundromat and asking for a restraining order against you.

There's a hearing scheduled, but I'm afraid over the holiday weekend, there's nothing we can do about it."

"Seriously? Those crooks!"

"You should call your lawyer. We all know this is bogus, but we have to follow Judge Head's orders and serve this on you—and Mrs. Smith." Eric sighed again. "I saw it and decided I would rather it be me than anyone else. I have a feeling . . . well, let's just say the word is out that you filed a complaint with Judicial Conduct, and some of us are expecting there's gonna be some blowback in your direction."

"Yes, I guess I should have thought of that, but . . . " I heaved an anxious breath. "But that would just implicate them even more, right? I figured they aren't that crazy."

"Ah, but you don't know who you're dealing with," he said. "They aren't innocent and responsible like you. I'm keeping an eye out for you, but you're going to have to watch your back, too. And, unfortunately, stay away until your lawyer can get this dealt with."

"How did you hear about the complaint?" I asked him.

"There's been an investigator snooping around. Long overdue if you ask me. So, shall I meet you at the building when you take your friends down? Where can I find Mrs. Smith?"

"Yes. I'll be there. Kat just left here. I'll phone her and let her know you're coming. She just lives down on Chesterfield Street, number 27. Does 6:00 p.m. work?" I thought about all the ramifications of having to stay away from the Lorrys when they were in that laundromat day in and day out, sitting in front of my door, even.

"See you then," Eric answered. "Hang tough."

Kat was appalled when I told her the news. She was ready to hold a rally and protest, alert the media, and if she could have reached Glen Michaels she would have. Though the closing was supposed to happen just two days after our little session with Carolyn, the paperwork was not correct and had to be sent back to the bank for revisions. The new date was set for September 6th, just days away.

The Lorrys, Mark Whitey, and Judge Head were all under the assumption that the closing had already taken place. In fact, while I was in the stairway outside the laundromat just a couple of days before I overheard a conversation between the village clerk, Lynn, and Carolyn Lorry. Lynn was telling Carolyn that she and Mark were so sorry but there was nothing more they could do. The closing between the Smiths and me was going through and that would tie their hands from assisting the Lorrys. I made a note of everything they said, the date, time, and background and sent it to Mark Rogers and Glen via fax, as per usual. I should have anticipated that without the mayor's help, the Lorrys would once again turn to justice Head for help.

Linda and Sonny, Marie and Tim, and I went to the inn for 6:00 and stood outside waiting for Trooper Eric. As he strode up the sidewalk to greet us, he stuck out his hand to shake with each person, before finally handing me the paperwork.

"Now, Judge Head has his own way of doing things, so there's a handout attached telling you his particular version of the rules," Eric eyed the reactions of my friends as he talked.

"Is that even legal?" Marie wondered aloud, concern on her face mirrored by all.

"It is what it is," I said quietly. "He's an unusual 'judge'."

"Well, what this means is you have to stay at least 500 feet away from the Lorrys at all times, at least, until you get this taken care of." Eric looked at me, searching my face for comprehension, I'm pretty sure.

"But that's impossible!" I gasped. "How am I supposed to run my business? I have guests coming in this week—it's fall foliage!"

"I think that's their intent," Eric acknowledged quietly. "You can't be in your own building because then you would be in violation of this restraining order, and you could be arrested."

"Oh my God!" Linda whined. "That's so unfair!"

"Yes. It is," Eric replied. "But we have to follow orders I'm on duty tonight, but off tomorrow and Monday."

"So these crooks who owe her over a hundred thousand dollars and won't get out of her building are protected and she has to stay away and not even be able to run her business!?" Tim asked, agitation in his voice and color rising in his face.

"I'm afraid that's so," Eric replied.

"Eric is one of the good guys. He's just the messenger," I commented. "Eric, I need to get in the building and get some things, but—"

"Take as much time as you need right now while I am here," he interrupted. "Get whatever you think you'll need until your lawyer can get this rescinded."

I showed my friends around, still feeling dazed. They were very impressed with all I had accomplished since they had seen it last, but it seemed a bit anti-climactic now. I went down to my office and checked voicemail, then grabbed my paperwork and schedule for the coming weeks. We all went back to the house for a bonfire with the kids, roasting marshmallows and playing games, and eventually I was able to let it go and relax again. It wasn't fair, but the holiday weekend meant there was nothing I could do but enjoy my friends.

THIRTY-FOUR

*Some men are gentlemen, others are Don Juans,
and still others pretend to be both.*

WHEN TUESDAY CAME, IT was closing day. We went to Mark Roger's office and proceeded to go over the numbers. The Village was seeking a pay off in excess of $186,000, over $40,000 more than I had borrowed. That was a last-ditch effort on the part of Mark Whitey to prevent the closing from happening. When Kat was told the new pay off figure just a week or so before, she refused to back down, and instead apparently borrowed extra money from her father. I insisted on an accounting, which was only provided to me the morning of the closing. It showed where they had re-amortized my mortgage twice, jacking up the interest rate by more than double, and still not reflecting cash payments I had made in the village offices.

"Mark, this payoff is wrong," I told him. "If they take all this money from me, I will walk away with not one dime, and still have to fight them."

"Yes, I realize that, so it's up to you," he replied, leaning over his desk earnestly. "The way I see it, you're already going to have to sue the village to be made whole, so you may as well get them off your back and at least they won't have any control anymore. This makes the foreclosure go away."

"Well, I suppose if Kat and Kenny have the money and want to go forward, then that will determine it," I told him, breathing a prayer.

"Speaking of the Smiths," Mark leaned back again. "Are they here yet?"

"I believe they're in the conference room waiting," I told him.

"Well, I got an interesting call from John Clute the other day. He said the village was willing to add the Smiths to your mortgage and renegotiate."

"What the—?" I gasped. "You've got to be kidding!"

"That's what I told him!" Mark laughed. "What do you make of that?"

"Well, did you get that fax I sent the other day? They thought the closing had already happened—on our original date. Anyway, I overheard the village clerk and Carolyn Lorry talking. The clerk was *apologizing that there was nothing more the village could do to help the Lorrys get the building back!*"

"You're kidding?" Mark looked stunned. "I didn't see that."

"Yeah, I faxed it to you and Glen Michaels. I noted the date and time. And by the way, what are we going to do about this restraining order?" I worried. "I have guests checking in tomorrow."

"I *did* get *that* fax. Absurd!" Mark replied. "That's one for Stephen Johnston to handle. He's best. I'll call him. I'm sure he will get it rescinded ASAP given how judge Head still hasn't issued a final ruling on your eviction of the Lorrys."

"Okay. Great." I pondered the whole proposal of adding the Smiths to my mortgage. "Isn't it just blatant? Their proposal to add the Smiths? It's like one dying wish for control."

"That's why I didn't even bother to call you," Mark chuckled. "I would advise against it. So, let's go over these numbers with the Smiths. The title agent should be here any minute."

Kat sat in the waiting room anxiously clenching and unclenching her hands. She stood to her feet as I came out of Mark's office. "Everything okay?" she asked, nervously.

"I think so. He says I have to get Stephen to handle the restraining order because justice Head still hasn't issued the final ruling on the eviction of the Lorrys."

"Stephen will kick ass," she said with determination. "Are we ready?"

"Mark wants to go over the numbers with us before the title agent arrives. Where's Kenny?" My eyes scanned the office.

"He said to text him when we're five minutes from starting. Something came up at work."

We made our way into Mark's office and sat down again. Mark handed us each a copy of his legal pad notes with the closing figures. Between the payoff being inflated and the fact that I was holding a second for all but $1,000 of the down payment, I would literally walk away from this closing without a dime. The legal fees and closing costs had to be paid. I wanted to cry, until I thought about the fact that this was a new beginning. An opportunity to get out from under the manipulative control of the devious mayor and scheming Lorrys.

"Well, are we moving forward today, ladies?" Mark smiled as he seated himself behind his desk again.

"Yes, we are," Kat said nervously, letting out a slow breath.

"Are these figures what you expected, Kat? Do you still want to go through with the closing and partnership?" I queried, seriously giving her an opportunity to change her mind.

"Karen Marie, what would you do if I didn't?" she asked rhetorically. "You need this. We do too. We're prepared. Next step, evict those bastards."

"Let's hope," I told her. "But seriously, if you want to change your mind, now is the time. I would understand." Mark watched us both intently.

"Let's do this!" she said determinedly, grabbing my hand firmly.

"Okay, then," Mark continued with preparations. "I explained to Karen Marie earlier that she will have to file a suit against the village based on all of this erroneous accounting plus what they owe her from before. In fact, I suspect a suit against the village and the Lorrys is in order. But what about this second mortgage between you which is the down payment? I assume it should be recorded."

"Well, it is supposed to go to Karen Marie's share of the partnership interest, so essentially, she would still be the majority owner," Kat told him. "So, does it have to be recorded?"

"I think if we have a provision where it gets recorded in the event of a dispute or a default, then that would be fine," I thought out loud. "Does that make sense?"

"Technically, it doesn't matter when it gets recorded unless it matters to you," Mark replied. "Procedurally we usually do it all at once, but—Is Kat going to make payments on the $36,000 note?"

"No," Kat answered. "It's just documenting more of Karen Marie's partnership interest at this point. She would have to be paid back, but our agreement is that she has the right to buy us out whenever she wants, so that would go to her ability down the road."

"I see," Mark continued. "So, for now, we won't record it." Just then the intercom buzzed. "Yes?"

"The title agent has arrived," his secretary informed.

Kat texted Kenny, and we made our way to the conference room.

After the closing, I went straight to Stephen's office; it was just around the block. He was in a meeting but came out to see me briefly. We agreed on a small retainer for him to handle the restraining order for both Kat and me. I promised to come up with it within the week, and he promised to get on it by the end of the day. He was very curious to hear more about the judicial conduct investigation, but so far, I had only received one call from the investigator asking me lots of questions, and of course, asking me to include him in every fax pertaining to the village, the Lorrys, and justice Head.

"How soon will these be taken care of? I have guests checking in?" I asked just before he went back to his meeting.

"Sorry, Karen Marie. It won't happen by tomorrow," Stephen replied. "Knowing Judge Head and the Lorrys, he'll make us work for this. I would say we could go to court next week."

"Court? Next week?" I moaned.

"Yeah. You had better cancel your guests. I'll get on it as soon as possible."

Fortunately, the guests that were set to arrive the next afternoon were by now friends. They had stayed so frequently since I opened that we usually had dinner together at least once while they were in town. I called them and explained what happened and they graciously rescheduled for three weeks down the road when they thought the foliage would be better anyway. The remaining guests however, were not pleased. I sadly explained that circumstances were beyond my control, offering to help them find other lodging.

Around 7:00 that evening, as I cleaned up the kitchen and looked forward to a glass of wine, the phone rang.

"This is William Meconi," he said brusquely. "I'm a partner of Mark Rogers. I'm going to be handling the restraining order for you in front of Judge Head."

"But I—" Confusion and anxiety gripped me at the end of a long day. "Stephen Johnston is handling that."

"I am handling it. It's one of the perks of being a client of our firm. No need for a separate retainer. I'll just bill you later." He talked quickly. "Stephen is slammed, and I am going to be in Judge Head's court next week anyway, so. . . . Mark tells me you're quite the Erin Brockovich."

"Excuse me?" My mind fumbled to keep up with him. "Erin Brockovich?"

"Yeah! You've seen the movie, right? Hell of an investigator and determined to fight for the underdog." He went on. "It's a compliment."

"I guess, so you have heard about the judicial complaint and investigation, too." I realized as I spoke.

"Hell yeah, but all that aside," he chuckled. "Do you have boobs like her?"

I suddenly realized that Mark's partner was very far from a gentleman. I hoped he was at least good in court and had some pull with justice Head. I didn't have all of Stephen's retainer, and the idea that he would bill me later was appealing. The silence on my end of the phone apparently didn't even confound him.

"Well, I guess I'll see for myself when I meet you next week. We have to appear in the village court on the 13th," he said.

"But, can't you do something sooner? I'm losing business!"

"No, he only holds court every other week now. I will be there at 5:30. You make sure you're there, we'll talk for a few minutes, then I will get this taken care of."

"And what about Kat Smith? You'll represent her, too, right?"

"Two-for-one special," he replied. "I'll see you next week."

THIRTY-FIVE

When evil is exposed, it is not prudent. It retaliates like a lunatic.

IN THE DAYS THAT followed, I struggled with feeling abandoned by Stephen. I trusted him more than any other lawyer, and believed he was the sharpest attorney with a keen conscience I had ever met. It bothered me that he would pass the case off to Bill Meconi without even calling to explain. As things dragged on, I got another call from Mr. Payette, the judicial conduct investigator.

He was in the village of Keeseville court going over the records of cases and came across several entries in the cases where I had filed against the Lorrys that had been "whited out". This proved to me that he was indeed investigating thoroughly, but also made me realize that now even justice Head would be made aware of it.

I had to rely on the kids to go into the inn and retrieve calls off the answering machine so that I could return calls from home. I got a partial rent check from the Lorrys, woefully inadequate, but Kat and I decided to return it, telling them they had no choice but to vacate, and that the amount was not sufficient. That hurt, but we figured, if the village could refuse my full payments, then we could refuse their minimal ones. It was time to get them out once and for all.

Finally, the evening of September 13th arrived, and we went to the courthouse. To my surprise, justice Head was not on the bench that evening. Rather it was justice Morrow. Bill Meconi approached me as I made my way to a seat in the hallway. He wore a plain white oxford, unbuttoned too far, and a grey suit, no tie.

"Karen Marie?" he inquired, sticking his hand out.

"Hello," I replied.

"Here's the deal, I'm going to go in and talk to Judge Head and you're gonna sit in the back of the court room as far away from the Lorrys as possible," he snapped.

"I have been here a while, justice Head is not on the bench tonight," I smoldered.

"He's here. I'm going to see him in chambers," he nodded toward the door just as Tom and Betty Lorry came out of it.

"This place is so corrupt," I muttered.

"Who's that?" Meconi asked.

"Tom and Betty Lorry, Don's son and daughter in law."

"Let me handle this," he replied, just as I saw Kat approaching from the other end of the hallway. He sauntered into the office of the clerk, and then beyond into justice Head's chambers as if it was his second home, closing the door behind him.

I waited for Kat to get close enough then motioned for her to join me in the back of the courtroom. We watched as misdemeanor cases were heard so abruptly it looked like an episode of "Let's Make A Deal," whispering occasionally to each other and watching the door for Meconi's return. After about twenty minutes, Meconi came out, motioning to us to join him in the hallway. As I approached he handed me a copy of the restraining order that had been marked "rescinded" and sealed with the justice's seal and date.

"How'd you do that so fast?" I gasped, then showed Kat.

"I walked in there and told him to stop fucking with my client," Meconi crooned.

"Ah! What a relief! Thank you!"

"Yes, thank you," Kat chimed in.

"Here's what's going to happen," he sobered, looking down his prominent nose at us. "You Kat Smith?" he asked. Kat nodded. "Okay, this is two for one," he said, holding up two fingers, then pointing only one at me. "Two for one special. You're going to agree to what's called adjournment in contemplation of dismissal."

"Which means exactly?" I asked.

"You will have to be on your best behavior around the Lorrys for six months, and—"

"And, nothing!" I interrupted him. "You know how twisted they are? If I sneeze in their direction they will call the cops!"

"She's right you know," Kat agreed. "This is bull shit, and she has a lot more patience than I do. They'll be having us thrown in jail every time we walk down the street!"

"Listen, this is what's going to happen. Do you want to get back in business? You agree to ACD status, and this will fall off the record in six months. You just need to stay the hell away from the Lorrys," he said firmly. "That's the deal." He pointed his finger at Kat. "*You* be the go between if necessary."

"But she is agreeing to the same thing as me," I pointed out. "If either one of us goes near them—"

"It doesn't make much sense to me," Kat told him. "I'm more easily angered than she is."

"*She's* the lightning rod as far as they're concerned," he told Kat. "*You be the go between.*"

Our case was called, and we went before justice Morrow. Meconi explained the situation and we agreed to the ACD status. I felt like I had won a battle but potentially lost the war.

We went by the inn to check on things. It felt good to walk back through the doors. Next, we went by Little Italy to tell our friends there what had happened. As we stood outside, talking, I noticed justice Head hiding behind a car in the parking lot across the street, watching me. Following my gaze, Kat and a friend also spotted him. When he realized we were watching him, he crawled behind the car, then pretended to be getting out of it, grabbed a shopping cart and started walking to the store. He came out minutes later with no packages at all, looking in our direction.

Later that night, I heard someone walking in the woods outside my house, and Luke wouldn't stop barking. I tried to get him to come in the house for the night, but even as darkness fell, he refused to budge from his post in front of our door. I played it nonchalant for the sake of the kids, but I was terrified. I looked out from various windows, eventually spotting justice Head's car parked off the road, partially behind a bush just in front of the house. My heart pounding, I went to every window and door, making sure they were locked. I tried again to get Luke to come inside, but he would not. I left lights on around the house, and never got undressed for the night. Sitting upright in the middle of my king bed, leaning against the wall behind me, I watched, and waited, cell phone in my hand, and house phone next to me.

"I can't call the state troopers," I told myself. "They'll never believe me." Still, as the hour approached midnight and I could still see his car silhouetted by the moonlight, I dialed the local barracks.

"Is Trooper Eric on duty tonight?" I asked the dispatcher who answered in the affirmative. "Oh good. Then can you please have him drive by my house? There is someone who has been parked just beyond the bushes since about 8:00 p.m., and he knows the backstory." The dispatcher took my phone number and address, then promised to alert Trooper Eric. Almost forty-five minutes later, I watched as he drove by slowly, then went to the corner, turned around, and started back toward my house, just as justice Head pulled out from the bushes on the side of the road and headed back toward the village. Eric pulled into my semi-circle driveway on one side, and continued out the other, following justice Head's car toward the village, too. About five minutes later he called.

"Are you okay?" Eric's voice seemed incredulous and urgent. "I didn't want to scare your kids by knocking on the door at this hour."

"Thank you so much. I'm scared out of my mind," I whispered into the phone. "That was—"

"Judge Head," he confirmed. "Kind of hard to disguise an official plate. What the hell happened?"

"He was forced to rescind that restraining order, but, more importantly, I think he knows it was me who filed the judicial complaint. The investigator has been in the court office going through files." I trembled and couldn't relax. "What am I going to do? I think he's just crazy enough to do something stupid."

"If the rumors are true, you're right. I am on until 7:00 a.m. Try to get some rest. I've got your back tonight, but first thing in the morning you need to get a hold of your contacts at the AG office, and probably that investigator if you can," Eric continued compassionately. "I'll keep driving by tonight. There's one other officer on that is concerned about the Judge Head rumors. I'll let her know to be on the lookout, too."

"Okay," I let out a long sigh. "Thanks, Eric. I appreciate it."

I went to the door to see if Luke would finally come inside. He did, but rather than going to sleep by Jonathan's bed as usual, he positioned himself at the end of the hallway, the only access to all our bedrooms.

THIRTY-SIX

*When you agree to something your gut tells you is wrong,
be prepared for your gut to be eventually found right.*

"WELL, WELL," GLEN REMARKED with amazement. "Maybe he's going to make this easy for us, huh? I mean, I'm sorry for your fright, but this moves things up a notch."

"Glen, if Trooper Eric had not been on last night—" Exhaustion and fear made it hard to even finish the thought. "What would I have done? I have my children to worry about! All of the others think justice Head is the greatest thing since sliced bread."

"Do you have a pen? Take my cell phone number, and my home number, for that matter. You can call me anytime, day or night. Don't hesitate." He rattled off his numbers for me and then continued. "I have a contact at the FBI who's interested in following up on this. Have you heard anything more from Mr. Payette?"

"The investigator? No, but Eric suggested I call him this morning," I replied.

"Do that. Fill him in. But then, I want you to file a police complaint against Head. We need to get this documented," he cleared his throat. "It may mean an eventual order of protection for you, and maybe we can get the Lorry case transferred to another judge for a final decision. You should also tell Stephen."

"Stephen didn't handle the restraining order," I replied.

"What? Why not?" Glen was evidently taken aback.

"I guess he was slammed. He evidently asked Bill Meconi to handle it."

"So it was Meconi that got the order rescinded? And told you to agree to ACD status?"

"Yes."

"Hmm. Well, get that complaint filed. And anyone else who saw him stalking you should file one, too."

Kat was shocked to hear about my night of terror. True to her personality, she was ready to launch a protest and alert the media. She agreed to meet me at the building to file the complaint. Our friends at Little Italy also offered to file statements as to what they witnessed the night before. One of them, Kelly, offered more information about justice Head.

"You should probably talk to Dale," she told me. "He has been abused by Judge Head. Says that in the past the judge made him do drug deals or else go to jail." Kelly whispered sheepishly under her breath at the counter, so no one else could hear.

"What? Justice Head made him do drug deals?" I watched her eyes widen as she nodded her head affirmatively. I could scarcely believe this preacher's kid had contacts like that.

"He's not the only one either, and there's more, but I'll let Dale tell you. He's the one most likely to speak up" She reached in her pocket for her cellphone. "Give me your cell number. I'll text him."

I gave her my cell number and then saw the state police cruiser pull up out the window. "Kelly, I have to go next door. Are you willing to make a statement about last night?"

"Sure. Just tell the officer to come over here when you're finished," she replied.

I greeted Officer Rebecca as she made her way around the cruiser toward the sidewalk. After we shook hands, I unlocked the building and we went inside to talk privately. Kat was due to arrive in five minutes, so I gave the officer the backstory.

"Yeah," Officer Rebecca nodded affirmatively. "Eric told me about the situation. "I'm pulling a double today. Did you manage to get any sleep?"

"No, not really," I sighed. "But thank you for having my back. So, where do we begin then? You know about the court appearance?" We talked about the investigation, and just as we got back to the way justice Head was seen squatting behind cars watching me, Kat entered. She looked more distraught than I had ever seen her.

"Are you okay?" I asked her, as she seated herself at the table with us.

"Yeah, just need to hurry and get an allergy shot in about a half hour." She turned to Rebecca. "I'm her partner, Katherine Smith."

"You were involved in the events last night too? Except at Karen Marie's house?"

"Yes," Kat let out a deep breath. "It's really creepy, isn't it? What kind of town is this? I'm starting to wonder why we ever moved here."

"Here's the form I want you to fill out describing the events as they happened. Be specific. If you took note of the time, write it down. Names of others present, describe what you saw Justice Head do, how it made you feel, whatever might help paint the picture of events for someone who wasn't there."

As she spoke her radio went off, she reached to turn it down, then handed the same form to me.

"Officer L10, you're needed at base, code 3. Over," the radio squawked again.

"L10, I'm taking a statement right now; not available. Over." She returned her attention to us. "I am going to see if I can get this pushed up the ranks for some more attention given other things I'm aware of. We may help you get you an order of protection, but I would have to see what court to pursue that in given the situation."

"L10, code 3. Over."

"What the?" Rebecca annoyingly pushed her blond bangs aside and grabbed her radio. "I'm sorry. This is not typical," she said, watching my reaction. "L10 to base. I'm taking a statement from a vic. Try L15. Over."

Kat stopped writing and looked at her watch nervously. "Can I bring this back later? I have to go."

"Sure. You can drop it off at the station, or—"

"L15 not available. L10 report to base. Repeat. Code 3. Over." Rebecca rolled her eyes.

"This is highly unusual," she told us. "I'm going to go see what's up and come right back. Will you be here?"

"Yes, I'll wait." I told her. "I'll fill this in while you're gone."

"I'll just go get my shot and come back," Kat informed us, grabbing her purse. "I'll be half an hour, tops."

"L10? Acknowledge last transmission. Over."

"L10. En route. Over." Rebecca barked in the radio with some measure of irritation. "Sorry. You said you have additional witnesses?"

"Yes, next door," I noticed a text message on my phone, as Kat made her way out the door.

"I'll stop in there when I get back, too." She strode to the door like an athlete who hasn't even begun to tire. Despite her long night into day, gear and body armor, she was svelte, energetic and moved with ease.

The text message was from Kelly. She said Dale would only agree to talk to me if Vern or Shannon talked, too. I had responded by asking who they are and was informed that they are also victims of justice Head. I asked her how I could reach them. She promised to forward my number to them. I sat at the table and wondered what on earth I didn't know about the justice, and all that seemed to be going on behind the scenes in this bucolic little village along the river.

Mr. Payette and I had a discussion while I waited for Kat and Trooper Rebecca to return. It seemed he knew about Vern. He told me that Vern had filed a complaint with Judicial Conduct in the past, he had been trying to locate him to follow up, with no success. He urged me to persist until I had his contact info and promised to put the word out to keep an eye on me with his in-the-know contacts in law enforcement. Rebecca called about an hour later.

"Between you and me," she almost whispered into the phone. "Something's fishy here."

"You mean with Justice Head?" Fear once again gripped me. Could she possibly be talking about the police barracks?

"Yes and *here*," she enunciated.

"Higher-ups? At the barracks?" I gulped.

"Mmhhhm. I am trying to push this up, give it credence, but I'm running into opposition and interference," she replied. "I can't go back there before my shift is over. Can you drop off your statements?"

"At the same barracks? Who should I give them to?"

"Put it in an envelope with my name on it," she replied. "I'll be in tomorrow. I'll call you later if I get a minute. I still have one more person to talk to about this."

"I'll drop it off in a half hour. But what about the others?" It was all too much for me to fathom, like a strange dream, not reality.

"Yes, sir," she said firmly, but not to me. "I'm on it. Gotta run!"

Kat came in as I hung up the phone. Blowing her hair out of her eyes through pursed lips, she pranced nervously around the shop.

"Are you alright?" I asked her.

"Yeah. Why?" she had the expression of a deer caught in headlights.

"I don't know, you just seem super edgy. Did you get your shot?"

"My shot? No," she replied. "Why?"

"Because I thought that's where you were going," she had me so confused, but I realized I was exhausted, too. Maybe it was me.

"Oh, well. I went, but ya know how doctor's offices are," she sighed. "So slow, and apparently someone else just had to be seen, and I told them after waiting forty-five minutes that I'd come back tomorrow."

"Oh, that's a shame. But, anyway, a lot has come up since you were gone," I told her. We proceeded to discuss the whole situation, then set up a date and time to have a meeting to go over our budget in time for the first mortgage payment to be made jointly. Eventually we got back around to the fact that we had to drop off our statements, and I left to do just that. She took hers home to fill out.

Upon returning home that afternoon in time for Jonathan to get off the bus I immediately sensed something amiss. I had this eerie feeling that someone had been there. I went to the dining room table where I had piled all the documentation Mr. Payette had requested in preparation for copying. Papers were strewn all over, not as neatly as I had left them. I let Luke out of the basement and he fussed about the house before prancing to the door to go out. Going into the living room I noticed one of the windows slightly ajar. Quickly, I grabbed my cell and called Glen Michaels.

"What's up? Did you get your complaint filed?" he answered.

"Glen, someone's been in my house!" I gasped. "And Trooper Eric isn't on duty. Who do I call? What do I do?"

"What? Are you sure?" his voice was measured but concerned.

"Yes! The screen has been broken for a couple of weeks, so I removed it, but I just checked all the windows last night—"

"So, someone came in a window?" he asked.

"Yes, I'm sure of it. It was locked like all the others last night, but this one is tricky, and I've been meaning to get it fixed. It's right by the porch, into the living room. Easy to climb in—and my papers are a mess!" Tears wet my cheeks, my heart felt like it would explode from beating too fast.

"What papers? Judicial Conduct stuff? Is anything missing?"

"I'm not sure. I called you right away. Jonathan will be getting off the bus any minute now—" I slumped into a chair, completely bushed and trying to settle my heart rate.

"What happened when you filed the complaint today?" I filled him in on what Trooper Rebecca told me, and how she got called away.

"I'm so sorry for what you're going through, and I agree with you, given the situation," he sighed, pausing a moment. "Given the way things are let's keep this close to the chest for a few days. And, as always, write this down, fax it in."

"Okay," I said, trying to compose myself. "Thanks, Glen."

"I'm so sorry, Karen Marie," he spoke tenderly. "I know you're tired and frustrated, but you've gotten the attention of judicial conduct now, and I think the FBI. We are moving as best we can on this. Are you going to be okay alone? Don't hesitate to call me if you need to."

"I sure wish I had my soldier home," I told him. "Isn't it ironic that he's on the front lines fighting for our country while I'm home alone fighting for my life and my children's futures?"

"Is there anyone you can call to come stand watch tonight? Let you sleep?" he asked.

"No. I'll be fine." But when I hung up the phone I realized that God saw my need. I got a call from a friend's son, Matt. He heard his mom and Laurie talking about what happened to me in Little Italy. He was only about nineteen years old, in the Army National Guard. He offered to come stay at my house and stand guard so I could sleep well that night. And I did.

THIRTY-SEVEN

To overlook evil because it hurts someone else more than you is to mock the love of God, who says "Love your neighbor as yourself."

NANA WAS VERY WORRIED about me, even though I didn't tell her everything. I didn't want her to be frightened, but I needed her support and prayers. She contacted her old friend, Sister Jeannie, a Carmelite nun who prayed for the whole situation and wrote me encouraging letters. I really appreciated the support since it seemed very few people in our local church understood what I was up against. Mostly they were critical of me and felt it was wrong of me to "disrespect the judge." One day as I sat down to read and pray, I happened upon a Scripture verse that read: "Have nothing to do with the fruitless deeds of darkness, but rather expose them." It was on a day that I needed to be reminded to keep up the good fight. The next thing that happened was surreal.

A black suburban with tinted windows pulled up outside my shop. Two men in dark suits came in, and abruptly flashed badges.

"Karen Marie?" One of them queried tersely as he removed his dark sunglasses.

"Yes?" My raw nerves fired, I immediately thought of my husband. "Oh my God! Oh No!" I began to sob.

"Ma'am?" the other man wondered aloud.

"My husband! Is he—oh no! Is he dead?" Queasiness crept up in my belly and my knees shook. Reaching out and putting his hand on my shoulder the first one, spoke again.

"Is he on active duty?" He glanced at the other man. "Oh. No. Sorry! We are not here about your husband."

"You're not? He's in Ramadi. I haven't heard from him in days, which is highly unusual." I tried to compose myself.

"I'm sorry, ma'am. No, we're with the Federal Bureau of Investigation. We're here about the investigation of town justice George Head."

"Oh," I let out a deep breath. The other man spotted a box of tissue on my desk and grabbed one, handing it to me.

"We're so sorry. We didn't mean to upset you. We appreciate your husband's service," he said.

The first gentleman reached in his pocket and pulled out a business card. "My name is Steve Weintraub, and this is Jim Spivey. We need to ask you some questions. Can we have a seat?" He motioned to the couch nearby and I sat down, as they each pulled up a chair and faced me.

For about twenty minutes they asked me to recount the events that led to this point and about what other officials I had met with. Just the previous couple of weeks I had also met with the Essex County District Attorney's Office because Glen had called them and asked them to hear me out, but I didn't think they were really going to do anything. When the agents were through asking questions, they asked me about other people I knew of that had similar complaints. Finally, they asked me to keep them in the loop, and especially to prepare a list of witnesses with as much contact information as possible and get it to them.

As if on cue, later that evening I got a compelling phone call.

"Are you the woman who's making Judge Head sweat?" he asked seriously when I answered the phone.

"Who is this?" I asked warily.

"My name is Vern. Kelly gave me your number."

"Vern! Yes! Hello! She told me you might call," I hoped that he had the information that would tie everything up in a neat little package for the various investigators and my life might return to normal. "Would you like to meet and talk?"

"I don't trust law enforcement. I'll meet with you, but I got beat up bad by corrections officers the first time I told about Judge Head." He sounded scared, and very serious.

"I'm so sorry, Vern," I said, as sympathy overtook me. I knew the feeling of being outnumbered and still trying to do the right thing. "I am happy to meet you alone, just tell me when and where."

"I can meet you about 8:00 tonight. At the gas station on Route 9 near the Plattsburgh Air Base exit off 87. I will stand under the street light. What do you look like? What car do you have?"

We exchanged info, and then I called my friend's son Matt to ask him to come hang out with my kids. I called Glen on his cell phone, explaining what had transpired that day. He hoped to meet with Vern if I could convince him.

It was already dark when I pulled into the gas station lot. I parked under the street lamp facing north. There was no one there. I worried that Vern might change his mind; that fear and past retribution would prevent him from following through. I prayed silently in the dark, car doors locked. After about five minutes a slender man in his mid-twenties walked by my car and perched himself against the guardrail below the street light. This was more than clandestine; it was the weirdest thing I had ever done. I was hesitant, but I needed the truth.

I rolled my passenger window down part way, leaned over and waved.

"Vern?" I asked. He stood up, looked around him, and then came over to the passenger side of the car, sticking his face in the window.

"You Karen Marie? The mom who's kickin' judge Head's ass?" He was dead serious.

"I am Karen Marie," I told him, unlocking the door. "Want to sit down?"

"Yeah, I wanna get away from anyone who might see us talking," he said, climbing in the car and pulling his hood up part way over his head. "This is hard."

"Yes. I understand. But, there's an assistant attorney general—he's actually the one who urged me to file the complaint with Judicial Conduct, Glen Michaels. He is trustworthy, and we could talk in his office if you want?"

"Tonight?" he asked, curiosity on his face. "Is he for real?"

"Yeah, I mean—" I sighed. "Without him I would not have made it this far. I have his cell. He said we could go there and no one will know about it at this hour."

"All right," he heaved a huge sigh and shook his leg nervously. "But I trust *you*. Any mom who's gonna face a fuckin' crooked judge is okay in my book. This AG guy, we'll just see."

When we pulled up to Glen's office, the street was deserted, and only somewhat lit by street lamps. Glen was just arriving, waving us over as he unlocked the door. We followed him up a narrow flight of stairs to an office I hadn't been in yet, which had a conference table and some comfortable chairs. He turned on a couple of desk lamps, and we sat at the table. I introduced them to each other and explained Vern's concerns.

"Let's see if I can give you some background to make you more comfortable," Glen offered, sitting back in his chair. He recounted how I had gone to him the previous December on the advice of my lawyer, and of how upon reviewing the facts and seeing things escalate, he had urged me to file the complaint with Judicial Conduct. He explained that now there was a full-blown investigation taking place, and that he understood Vern had himself filed a complaint in the past. "So, maybe you could tell us a little about how that went? Did you go to Albany to testify?" Glen finished.

"Hell yeah!" Vern snapped anxiously. I realized he was not as comfortable as he had been when it was just the two of us. "I got the shit beat out of me by two fuckin' CO's!"

"Vern, can you back up? I know this is painful. I mean, that was so wrong, but, how did you get that far to begin with?" I asked.

"Judge Head had me thrown in prison because I wouldn't deal his shit anymore. So, I filed the judicial complaint. I wasn't the only one either. Other people filed, and they called me down to Albany to testify to the Commission." He drummed his fingers nervously on the table. I watched as his eyes filled with rage and tears and his neck veins bulged. "Those fuckin' bastard CO's—they had me in a holding cell and they beat me up bad. Told me I had better not testify or they'd do worse."

"So, no one realized what was happening? There was no one you could turn to?" I knew he was telling the truth, but it seemed unbelievable to me that no one realized what was going on.

"Judge Head has a lot of power. He runs a fuckin' crime syndicate up here! Cops, CO's, hell even border patrol agents and ADA's. No one has the balls to stand up to him," he said. "Except you." He looked at me sincerely. "And that's why *this time*, I won't back down! You better fuckin' go all the way lady, or we're both dead." Glen leaned forward soberly, compassionately.

"Vern, I believe you," he said with deliberation. "It would help Karen Marie and you a lot if all of this comes out now. Do you mind if I take some notes?"

"Go ahead. I'll tell you anything you need to know," he settled back in his chair, more confident, as Glen got up to retrieve a legal pad off the desk. Vern went on to tell us that when the Commission finally called him to the room to testify, he could scarcely breathe his ribs were so busted up, and when they questioned him about the specifics of his complaint, he said nothing. Eventually, the complaint was dismissed, and he was let out of prison on parole. He talked of all the young kids that justice Head molested, and how he even videotaped himself abusing them in order to watch again later.

"The first time he tried to get at me," his face turned red. "This is so fuckin' embarassin'," he gulped. I reached across the table and put my hand on his, my stomach convulsing from the grotesque things he had been describing, my heart literally aching for him.

"It's not your fault. You were just a kid," I told him. "You're doing something about it now. That's nothing to be embarrassed about. That takes guts."

"He has his own 'judge's probation' he calls it. I was barely sixteen years old. A bunch of us guys got in a food fight in the school cafeteria. Instead of just sitting us in detention, they called the fuckin' cops!"

"For a school food fight?" Glen remarked.

"Yeah, man! Crazy, right? But that's how Judge Head operates. He has us all lined up in his courtroom and sentences us to judge's probation. There was a young punk public defender and he said it was the best deal. So, we did all these odd jobs at the judge's house, or in the court offices. And he would show us his folders. He had a folder for each of us, and he kept track and made notes. If we didn't do what he said, he'd pull out the folder and tap his fingers on it. Threaten to send us to jail instead of his probation. We were too young an' scared to know anything." His hazel eyes were wide and deeply expressive as he spoke, he moved his hands with gestures of exasperation.

"So, he molested every one of you?" Glen asked. I felt nauseous as bile rose in my throat. I looked around the room for a waste basket, fearful I would vomit the more I listened.

"Eventually he got us all, that fuckin' pervert!" He slammed his fist on the table as tears escaped his eyes. I let mine fall, too. "At first I was able to avoid him. He would slide his hand up my thigh, or rub my shoulders, and I would tell him 'I like women, man.' But after a while he told me about the first time he had sex with a dude, and how only a man knows what a man likes and stupid shit like that."

"When did this happen? You were about sixteen?" Glen asked, making notes furiously. "Did this take place at the village court?"

"At first, we were always at the court, and he would tell me I was smarter than the other guys. He told me I had a good mind and offered to help me get into college. He would have me do paperwork and shit in his chambers. Then he had me thinking that he was really gonna help me go to college. He said he was going to get my probation lifted and make it so there was no trace of it—an' I didn't even know it wasn't a legit probation, just his pretend probation!"

"So, he stopped getting physical at some point?" Glen asked, looking over at me. I must have looked as ill as I felt because he asked, "You okay?"

"I'll be okay. Maybe I'll get a glass of water," I eyed the water cooler in the corner. Before I could get out of my seat Glen was at it, bringing us each a glass. Vern kept talking.

"So, he eased up and told me he respected me for speaking up. He told me that he was going to introduce me to someone that would lift my probation, and then he was going to help me put in some college applications. Next day, he calls me and tells me to be at his house to have dinner with this dude and go over things. I showed up, and there was no one else there. He put on a gay porno flick and said he had to go make a phone call to see where the dude was."

"So, he tricked you into going to his house?" I gasped.

"Fuckin' bastard! Then he comes back and says 'dinner is almost ready'. I asked him where this person is that's supposed to meet with us and he tells me he can't make it. 'Something came up' he says. He went back in the kitchen and I thought I was gonna puke watching that video, plus, I figured something was very wrong. I looked to see if he had anything else to put in the VCR. I opened the cupboard and there had to be a thousand videos, some of them with names of boys I knew."

"What did you do?" I wondered aloud.

"I went in the kitchen and told him I wasn't hungry, but he put a plate of steak on the table and motioned me to sit down. I noticed there was a steak knife there, so I sat down. I kept thinking, if I have to use it I will. Then he told me about all the places he's been in the world because he was a Marine. How he discovered that he liked sex with guys, but back then no one dared come out, and I told him I didn't have any interest. I tried to bring up the college thing, and the probation thing, but he kept changing the subject. He told me he was attracted to me and I wouldn't know unless I tried it. When I tried to tell him I didn't need to try it, he asked me, 'Did I ever tell you about the first time I killed a man?'"

"He said he killed a man?" Glen asked, plopping his pen onto the pad and leaning closer. "Do you think he really did that, or was he trying to intimidate you?"

"I know he was tryin' to intimidate me but, I think he did it. He said he never felt such power until that moment; said it was like the greatest feeling, being that powerful over another person."

"Where did he say this happened? When?" Glen was as shocked as I was. Retrieving his pen, he scrawled across his legal pad furiously, flipping page after page to continue. I glanced up at the clock on the wall: 10:20 p.m.

"When he was in the Marines, but it was when he got in a fight with someone, not because of his duty. Said he was lucky to be transferred right after so no one knew it was him."

"The *first* time?" I muttered, realizing that he had probably done so more than once—and if he enjoyed it so much, what would stop him from doing it again?

THIRTY-EIGHT

While it's best not to live in fear, respect for fearful situations is prudent.

MORNING CAME QUICKLY, AND once again I had not slept. Thoughts of Justice Head's activities, and of what he might do to protect his "reputation" wearied me. Every time I fell asleep I had nightmares and would wake up in a cold sweat, afraid to go to sleep because of not only the dreams, but the fear of not being alert to protect my kids. Glen had the same concern evidently, because he called me very early.

"I think it's time for you to reach out to the Red Cross and have your husband brought home," he stated more as a friend than an official. "Now that we know what we're facing here, or even some of it, I don't think it's good for you to be home alone."

"Glen, I—" I broke down. I couldn't help it. "I am so scared. I mean, what if—"

"I know," he said soothingly. "But you can't go on like this without some support. You need to sleep, and it's just too much to handle by yourself. Let alone you must be beside yourself with worry over your husband!" He paused for a moment and I tried to compose myself. "Do you have a family support officer? I am going to reach out to Senator Little's office."

"I do, he called last week," I dried my tears, sniffling. "I have his number here somewhere. But, you say I need to contact the Red Cross?"

"I think that's the protocol. I will talk to Senator Little, and draft a letter of support for the request," he continued. "I can't say too much, but I will make a strong enough point of what's been taking place, and we'll see if we can get Dave home. Then, he can put in a hardship request to terminate his active duty status. It's only right."

The thought of having Dave home was a huge relief. He called me later that day and I explained what had been happening. He said he would tell his Sargent to expect a message. Although he was very worried about me and the kids, he wrestled with feelings of guilt for abandoning his brothers in arms. That upset me, but I also realized he didn't fully understand what was happening at home.

"Babes," Nana sighed into the phone. "I think it's high time Dave comes home. You're on your own front lines here. I will worry a lot less when he's there with you."

"I know, I know. And, I don't mean to worry you, but," I hesitated for a few seconds, trying to determine how much to tell her. She knows me so well, I really can't keep much from her anyway. "Now that we know what's going on behind the scenes here, it makes sense. The Lorrys have obviously been bribing justice Head and that's why he won't sign the ruling and make it official."

"Do you know what they've got on him?" she asked, surprising me with her blunt acknowledgement.

"Yes," I exhaled heavily. "We do, and it's just the tip of the iceberg. In fact, I'm not sure I want to know anymore. Last night was hard. I feel so sorry for his victims. And there's more to know, like about who some of the corrupt correction officers and other agents are. Vern said that justice Head used his official car to transport drugs over the border because they all know him and wave him through."

"That's awful," she clucked. "Then he made the young kids deal them?"

"Yes. Vern said he even asked him one time, 'what does a judge want with all these drugs?'"

"What did he say?"

"He told him it was for bribing lawyers and DA's," I replied. "I had heard about a former DA in Plattsburgh who is heavy into cocaine. I never believed it until I saw her a few weeks ago at local café. It was a Saturday, and she was with another woman having a beer and eating cheese, her nose was so red and flared, eyes glazed over——I couldn't imagine how she could drive her pricey convertible!"

"Wow. People are strange, sometimes, huh?" Nana commented rhetorically. "You just never know; can't trust anyone nowadays."

Hours later I got a return call from Sargent Mike, my family officer. He then put in a call to the Red Cross, called me back, and told me to expect to hear something in two to three days. Meanwhile, Senator Little's office called expressing support and giving me contact info in case I needed their assistance. As if not to be outdone, a few hours later I received a call from Senator Hillary Clinton's office. I wasn't sure why, since I was not in her district.

"Senator Clinton wants you to know that if you need anything at all you can contact us here," the woman on the other end of the line assured me professionally. "Is there anything you need? Can you tell us more about the events that have led to this point?"

"Well, I—" I was completely taken aback at her call. "I am not sure who contacted you, but Senator Little's office has already been in touch," I told her. "I guess maybe you heard from the Red Cross?"

"No, I don't think so," she replied. "But, we understand there's some threats to you personally? Do you feel safe?"

"No, not really, but…" I was confused. "But it is all under control now. I will be fine." She gave me the office phone number and insisted I use it if necessary. I thanked her and hung up the phone, still wondering why she called, or how she even knew to call.

The next few days were a flurry of phone calls, compiling the requested list of information and witnesses for Agent Weintraub, and more victims coming forward to tell their stories, all this amid fall tourism and Jonathan's soccer season. If I had the chance to sit down, I fell asleep, except for at night, when I was consumed with terror.

I spoke with Officer Mike after a couple of days and asked him what the progress was on Dave's emergency leave. He told me that the message had been sent to Dave's command, and Dave should be boarding a flight home within twenty-four hours. When I spoke to Dave that evening he told me his CO informed him he had not received any message and he wasn't going to be released. This resulted in another flurry of phone calls. Finally, two days later I got a call from another officer who told me that the Red Cross message had been received, but Dave didn't *want* to come home.

"Excuse me?" I felt my face flush and heart sink.

"Your soldier doesn't want to abandon his brothers here on the front," the officer repeated. "We can't have our families sending emergency requests over broken dishwashers and windows. This is serious business. You know what you signed up for," he spoke gruffly. I could scarcely believe my ears. Fatigued to the bone, I pinched the back of my hand to see if I was awake.

"Uh, I think you must be calling the wrong spouse," I told him sheepishly. "This is not about a broken dishwasher. Our house has been broken into, I have been stalked, and there's an investigation going on. I'm a whistleblower and I'm being retaliated against."

"Can I pour you a glass of wine?" Tom asked me as Shirley unwrapped the rotisserie chicken and put it on a platter.

"No thanks," I replied. "I haven't dared have a drink in case—"

"We're here with you, now," Shirley interrupted me. "Have a glass of wine and relax a little." She scooped mashed potatoes into a serving bowl, and Tom poured us each some wine. "Kids!" she called Jonathan and Katlyn. "Dinner's on the table!"

We made small talk as we ate, including the kids in the conversation, until they finished and asked to be excused. Then the conversation turned to the situation at hand, and the heaviness in my heart over the message that Dave had refused to come home.

"You don't really believe that, do you?" Shirley searched my face.

"I don't know what to believe. The last time I spoke with him, he seemed like he couldn't wait to get home, but the time before—" I reflected on his concern and a lump came up in my throat. "Well, he said he was conflicted and felt guilty leaving his post."

"Naw," Tom shook his head negatively as he spoke. "I think he might feel guilty, and I can understand that, but he loves you and he wants to be here. Something else is going on."

"I don't know," I wiped my eyes as Shirley reached for the wine and poured me a little more. "Dave is easily conflicted, and I'm not so sure." I thought about how he was manipulated so badly by his former girlfriend, and how the military bravado can pull the same stunts sometimes. We sat there talking, with them asking many questions about the victims, and all that had come to light.

"You're a true Joan of Arc of the region," Shirley said, but before I could ask what she meant the phone rang. Tom jumped up and got it as I watched with anticipation.

"Dave!" he exclaimed into the phone. "Yeah, this is Tom. Great to hear your voice!" I exhaled deeply, Shirley reached over to pat my arm. "Yeah, I bet your time is limited. Here she is!" He handed me the phone.

"Hi! How are you?"

"I'm doin' okay. Worried about you. What the hell is happenin' with this leave?" he asked, agitation in his voice.

"I have been wondering the same thing," I told him. "An officer called two days ago and told me that you don't want to come home."

"What? That's bull shit!" he snarled. "Are you kiddin' me?"

"No. That's what he said," I wondered if he was being honest with me. "And, after you told me a while back that you felt guilty leaving your buddies—"

"Yeah, I feel guilty, but you come first!" he exclaimed. "I mean, we're facing death every day here. It's intense," he paused a minute, but I had no words, just hot tears trekking down my cheeks. "We lost another guy two days ago, so we had a blackout. No communications until the family could be notified, you know how it works…You go through stuff with these men—horrible stuff, and they become your brothers. It's hard seeing him all laid out, paying last respects . . . but he's not my wife and kids."

I still had no words. Shirley got me a box of Kleenex and sat back down next to me.

"Did I lose you? Are you still there?" Dave asked.

"No, I'm still here," I told him.

"Ah, honey," he sighed, obviously aware of my pain. "I love you. You are the most important person in my life. I want to come home and be with you. I will talk to my Sargent and see what I can do from this end, okay?"

"Okay," I replied. "I hope to see you soon. I'm so sorry about the circumstances."

"You can't help that! It's not your fault. It's those damn Lorrys," he snapped. "And judge Head. But you're doin' the right thing an' it's all gonna work out. I just need to be home to protect you 'til it does."

"I need that," I confessed. "I haven't slept…"

"Yeah, I know. I am not sleeping much here for worrying about you there," he replied. "Scooter noticed and keeps reminding me it's not good for me to be out on the machine gun all day and not sleepin' at night." Scooter is Dave's best friend, roommate, and platoon buddy. The two are inseparable, as only other soldiers understand, they are brothers. I feel better knowing David has such a close friend over there. "I'll call you tomorrow when I get back from my mission, okay?"

"Okay. I love you. Stay safe," I told him earnestly. "Don't worry, just stay safe."

THIRTY-NINE

The righteous perish, and no one takes it to heart; the devout are taken away and no one understands that the righteous are taken away to be spared from evil.
ISAIAH THE PROPHET

ALMOST THREE WEEKS AFTER the first Red Cross message, on September 20th, Dave boarded a helicopter to begin his journey home on emergency leave. He called me minutes before and said I would get a phone call from our family officer about when to meet him in Burlington. Indeed, Sargent Mike called me the next morning, offering to come and get me in time for Dave's arrival. While I appreciated the offer, it made no sense since then he would have to drive us all the way back and return to Burlington again. I opted to take my own vehicle. Just as I was leaving the house, he called again, repeating his offer.

When I got to the airport later, I was surprised to find not only Sargent Mike, but another officer waiting for Dave as well. They greeted me very professionally, but I sensed something was wrong. Although I asked them, I was assured this was standard protocol. The wait was intense. Finally, a camouflage-painted airbus landed, and in what seemed like an hour later I spotted Dave walking toward the terminal with his gear. Once inside, he spotted me and quickened his pace. As we embraced each other he dropped his gear and held me so tight I felt safe for the first time in months. "I love you, Karen," he whispered before kissing me passionately. After a couple of minutes, Sargent Mike and the other soldier approached and asked if they could have a word with Dave.

"What's goin' on?" Dave asked suspiciously. He motioned me to stay there and moved closer to them. As they spoke in low tones I couldn't decipher, I watched as his face changed from tired happiness to sheer sorrow in an instant. His face turned red and I noted that unmistakable quiver he gets in his jaw when he's trying to hold back emotion. After a couple of minutes, he turned back toward me, his eyes brimming with tears. I reached for him, hugging him tightly.

"Dave? What's going on?" I queried softly.

"Scooter's dead," he mumbled, burying his face in my hair, crying softly.

"Oh my God! Dave! I am so sorry!"

"I can't believe it," he told me, wiping his eyes. "I just can't believe it."

"Sweetheart! I'm so sorry!" I suddenly felt as if we were targets in an unseen war. "But, how? What? What happened?"

"His first time taking my place on the gun, he was shot. It should've been me. Any other day, it would've been me."

It was a few days before I could accurately reflect on the gravity of the invisible conflict we were embroiled in. The unusual way in which Dave and I had to fight to get him home, when it should have been a matter of two days, the stalking, the break-in, Judge Head's bizarre behavior, Scooter's death. The first few nights he was home, I really slept. He was filled with grief, and didn't sleep as well as I. Yet, in a paradoxical way, he was so happy to be home with me and the kids. The leave was only for two weeks, so there wasn't any time to waste in applying for a hardship discharge. He felt shameful about it, but at the same time, knew it was the only way I would really be safe. His shame was compounded by Scooter's loss. The fact that had it been a day earlier, Dave would have been in the crosshairs of that sniper beleaguered him.

"I just don't understand it," Dave whispered to me in the wee hours. "How could God let this happen? Why would he take such a good man like Scooter? He didn't deserve to die."

"I wish I knew, honey," I told him groggily. "Sometimes I wonder is it really God that does that? Or is it sheer evil?" I snuggled up even closer to him, as he brushed my hair off my face and caressed my cheek.

"If it's God, then I'm mad at him," he said. "If it's evil, why would it have the last word?" His words stung me, arousing me to contemplate.

"God is more powerful," I offered, "but man has free will. He doesn't violate free will."

"But Scooter was a good Christian. He really loved God, loved others, his wife, his children. . . . Shouldn't God have protected him? Yeah, that sniper has free will and he was bent on killin', but Scooter's free will was bent on loving—God and people."

"I don't know all the answers," I told him. "I wish I did, but I will pray that God gives you peace and understanding."

"I need that. I feel so guilty enjoying being with you, being home, knowing he's gone because he took my shift." He paused for a minute and I stroked his face in the moonlight, cupping it in my hands and peering into his eyes. "I'm sorry, honey," he whispered softly. "I am sorry I'm so torn."

"You have no need to apologize," I assured him. "I understand. Just pray for insight, and trust Love."

The next morning in my prayer and reading I asked God for understanding. I asked for peace. Then as I was reading I came upon the words of the Prophet Isaiah: "The devout are taken away and no one understands that the righteous are taken away to be spared from evil." The words seemed to leap off the page directly into my soul. Instantly I realized how small my own understanding is. I showed the verse to Dave, hoping he would find the same solace in it that I had, but it had little effect.

We went about the day setting in motion the hardship discharge, gathering documentation, and identifying procedures that lay ahead. He would have to report to Fort Drum from the day his emergency leave is over until the day his hardship discharge is granted. We had no idea how long that would take, but it was better than Ramadi. Glen Michaels drafted a letter in support of the request.

Kat wrote out a statement in support as well. All told the package we put together in support of the hardship discharge was in excess of eighty pages, including the judicial conduct complaint, various inquiries from state officials requesting more information in order to investigate, and even a letter from Senator Little. We submitted it by fax to the office in Fort Drum, then prepared to spend the next day in Vermont for Scooter's funeral.

We drove in silence, except for the ferry ride across the lake, when we took advantage of the fresh air and opportunity to stretch our legs. Leaning against the railing, a gentle mist hitting our faces from the waves, I tried to encourage Dave for the day ahead. But he was still wrestling with guilt and confusion.

"The last time I saw him he told me, 'If I don't see ya in two weeks I'll see ya when I go home'. I don't think he meant this way," Dave spoke soberly. "I still can't believe it."

As we made our way closer to the community church that Scooter

State of New York
Office of the Attorney General

Eliot Spitzer
Attorney General

Regional Office Division
Plattsburgh Regional Office

September 27, 2005

For Pick-Up
Karen Marie
20 Thompson
Keeseville, NY 12944

Re: <u>Complaints Regarding Officials of the Village of Keeseville</u>

Dear M

You have asked me to recount the interaction between yourself and our office in recent months. I am happy to do so. Earlier this year you contacted our Plattsburgh Regional Office, which covers Clinton, Essex, and Franklin Counties in New York State. You complained regarding the conduct of certain officials of the Village of Keeseville and supplied copious documentation. I informed you that the Attorney General did not have jurisdiction absent a request from the New York State Comptroller. We have forwarded your complaint and materials to the Comptroller.

Subsequently, you complained to this office regarding alleged misconduct by certain judicial officials and provided written documentation and other evidence to our office supporting the complaint. At my urging, you filed a complaint with the New York State Commission on Judicial Conduct, which, I am informed, is investigating. In addition, pursuant to my suggestion, you have met with officials from New York State Police Bureau of Criminal Investigations and the Essex County District Attorney's office. Officials from these offices have been in touch with me.

At this time, it remains the case that the Attorney General has no jurisdiction with respect to the subject matter of your complaints. However, I believe that they may have significant merit, and therefore, I urge you to continue to pursue these with appropriate State officials and to provide me with periodic updates. My understanding is that your husband may be able to obtain leave from military duty to provide support and protection for you during the remainder of this investigation. If military officials should require verification of the subject matter of this letter, please write me at the address below or phone me directly at (518) 562-3291.

Sincerely,

Glen Francis Michaels
Assistant Attorney General

70 Clinton St., Plattsburgh, N.Y. 12901 • (518) 562-3282 • Fax (518) 562-3294

loved, we could hardly believe the cars everywhere. There was no place to park, but we were directed to an empty lot about a mile away, where a shuttle bus would bring us back to the church. When we made our way back, the line to get in was out the door and down the sidewalk. It was then I realized that Dave was not the only one who truly admired Scooter. And when, during the course of the service the pastor read a letter he had recently received from Scooter, I realized that verse from Isaiah must surely apply. Dave wept as he listened, and I held his large hand in both of mine.

"You never really come to terms with loss of a loved one," the pastor said. "We all seek answers. We all want to understand how this could happen. Why this bright, energetic, loving father and husband, brother and friend, soldier and confidant, could be gone from this earth in the prime of his life. Scooter believed in Jesus, and he laid down his life for his fellow man, like Jesus. But because of Jesus, because of his victory over death and the grave, Scooter is not merely gone from this earth. Scooter believed that to be gone from this life is to be present in another life. Scooter believed it is not really death, but a continuation of life without the trappings of mortality, the anguish of sorrow is temporal if you have the love of God in your heart, for eventually, you go home where your soul is always at rest. Always at peace. Scooter believed that Jesus' victory over death applied to him. And it applies to you.

"So, we still have our sorrow, but God is comfort. We may have our questions, but God has answers. When I was preparing for this celebration of Scooter's life, I couldn't help but wonder like many of you, *why?* Why would God take this exemplary man from this life now? A man so young and full of promise?

"As I read and prayed I came upon this verse which spoke to my soul, and provides us some insight into things well beyond our knowing:

> The righteous perish, and no one takes it to heart; the devout are taken away and no one understands *that the righteous are taken away to be spared from evil.* (Isaiah 57:1, NIV)"

Dave squeezed my hands then wrapped his arm around me. Pulling me close he whispered in my ear, "That verse! I get it now!"

FORTY

If I call you friend, and you plot to betray me, either I have been too quick to trust or you have been too quick to deceive.

"IS THIS KAREN MARIE?" came a scratchy male voice on the other end of the phone.

"Yes, how can I help you?"

"My name is Bill Glaberson. I'm an investigative reporter with the *New York Times*. Do you have a minute to talk?" My thoughts raced.

"Who is this *really*?" I asked warily. I imagined some sort of Don Lorry prank. He had already called ABN AMRO and asked for information about buying my house, telling them he was an authorized representative. I trusted no one, and Dave was still at Fort Drum so I was especially wary.

"Really," he laughed on the other end of the phone. "Aren't you the woman who is single-handedly taking on Judge Head?"

"Well, I wouldn't put it that way," I retorted, still not wishing to say too much for fear of who I might be talking to.

"I really am Bill Glaberson, an investigative journalist for the *Times*. Check me out. Look me up on line," he coaxed.

"Anyone can do that," I told him. "Anyone can read the *Times* and see your name and try to fake me out."

"Okay, listen. I got a tip. A reliable source gave me your name. I've been doing an investigative reporting series for the past nine months already on the small town and village court system in New York," he paused. "Are you still there?"

"Go on," I replied, intrigued.

"I bet you would agree with me that the system must be changed. It's rife with corruption, right?"

"Yes . . . and?"

"And, I would like to meet you in person and discuss this more. Specifically, I'm investigating Justice Head now. I'm actually in town today," he said. I noted that he—like me—referred to him only as 'justice,' not 'judge' like everyone else around Keeseville."

"So, how am I supposed to be sure of all this? Like I said, anyone could say they are you." I genuinely wanted to know more and hoped that the exposure would help me to get some *real justice* after all.

"Check me out online. There's a bio with my picture. We can meet in person after that and you'll see it's really me," his voice was earnest. "Do you have time later today?"

"Okay. Give me your phone number. I'll call you after I check things out," I assured him.

We hung up the phone and I went to my laptop. He had already written a couple of articles on the abuses and ignorance of the small town and village court system. I read them, then called him back, agreeing to meet him.

Kat had gone to the town of AuSable court to inquire about what forms to fill out to evict the Lorrys as "new owners." The grapevine travels so fast that before she could even get them filed Evan Tracy sent a letter stating that the Lorrys had rights that extended beyond the new ownership and would not be vacating the property. She was devastated, and very angry. She called me to explain what happened, and I told her about Bill Glaberson.

"I want to go with you," she gasped excitedly. "This is just what we need!"

"Maybe," I still felt cautious. "We'll see. But tell me, didn't you just go to the Ausable Court yesterday?"

"Yes! Can you believe it! She must have picked up the phone as soon as I walked out the door!"

"And Evan is always happy to oblige with continued harassment," I sighed. "Well, at least we are moving in the right direction. We need to open up the partnership bank account so we can put the mortgage and bill money in it. Want to try for Monday?"

"Maybe. I'll have to check my schedule," she sounded weary. "It would be nice if we had some rent money to put in there!"

"Yes, it would. I just paid the electric bill and fuel bill out of my business account, but we really need to keep things straight to be fair. Anyway, I had better get off the phone if I am going to meet this reporter on time." I looked at the clock on the wall and searched for my purse as I spoke.

"Where are you meeting him?"

"At the bar downtown," I informed her with a laugh. "I swore I'd never go in that dive, but I figure it's the middle of the day, and no one would expect me to be in there!"

When I arrived at the bar, Bill was already having a discussion with someone about Justice Head. He informed me that in fact it was a local lawyer who represented many of the young men sentenced to "judge's probation" who had referred him to me. The young person he was speaking with left, so I asked him if he would rather talk at the inn.

"I know the walls have ears here," I explained, as we headed out the door. He lit up a cigarette as we made our way down the block. He told me that he needed more proof of illegal activity, and especially a victim willing to go on the record.

"The thing is, I can smell the wrong doing here, but these boys they don't seem to understand how badly they've been abused. They don't know how the justice system is supposed to work, I guess."

"Believe me, I get it," I empathized. "People around here are so uneducated about how things should work, and so accustomed to abuse that they feel they're disrespecting "the judge" if they speak up. And, the ones that want to speak up are ashamed of what happened. They feel as if they contributed to the abuse they suffered, so they should just shut up and deal with it."

"You don't know anyone who might come forward?" he snuffed his cigarette out as we headed into the inn, where Kat joined us. "I hear you're like a magnet to these victims."

"Lately it seems that way," I replied. "I can tell you about Vern, but the others—" I let out a big sigh, shrugging my shoulders. "They seem to have a lot to say to me, but when I try to get them to talk to Glen Michaels, or the judicial conduct investigator, they clam up. Twice I've had group sessions organized thinking it would be easier for them *en masse*, but each time they don't show, after telling me they will."

"It's been really frustrating," Kat moaned. "I'm Katherine Smith, Karen Marie's partner." She stuck out her hand and Bill shook it.

"I bet! I'm having a hard time of it, too," he replied. "But, we'll keep on it no matter how long it takes. I've been investigating this ridiculous small town and village court system for a while now. I don't intend to stop. Who's Vern?"

"You haven't talked to him yet?" I wondered.

"No. What can he tell me? Can you introduce me?"

I explained about the late-night interview I was involved in recently, and all of the sordid details that came out.

"Basically, it's worse than we imagined. And what I'm realizing now is that my tenants knew about this, and that's how they are bribing justice Head to keep him from ruling in my favor—despite the facts."

"Do you have proof of that?" Bill asked, curiously tilting his head and brushing hair off his face.

"Not yet, but I'm working on it. Vern said that Don Lorry absolutely knew about the molestations—he even teased Vern about it; degraded him."

"Well, if Vern will go on the record then that would be big for both of us," Bill exclaimed. "Do you think he'll talk to me?"

"I hope so, but lately he's been very sheepish. I think he's nervous now that he's spilled his guts," I thought about how badly he had been retaliated against before. "And, he has reason to be. The last time he went before the Commission on Judicial Conduct two corrections officers beat the crap out of him."

"I've been told Head's well protected. It seems like he's one of a few kingpins up here that are all connected." Kat's eyes widened in shock. She shifted her weight from one foot to the other nervously, clenching and unclenching her hands in front of her.

"Connected to what?" she asked. "The mob?"

"So I've been told," he replied matter-of-factly. "But I need the proof."

"The mob? Really?" I had never really thought about it before, but it made sense.

"Where there's drug trafficking, human trafficking, and money laundering, don't you suspect the mob?" he queried.

"I suppose, but I never thought of it in those terms. I mean . . ." I fumbled for understanding as much as for words. *How could the Lorrys, or anyone in Keeseville for that matter, be connected to the mob?* "I came here to raise my kids away from big city problems, and I end up running right into them?"

"The Adirondacks are New York State's dirty little secret," Kat shrieked. "The friggin' backwoods rednecks are just pawns."

"Will you give me contact info for these victims you referred to?"

"Yes," I exhaled slowly, nervousness gripping my chest. "Yes, I will. And I will look at things differently from today on."

FORTY-ONE

Ignorance and insecurity knock a person down to build another up.
A secure and loving person knows that love is humble and kind.

DAVE WAS FINALLY RELEASED from Fort Drum with his hardship discharge approved. He tried to go back to his job, but with the downturn in the economy, they could only take him back part time. His boss suggested he file for unemployment until he could find something else. It was yet another blow financially, but it made sense to him to find a better position. He spent his days job hunting, sending out resumes, and catching up on repairs around the house. It was slowing down at the inn, which didn't help financially, and I was still paying the bills myself since Kat and Kenny had been unable to start their business while the Lorrys were still in there.

Our first mortgage payment under the new partnership structure was due November 1st, and Kat had been putting me off about the joint account. It seemed she always had an excuse that tugged at my heartstrings. The worst one happened around the third week of October, just after Dave had come home.

"Karen Marie, I just can't think about this right now," she cried into the phone. "I'm so upset with Kenny . . . I'm thinking about getting a divorce."

"What? What happened?" I knew their relationship was more transactional than romantic, but this caught me by surprise.

"Do you have time to talk?" she asked, sniffling.

"I'll be right over," I replied. "Are you free to talk there?"

"Yeah. Thanks." Her house was just one mile down the road. We made the trip back and forth often, and I passed it every time I went to the inn. The door was open when I arrived a few minutes later.

"Kat?" I inquired as to her whereabouts as I walked in.

"In the kitchen," came the reply. "How about some tea?"

We sat at the table and she told me of the dreadful events of the night before. She and Kenny had gotten into an argument, which seemed to be happening more and more lately. He then got drunk in his basement mancave, and a couple of hours later came upstairs, dragged her by the hair up to their bedroom and demanded sex.

"He dragged you by the hair?" I was shocked and upset. "After all that he demanded sex!? Kat, you can't put up with this!"

"I know. It's horrible," she whispered nervously as if he could hear her. "Lately he's been getting drunk every night down there. When I try to talk to him about it he tells me that we made a deal and I had better stick to it. He tells me to buzz off, stuff like that."

"A deal?"

"Yeah," she moaned. "When we decided to get married, we made a deal." She looked into my eyes, as if seeking my understanding of something she hadn't explained yet. I was clueless. "He told me, 'You give me what I want, *every night,* and you'll never lack for anything. You don't even have to work unless you want to.'"

"And you agreed to that?" I wondered.

"Yes. I mean, it seemed like a good idea at the time, but now it seems as if he thinks he can do whatever he wants and I'll still hold my end."

"And of course, that's not what marriage is all about," I told her, sensing the familiar pain of abuse keenly.

"I know, but it is about compromise," she said thoughtfully. "I mean, when things are good, when there's less pressure, the arrangement works out just fine."

"Is he into pornography?" I asked, hoping the answer was 'no'.

"Yeah, but not in front of the kids," she said, as if that made it acceptable. "He prefers live action, but I know that he watches it while he drinks down there, when he isn't watching golf or practicing putting."

"Live action? Like dragging you around by the hair?" I retorted.

"Like, well—" she heaved and gulped her tea before continuing. "That's why I have to stay in perfect shape. That's why all the yoga, and exercise, and dieting—I have to be in perfect shape. If he sees one bit of fat, or if I get one dimple of cellulite, he's merciless."

My heart was heavy for her. This woman whom I thought was savvy and self-confident, was really a hurting child willing to do anything for the approval of the man who held all power over her. I wondered if it was just for financial security that she made the 'deal'.

"Kat, that's no way to love," I whispered softly. "Marriage is supposed to be much better than that. You deserve better than that."

"Sometimes when I am dancing on the table in one of the whorish outfits he likes I think the same thing," she said quietly.

I tried to encourage her for a while. After another cup of tea and some more talk of marriage and real love, we set a time to meet in a couple of days for business.

When the day came, I went to the shop and waited for her. After a half hour, I tried calling, but only got her answering machine. I swung by the house, but her car was gone. Later in the day, I tried calling the house, assuming something must have come up with one of the kids, but that she should be home for dinner. I left another message. This continued for two days: no response to texts or messages was received. I worried about her safety and wellbeing, *Could Kenny have really flipped and hurt her?* Finally, at about 7:00 p.m. the third day, someone answered the phone.

"Kenny!" I exclaimed, happy to have finally reached a live person at their house. "How are you? Can I talk to Kat please?"

"She's not here," he replied tersely.

"Oh. Where is she? What's a good time to call back?"

"I don't know," he told me. "She took off a couple of days ago. I haven't seen her or talked to her."

"What?" Surprise and anxiety struck me to the core. "Um, I mean. Aren't you worried about her?"

"She does this sometimes," he said flippantly. "She's a bit neurotic, in case you haven't noticed. Gets herself all worked up and needs some space. She'll call me eventually."

"Well, I guess if you're not worried—" I could scarcely gauge this turn of events. I wondered if he had hurt her worse than the hair dragging episode. "But the mortgage payment is due in two days, and we need to make arrangements to get that paid."

"It can wait 'til she gets back. I'm not worried about it." I thought maybe he was drunk and his senses dulled. "I'm sure I'll hear from her in a day or two."

"Well, if she calls you, please ask her to give me a call, okay?"

"Yeah. Sure. Bye." He hung up the phone. I sat there in utter astonishment and concern, not knowing what to do.

A day later Kat called me from Ocean City, New Jersey.

"How are you? Are you okay?" I gasped.

"Yeah, I'm better now," she said soberly. "I needed a break, I guess,"

"But—? Did Kenny hurt you again? What happened?"

"We had another argument. I guess Don Lorry contacted him at work and is putting the pressure on for us to deal with him. It was infuriating to me."

"That creep! You're kidding!" Don's meddling had risen to new heights of offensiveness in the previous couple of months. It was worrisome and very unsettling. "But surely Kenny knows how corrupt he is? And besides, our partnership dictates. Kenny didn't want any part of the partnership, just the tax breaks."

"Yeah. I reminded him of that, but he said that he was my partner long before you ever were, and he wanted to hear Don out." She paused and I heard her let out a long deep breath. "We met Don and Carolyn for dinner, and afterward Kenny and I got into a big argument, and he got drunk again."

"You what?" I could scarcely believe my ears! "Kat! How could you?"

"That's what we fought about," she exclaimed. "I didn't want to do it, but he hasn't been in on all of our conversations, and Don was schmoozing him. Kenny said we had to at least hear him out."

"I am so disappointed," I stammered, my mind spinning and my heart aching.

"That's why we fought. I knew you'd be upset, but I also thought once Kenny saw what a jerk Don was, it would be over."

"But he doesn't want to deal with the Lorrys now, does he?" I implored.

"No. He made me go to dinner, and they made up a bunch of bullshit, but I know the whole story. I tried to tell Kenny that night, but he was too drunk," she said woefully.

"Did he hurt you? I mean, I thought maybe . . ."

"It wasn't pretty. But I'm doing better now. I talked to him this morning and he apologized."

"Apologies are great, but is he going to change? I mean, he can't abuse you like that! And what about the Lorrys?"

"I told him that," she said, calmer than her normal self. "This morning he said he understands what Don is all about, so it's all safe. And honestly, you know how hot tempered I can be at times. I didn't exactly handle the whole thing well. I have been thinking and relaxing, just doing some yoga on the beach and reading. I'll head home on Friday."

"The first mortgage payment is due tomorrow," I reminded her. "I plan on paying half, but we will have to overnight it—"

"Yeah, but it isn't considered late until seven days after the due date, so we can do that when I get back. Kenny told me that you were concerned."

"Yes. I just want to make sure everything is done properly. By the way, I got another call from Steve Weintraub—he wants me to go in for a lengthy interview next week."

"Weintraub? Who's that? You have a job interview?" she seemed surprised. "I know David is looking for work, but—"

"No. He's the FBI agent that was in touch last month. I finally finished my list of witnesses and other info he asked me for a couple of weeks ago. Anyway, now he wants me to go in and be interviewed. I guess they're beginning to investigate after all."

"That's great news! Maybe we can finally get some closure on this whole Lorry-Judge Head thing!" she exclaimed. "I hope they stick it to them!"

"One thing I've noticed is that all these investigators work at a much slower pace than I do, or would like," I said. "But it is better than nothing. I'm happy they are taking this seriously."

"Me, too. Sorry I have been so out of touch," she spoke sincerely. "I'll see you when I get back and we'll get everything on track."

FORTY-TWO

Caving into fear and intimidation creates only more of the same.

ON DECEMBER 8TH, 2005, I headed to the inn as usual to retrieve messages and mail. Being winter time with no business to speak of, I had set the heat to fifty degrees Fahrenheit, and only stopped in to check on things every day. Without thinking much about it, I stuck my key in the door, but it wouldn't turn. I tried fiddling with it for a second, but then I noticed a note taped to the window from the inside.

> Karen Marie. This is the only way I can get your attention.
> This is serious. We need to talk. Kat

Furious, I thought about the many times I had tried to call Kat in the previous weeks. The many emails, text messages, and now she is locking me out claiming she can't reach me? I looked for signs of life in the windows, but there was no one there. Even the laundromat was closed. I stood on the step and dialed her cell, and again the call went straight to voicemail. I tried her house phone and had to leave a message there, too. I headed home and placed a call to Glen Michaels.

"Karen Marie! What's going on?" he asked as he answered. "I had two very strange calls from Kat Smith about you."

"You—what?" I wondered, body trembling, my mind swirling with thoughts of betrayal and loss. "From Kat?"

"Yes. Is she a little crazy, or what?" he was serious. "She left me a voice mail the other day ranting about how you need to be reined in because the Feds aren't going to really investigate. She said you've gone off the deep end and asked me to talk to you."

"She said that? Oh my God!"

"Yes, what is going on?" he wondered.

"She locked me out of the building! I just tried to go as usual to get my mail and messages, check on things, and she has changed the locks and taped a note on the door."

"You're kidding! She did?" Glen was as perplexed as me. "What is she afraid of?"

"I think she got intimidated by the FBI interview," I told him. "I mean, she insisted on coming with me, and it was a grueling day. I was there almost eight hours, with only a quick break."

"She went with you? Why?"

"Well, she and Kenny had been fighting over the Lorry situation, and I guess he insisted that she be present at that interview. When I asked Agent Weintraub if that was okay, he indicated that if she might have something to add, she was welcome."

"But I got the impression that they thought the interview went well," Glen countered. "They have begun investigating in earnest, you know."

"I had hoped, but I wasn't sure," I told him, trying to steady my nerves. "It was difficult. They are not charming guys, and they questioned so much—I guess Kat thought they questioned in a way that was insinuating there was nothing to investigate. You said she called you twice?"

"Yeah, the second time was to try to convince me what a horrible person you are. She said that you were fighting a battle that 'isn't there', or something like that. I told her that I am in possession of facts that say otherwise, and I know you well enough by now to know you have a good head on your shoulders. I reminded her you are very kind. After all, the average person doesn't help the victims you've been helping. I know you. But . . . " he paused for a second and let out a sigh. "But now on the deed, are you both on the deed?"

"Not yet," I moaned, knowing full well what he was getting at. "We kept the building in the Smith's name so as not to conflict with the existing eviction proceeding. We—"

"Yeah. The one Justice Head still hasn't issued a final ruling in. But didn't they file their own eviction proceeding against the Lorrys?" I could hear the problem-solving angle in his voice.

"They tried, but the first time, Evan Tracy wrote a letter stating that the Lorrys have rights which supersede the new ownership; they got nervous and decided to consult a lawyer. The second time, I am still confused as to what happened. It was just a few weeks ago, and Kat said something about how the town justice said the paperwork was wrong. Sound familiar?"

"Too familiar! Was that in the Keeseville court?" he inquired.

"No. It was in the AuSable court, but you know how connected they all are." Anger welled up in me as I thought about how illegitimate these little courts really are, and of their overreach and harm. "So, without my name on the deed, I can't just go change the locks again, and there is still no closure on the Lorrys. Justice Head issued an unsigned ruling saying that they owe me money and that they indeed caused damages, but he has yet to sign it. Don Lorry has been pestering Kenny at work asking him to make a deal—and Kenny isn't even involved in the partnership! I am beside myself, Glen! I don't know what to do."

"What's that reporter up to? Has he got enough for a story yet?" Glen inquired. "Sometimes a little public attention spurs things along."

"I don't know. I haven't talked to him in a couple of weeks." I sighed. "I guess I need to get someone to handle this now. Another retainer!"

"You may want to consider filing bankruptcy. Chapter Thirteen would give you some protections while this gets sorted out," he said in typical lawyerly fashion.

"I don't know about that," I said sheepishly. "I don't want to be a deadbeat. I just want what is rightfully mine! And to be able to keep my home and run my business without all this harassment!"

"Think about it. You have a paralegal background. Chapter Thirteen means you make payments until it gets sorted out. It gives you some much needed protection."

Dave had been working with a friend while this debacle unfolded. He had a job interview scheduled for the next day, which he was anxiously anticipating. When he got home I told him all that transpired. To say he was angry would be an understatement.

"That bastard Don Lorry had something to do with this! You can't trust anyone around here!" Suddenly I realized he was probably right. Kat and Kenny made a deal with the Lorrys. They must have decided if they can't beat them, join them. As I was reflecting, the phone rang.

"Hello?" I answered.

"Hello. May I speak to Don Lorry, please?" came a voice on the other end.

"Excuse me?"

"May I speak with Don Lorry, please?" the voice repeated.

"Who is calling?" I asked, smarting.

"This is Lucy from ABN AMRO, returning his call."

"Don Lorry doesn't live here, and he should have nothing to do with my ABN AMRO mortgage. How did you get his name?" Hearing me Dave came over to the phone and hit the speaker button.

"Huh, hold on one minute please," the woman replied. I couldn't help but think how hard it was to get a live person to talk to at ABN when I needed one, and now they're calling Don! "Okay, who am I speaking with?" she asked.

"This is Karen Marie Dion," I told her. "I am the substitute mortgagor and owner of the house. I have been working with Linda Maas to assume the mortgage since my divorce."

"Oh, No, we're not authorized to speak with you. Only Robert Davis or Don Lorry," she replied customarily.

"Wait! You have authorization to speak with me *and have been speaking with me*. I make the payments! I have a court order that says the house is mine—"

"I'm sorry ma'am, but that authorization has been rescinded. We have a new authorization to speak with Mr. Lorry. Goodbye."

"But wait!" It was too late. She hung up.

The next day I got a hold of Linda Maas. She checked into what had transpired. Bob had indeed rescinded the authorization and given ABN authority to speak with Don. My gut twisted as we talked. I explained who Don was and how he and my ex could only be up to no good, begging her to use the court documentation as authorization instead. She notated the file and promised to let me know if Don tried contacting them again.

Dave and I didn't sleep well. It helped that his interview was with a man he had met at church. By the end of the day he was hired to be a fuel delivery person—a far cry from what he wanted, yet we were both happy he had work. I tried calling Kat again, and finally penned a letter. I dropped it in her mailbox on the way by, and then as I drove by the inn noticed she was in the laundromat talking with the Lorrys. My heart sank, tears rolled down my face uncontrollably. All my hard work. The long nights. The grueling days. All the effort I put into that place, to provide for my kids flashed before my eyes. I was overwhelmed with sadness and felt hopeless.

The next day I received an email from Kat:

Geesh! The things I have to do to get your attention! I got your note. I understand you're upset. But we can't keep going like this with Kenny and I paying all the bills. Something has to give. I will go check your messages and get your mail and drop it off later. Kat

I replied:

Kat, I have been trying to get *your* attention for two months. Every time we plan a meeting to sort out the financials, you cancel or disappear without notice. I have been paying the bills. I tried to pay half of the mortgage and still don't understand why you are claiming it was not due yet. I have paid the electric bill—$436, the phone bill, filled the fuel tank, and paid the water bill. All of this even though you have blown off our partnership account set-up. We have an agreement and you need to abide by it. If you're so worried about money, locking me out of my business is not going help that. Neither is not pursuing the eviction of the Lorrys. I look forward to talking later.

She never dropped off the mail, or messages, but I did get another email. She stated that she had tried to call the house phone repeatedly but was sure we were leaving it off the hook because it was always busy. In fact, we had dial up internet, and we spent much of the day online job hunting.

FORTY-THREE

*Seeking protection is beneficial at times,
but don't let it instill a false sense of security.*

"BABES? WHAT'S GOING ON over there?" Nana asked anxiously when I answered the phone.

"Oh Nana! You just wouldn't believe it if I told you!" I moaned, tears flowing freely at the sound of love and concern in her voice.

"I might," she said. "I got a very upsetting phone call from your partner."

"Kat? Are you serious? What did she say?" I wondered.

"She said that this whole investigative thing is a bunch of baloney and that you're going off the deep end. She asked me to talk some sense into you, said she is worried that you're losing your mind and maybe should be hospitalized." Nana let out a long sigh. "It was very upsetting."

"Oh my God! Nana! I am so sorry! I can't even believe she would stoop so low!"

"She is a nut case! I know that you've got a good head on your shoulders, Babes. I just hope the investigators hurry up and put an end to this! My blood pressure is up!"

"Oh! I am so sorry! I wish I knew what to say. I can't believe she would do something so awful!"

"Can you get rid of her?" Nana asked seriously.

"No, she is trying to get rid of me, I'm afraid." I went on to explain what had transpired, which was even more distressing to Nana. I felt horrible that my situation was now affecting her.

That weekend when I went to church, I discovered that Kat had been putting her own spin on things with people there, too. Even though the pastor and several others were aware of the ordeal I faced with Justice Head and the Lorrys, they were hesitant to get involved except to listen to her rant. I was so wrought, I contacted a mediation expert, and arranged to pay him to deal with the situation.

We had our preliminary appointment by phone after I filled out countless pages of a questionnaire he had sent me. He then contacted Kat and Kenny a few days later. They put him off repeatedly, until finally just days before Christmas Kat agreed to have a conversation with him. He called me afterward and told me he had never encountered such a vicious, non-conciliatory person.

"I am very sorry to have to tell you this," he said empathetically, "but mediation is not going to work in this case. You're dealing with a stubborn, unwilling, and unrepentant person in Mrs. Smith. She is determined. If I were you, I would hire a lawyer and litigate." He refused to take my money and wished me well. My hope had only been a flicker of flame on a candle without much wax left up until that moment. Now, it was snuffed out by his assessment.

I had driven by Kat's house plenty in the days leading up to that, but hardly saw any sign of life. One night before Christmas, Dave was driving home and saw her truck and Kenny's car out in front of the inn, and all the lights on upstairs. Seizing the opportunity, he went up the staircase to inquire but as he entered the hallway, was met by Kat, shrieking at him, threatening to call the police.

"Are you crazy?" Dave retorted. "This is my wife's business! You had a deal, Kat! What are you doing?"

"This is my *house*!" she yelled, eyes bulging. "Get out! Get out of my house! How dare you just walk in here!" She yanked him by the shirt as if to forcefully remove him. He slapped her arm away. Looking into the room beyond he noted dishes piled in the sink, and lumber was stacked on one side of the hallway. Her kids came out of separate suites to see what was happening.

"What are you doing here?" Dave fumed, exasperated.

Pulling her cellphone out of her pocket she shrieked again: "Get out of my house! This is MY HOUSE!"

Trying to come to terms with how they could abandon their new house, less than a mile away and move into my business as if it was their personal residence was not easy. It made no sense. They complained about money, and yet they installed a new door, and were obviously up to something in my nicely renovated, perfect space. Wouldn't the smart thing be to let me run my business? I had already turned away numerous requests for March reservations, and when it became apparent that they were now living in my beautiful inn, I gave up. I contacted the phone company and asked them to forward the calls to my house but disconnect the line at the building. I sent Kat a notice that I was terminating the electricity. If she and her family were going to live in my business, they would not be subsidized by me. She was furious. She filed a police report against Dave for "trespassing," but fortunately it came to nothing.

As the winter dragged on, I searched for a job, and a new lawyer. Mark Rogers indicated he would require a $40,000 retainer to pursue my case further. Of course, I didn't have it. Vern seemed to disappear, and I wondered if he was also suffering retaliation. ABN AMRO continued to vacillate and cause me even more anxiety. I had flashbacks to Bakersfield; to our possessions being auctioned off on our lawn, and of leaving all I loved, against my will at sixteen years old. Some of the bitter memories of that time came into clear recall for the first time since, haunting me, making me sweat through the night, and tremble at the least little thing during the day. I was filled with anxiety at the thought of putting my kids through the same thing. It was a bleak, cold season.

By the time Easter arrived, I was recovering a little, and trying to fan the flames of hope in my soul. I finally found a lawyer who was not seeking an exorbitant retainer, and I hoped he could quickly bring about resolution.

Easter Sunday morning, as we made our way to church, we were assaulted by huge signs Kat had plastered in the storefront windows of my building. "GOD MAY FORGIVE YOU, BUT I DON'T." The "I" was crossed in a red "x" and "We" was written in smaller letters above it. In another window, there were smears of all kinds. My children were deeply troubled by it. I tried to remain calm, but it reopened a still festering wound. I didn't get much solace from the people at church either—just a lot of preaching at me how I should respond, etc.

The next day I had an appointment with Glen. I was hoping he would have more news, some insight, that would help me get over the hurt and on with the resolutions I longed for and sought after.

"How is that going to help me now?" I asked Glen as he relayed the current status of investigations. "I am meeting with a bankruptcy attorney this week and I wish I didn't have to."

"Who are you meeting with? I told you a while ago, it's a good thing to get some Chapter 13 protections in place."

"Richard Weiskopf," I replied. "He apparently was the chair of the Bankruptcy Bar Association for many years. He says that he will get me into a protected plan so that I can pay my obligations and litigate the Lorry and Village matters in the bankruptcy court at the same time."

"Out of Albany? Yeah. He has a stellar reputation. I think it's a good idea. The Lorrys shouldn't get away with their tactics in a federal court, and your assets will be protected until justice can prevail."

"That's Richard's plan," I said wistfully. "I have to admit; the thought of filing bankruptcy really bothers me. It's just that now with my home mortgage company being so uncooperative, everything I own and have worked hard for is threatened. I have to protect myself and my kids."

"Did you ever get your back child support and alimony?" Glen asked as he finished scribbling some notes on his legal pad.

"A portion of it, but it wasn't enough to complete the refinance of my house, like I had hoped."

"Why not?"

"By the time ABN AMRO—the home mortgage company—got around to the paperwork, the only deal they would approve was one where I would have had to pay $36,000 cash."

"But I thought Bob owes you more than $44,000," Glen said somberly, removing his glasses and tossing them on the yellow pad in front of him.

"Yes, he does. And beyond that, about $5,000 in court ordered medical reimbursements," I sighed long and low, holding back tears. "But he said he could only come up with $20,000, and that would be if he took a loan from his retirement."

"And ABN wouldn't accept 20K?"

"When we began the process with Vicki Lester, she agreed to that, but now there is someone else in charge and the assumption department is insisting on $36,000."

"You're using a CPS lawyer for the support, right? What does he suggest?"

"He suggested that I could take Bob to court and fight for all of it, but that would take up to a year, and there are no guarantees. He said he thought I had a really good case, lots of hard evidence, but Bob puts on a good sob story—which of course I know too well…and it depends on which judge hears the case." I reached for a tissue on the corner of his desk and dabbed my eyes. "I was under the impression the $20,000 would save my home, so I agreed to accept it and forgive the rest with the provision that going forward his wages are garnished for support."

"You were too kind," Glen replied abruptly. "And now how far will that money go for you?"

"When I couldn't convince ABN to take it and let me assume the home mortgage, I used it to pay for some repairs needed at home and pay off debts. I had become very behind with Bob withholding support and the Lorrys still owing me, plus being locked out of my business and not finding a job yet. I wanted to set some aside, but if I am to refinance the house, or get the business back, I must protect my credit. Then I had just enough to hire Mr. Weiskopf. There's nothing left."

"Let's hope Mr. Weiskopf can pull off everything you need in bankruptcy proceedings," Glen sighed.

FORTY-FOUR

The thing about fear is, it entraps you. The very thing you fear is enabled to come about; it sets itself up as "fact" and "experience," then next time your fear seems responsible and prudent.

AT THE END OF APRIL Richard Weiskopf filed my chapter 13 petition and received an automatic stay of the ABN AMRO foreclosure against my home. My whole body seemed to breathe one enormous sigh of relief. The typical protocol meant that in a few weeks' time I would have to present myself to the Trustee and verify that I am who the papers said I am and go over the elements of the plan. Richard was associated with a firm in Plattsburgh, O'Connell & Aronowitz, and since the trustee held the simple verification sessions there once a month, he decided it best to have one of the local counsel attend the preliminary formality with me there. Fred Fiss was the attorney assigned to attend with me. He confirmed the day before by telephone, stating that it should only take about ten to fifteen minutes, but reminding me that I needed to bring proof of my identity.

Dave took part of the day off so he could come with me.

It was a sunny, mild day in May when we pulled into the parking lot of the federal building on Brinkerhoff Street. Mr. Fiss was standing outside on the sidewalk as I approached the entrance.

"Karen Marie Dion?" he asked, stretching out his hand to shake mine. I nodded nervously. "Fred Fiss. Nice to meet you in person."

"Hello. Thank you." Was all I could manage to say. Dave realized I was nervous, put his arm around me and stuck out his other hand to greet Fred.

"I'm David," he said in his adorable drawl. "Nice to meet ya."

"Fred Fiss. Pleasure," he reciprocated. Then looking at me, "Are you okay?"

"I'm a little nervous," I confided quietly.

"This is really simple," he assured me. "Nothing to be nervous about.

We will go in and confirm your identity then answer a few questions for the Trustee. It's a mere formality." As he finished speaking I noticed Bob come out of the building, lean against the wall and light up a cigarette. I had not seen him in quite some time. His hair was long, obviously died jet black, and very stringy. He had a tiny little line of a mustache above his lip that made him look cartoonish.

"What's he doing here?" I wondered aloud. Fred turned to follow my gaze, and as he did I noticed Kenny Smith joining Bob. The two of them were smirking and laughing, pointing in our direction.

"Who's that?" Fred seemed to instantly sense trouble.

"That bastard's a troublemaker," Dave snapped.

"My ex-husband, and my former partner's husband. I don't understand."

"That's not a good sign," Fred replied. "But I can't imagine what they think they can accomplish here. It's a mere formality. Nothing to be decided. Stick close to me. Don't say anything."

We made our way through security, and as we turned to go down the long hallway that led to the stairs, Don and Carolyn Lorry approached, giving me and Dave menacing glares as they did. Fred noticed, took me by the arm and pulled me aside.

"Who are they?" he asked instinctively. "Are you okay?"

"The Lorrys. My tenants that owe me about $136,000 now," I replied. "Sleazy." My stomach convulsed, my body trembled as we continued down the hallway. Fred kept his steadying grip on my arm. I worried that Dave might go off on them. Apparently, Don Lorry hoped he would. As we rounded the corner at the bottom of the stairs, they all lined the wall, along with two other 'friends' who had betrayed my trust, and Kat. I was walking a gauntlet.

Don moved stealthily toward Dave, sneering in his face, which was more than Dave could handle. He thrust his index finger in the direction of Don's face, wagging it in the air as he spoke: "This is dirty! You're all up to no good! If you would pay her what you owe her everything would be fine!"

Don jumped toward him even closer, his face inches from Dave's, chest to chest, they glared at each other. After a tense thirty seconds Don cajoled "Hit me. Come on, hit me . . . you know you want to!" Fred grabbed Dave by the arm, calmly telling him, "This is what they want. They want to make a scene. Don't give it to them."

By now I was barely functioning. Walking through them all to get to the courtroom was grueling. They snickered and jeered like schoolyard bullies. I just wanted to get my life back, what was rightfully mine. I wanted to move on, and they obviously wanted me to grovel and be intimidated. No matter how much I tried to remain calm, I was a wreck inside. They had sucked the strength out of me—each one of them in several ways, over a period of years and now they had combined efforts to reduce me to ruin.

The trustee, Ms. Celli, didn't see what took place in the hallway, but she eyed each of them with suspicion as they traipsed in. They took seats facing her, and I was called to the front of the room to sit at the table with her. Fred accompanied me. I pulled out my identification and she began to go over the elements of my plan. She began reviewing my list of assets.

"Did she list a diamond ring?" Bob said aloud from his seat, smirking. "She has a diamond ring."

"Please don't interrupt this meeting," Ms. Celli asked politely. We continued to go over the plan, and she asked about my ability to make payments under it.

"Ms. Dion is in the process of trying to collect debts owed to her and will of course be making some amount of payment under the plan," Fred answered on my behalf. "I believe Richard Weiskopf explained that in his cover letter?" He pulled a two- page letter from a file folder and handed it to her. "I know it's addressed to you but thought you might not have had time to read it yet."

"True," she said. "He said something about fraudulent conveyance—-is that of her home?" She continued skimming the pages as she asked.

"No," Fred replied quickly, eyeing the Smiths who squirmed in their seats. "That was of her business property. She has been precluded from making a living due to that and has been searching for work."

"I wonder how hard she's been looking," Don Lorry muttered, pretending he didn't want to be heard. The Smiths, Bob, and Carolyn let out vicious laughter.

"I will ask you one more time to keep quiet," Ms. Celli requested, looking up at them and then over at me. After another minute, she asked me, "Do you have a resume?"

"Yes, Ms. Celli."

"I would like to have a copy of it," she continued. "I usually—"

"She had better check to be sure it's legit," Bob said to Kenny folding his arms across his chest. He gave me the same menacing look I had been so afraid of when we were married.

"Exactly what is your purpose for being here?" Ms. Celli demanded.

"She's a fraud!" Kat snapped. "She shouldn't get any bankruptcy protection!" The rest of them made grunts of approval at her comment.

"These parties are responsible for defrauding Ms. Dion, including her ex husband, former partner, and tenants," Mr. Fiss responded coolly and professionally, but I could sense his tension. "I surmise their purpose here is to continue to intimidate her, as well as sabotage these proceedings."

"I am in charge here, and I will not have it," Ms. Celli replied. She watched them for a few seconds, then turned her attention back to me and the asset list in front of her. "Are any of these assets personal in nature? Any that fall under the exception—"

"She has a diamond ring!" This time it was Bob again.

"What exactly is that to you?" Ms. Celli snapped.

"She shouldn't be allowed to keep things like that!" Kat and Bob said simultaneously.

"Ms. Dion, do you have a ring?" Ms. Celli asked. I nodded my headed, confused as to why that mattered, feeling like I was the one being treated with suspicion instead of these characters who had completely robbed me. "May I see it please?"

I held out my hand for her to see the diamond attached to my wedding band. It isn't large, in fact very conservative, so I wondered what the purpose of this was.

"Thank you," Ms. Celli noted. A few minutes later she had checked everything off her list and began to inform me of the next steps. When she mentioned the meeting of creditors, once again Don Lorry piped up.

"We can attend that," he noted, feigning an air of knowledge and superiority.

"Are you a creditor?" Ms. Celli asked.

"Well, that is still being determined," Don replied. "But the public is allowed to attend, right?"

"That would not be normal procedure, but—"

"These people actually owe my client money, Ms. Celli," Fred Fiss interrupted. "Not the other way around."

"I see. Well I suggest they obtain counsel," she replied. After that she abruptly ended the meeting. I returned to my seat next to Dave and Mr. Fisss motioned for us to remain there until the others left the room. We discussed how unusual their behavior was, as he asked specifics about each one. After about five minutes, we left the building. Thankfully, they were all gone.

A few weeks later I got word from Richard that the Lorrys had filed a claim against me, as did Bob. The audacity was astounding to us. He had spoken with the trustee, showing her facts and documentation as to what had taken place and she agreed to join in the suit for fraudulent conveyance against the Smiths. Once those papers were filed, a torrent of retaliation flowed in my direction.

Frequently after that, as I drove past Kat's house, I noted Bob's car, my friends' car, and the Lorrys' parked in their driveway, especially just before a court date.

One morning in early summer I awakened at about dawn. It had been a very windy night, and I was tired because I hadn't slept well, but was drawn to get out of bed, though I didn't know why. I meandered down the hall to start some coffee, but the smell of smoke made me curious. It was still dark, so even though I looked out the window, I couldn't see much. I checked the house; everything appeared to be in order. Going back to the kitchen, I made the coffee, then decided to go out on the deck while it brewed. As I opened the door, smoke hit my face I noticed spots of fire all over my deck. The chimeneas had been smashed into pieces on both upper and lower decks. There was charcoal spread out on the ground below, as well as on the decks, the pressure-treated wood was still smoldering in places. I ran to get Dave, and buckets of water, even as I realized that with the wind the fires should have engulfed the whole house.

After we doused everything with water, we sat down quietly in the living room, the kids still sleeping in their rooms.

"I don't understand why the house didn't burn down" Dave said soberly.

"I don't either, but, thank you, God," I said.

"I know it was either Lorrys or Smiths," Dave said. "I guess we should call the police."

"Yeah, or one of Justice Head's cronies," I whispered. "This is freaky. I am so tired of this harassment all the time."

"Me, too. When is it gonna end?" Dave whined.

FORTY-FIVE

If you want to enslave a person, you must first alienate her from love and support, so that she wilts like a flower without sun or rain. If you want to conquer an honest person you must lie and lie and lie until the truth seems irrelevant. But in the end, you must live with your conscience.

MY FIRST MEETING OF creditors was held in Plattsburgh also; it proved to be yet another opportunity for the Lorrys, Smiths, and Bob to again try to intimidate and harass. As we approached the guard detail to go through security, one of the officers came over to speak to Dave. Fred ushered me down the hallway, so I was unaware of what was detaining him. This time I was prepared to at least greet my enemies with kindness. I had borrowed a book from my "friend" Carol previously and hadn't had the opportunity to return it before she turned on me. I had wrapped it up in pretty paper and ribbon, and placed a handwritten card inside: "Carol, no matter what has transpired to turn you away, I want you to know that I appreciated your friendship while I had it." She wouldn't take it from my hand, so I placed it on the table in front of her as all eyes gaped at me in curiosity mixed with surprise.

Next, I gave Bob a framed picture I had found of his family, also wrapped and tied with a bow. As I did, he scoffed, "Probably a trick. Poison or something." A faint chorus of nervous laughter ensued. Fred and Ms. Celli watched with keen interest as I then took my seat and waited for the proceedings to begin. Things went along in a tense manner, with Bob recording the whole proceeding on his laptop, and Don Lorry interjecting every other two or three minutes, usually off-the-wall comments and baseless accusations. What bothered me so much was how seriously Ms. Celli seemed to take him, even though we had provided her with an accounting of the now $168,000 the Lorrys owed me. Kat sat angrily at the end of the table where Bob had positioned himself, and Kenny sat next to her. They heckled and scowled through the entire proceeding. When it was finally over, Fred insisted I wait until they had all left the room before speaking or leaving. I anxiously wondered why Dave had not come in the whole time as he was supposed to.

"Ms. Celli," Fred spoke quietly as he approached her desk after the last person had shuffled out into the hallway. "I understand that there is a hearing planned on the fraudulent conveyance. Can you tell me what it is you need to see to also prove to you that the Lorrys are not creditors? That they are just playing games with the court?" The two of the them spoke in hushed tones, and I sat frozen in fear and contemplation at what might be transpiring with Dave, and why my former friends and former husband could turn so vile. After a couple of minutes, I realized Ms. Celli had addressed me.

"I'm sorry," I told her as I became aware. "Can you please repeat that?"

"Have you provided Richard with documentation outlining why you feel the Lorrys owe you this money?"

"Yes, I have. I thought he had already submitted it to you," I paused for a second to regroup. "I don't just *feel like* they owe me, they actually do. Ms. Celli, I am not sure if you're aware of all that is going on behind the scenes. I have been targeted since I became a witness to Judicial Conduct, the Attorney General, and now the FBI. The Lorrys, my former tenants, were bribing the local judge when I filed to have them evicted. The judge still hasn't issued the final ruling in the case, though even he admits they owe me money. And, if I may say, it seems highly unprofessional that all these characters, with their entirely fabricated claims, are represented by the same attorney who assisted the Lorrys in defrauding me from day one."

"And who is that?" she asked, making some notes on a legal pad.

"Evan Tracy."

"In fact," Fred concluded, "I called Evan and told him he had a serious conflict of interests here."

"Duly noted," she said coolly, putting her pen down and closing the folder in front of her.

As we made our way out of the room and down the narrow hallway, I looked around for Dave, but didn't see him anywhere. Fred and I made our way up the stairs and through the main foyer toward the front entrance, still not seeing Dave we stepped outside to discover him leaning against the side of the building.

"Dave! Where were you?" I exhaled fretfully. He came toward us quickly, visibly distraught

"I was arrested," he said.

"What?" Fred's eyebrows raised in a surprised arch as he spoke.

"They took me off to the side in a small room and presented me with this," he said as he handed Fred a citation. "They said I was under arrest for harassment and disorderly conduct in a federal building."

"What the—?" I felt as if I had been shot in the stomach.

"Lorrys?" Fred asked, his eyes scanning the document.

"All of 'em," Dave replied. "The bastards swore out affidavits that it was me who provoked Don last time, not the other way around! Said I threatened to beat him and kill him. Not that I wouldn't like to but, that ain't how it happened!" His jaw quivered as his neck veins bulged and face turned red.

"So they let you go with an appearance ticket—"

"But why didn't you come tell us? Why did you stay away?" I queried, tears brimming my eyes.

"They told me that if there was another incident, I would be put in jail, and—"

"He has to stay away," Fred admonished. "They lie about everything, but they are banded together. They will make up stories and swear to them, and then it's the two of you against the whole group of them. All they have to do is agree that Dave tried again and he's in jail."

"Oh my God! This is sheer evil!" I moaned.

"I'll go make a copy of this. Our firm will represent you on the court date," Fred walked toward the entrance again. "Be right back."

"These jerks won't stop, Karen," Dave snarled. "They won't stop 'til they destroy you. It's not right."

"They want to make me face them all alone," I pondered. "Are you okay?"

"Yeah. It was humiliating. They fingerprinted me and everything!" He shook his head. "Now I can't be with you—it could hurt you more!" He reached out to hug me tightly. "I'm so sorry, sweetheart. I really tried my best. I'm so sorry."

I barely felt his hug for the numbness that beset me. What wasn't numb was trembling.

As we arrived for Dave's court appearance a few weeks later I had an eerie sense that true justice would elude us. The federal judge presiding was named Judge Lewis. The same Lewis of Lewis, Rogers & Meconi, PC— my former counsel. In fact, the hearing was upstairs from their offices, in a tiny make-shift courtroom. Although I hoped that Fred's associate who was handling the case would explain the facts and Dave would somehow be exonerated, that's not what happened. Instead, she called Dave to stand by her side and asked the judge to accept adjournment in contemplation of dismissal. I winced, as I sat there trying not to explode at the injustice. After a stern, condescending lecture from the burly judge, Dave was subjected to a full year of being on his best behavior and staying away from the Lorrys, Smiths, and group or he could be thrown in jail at the least provocation—or lie. At the end of a year, the charges would be dropped as if they never existed, so long as he was not found in violation.

Same game, different court.

By now I pondered the connections these people shared. I wondered how many of them were in fact part of the corruption I had stumbled upon.

Aunt Shirley gave me some GABA to take before my next court appearance in Albany. I would have preferred a supportive companion, but no one volunteered. I made the two-and-a-half-hour journey alone, praying, brooding, and anxious to get the whole ordeal over with. I made my payment under the plan then went to wait for Richard near the court room. I watched as he spoke with Ms. Celli, standing closer than typical colleagues, he even touched her arm a couple of times as she met his admiring gaze with a smile. Eventually he made his way over to me.

"We're going to go in and sit in the back now," he said. "Ms. Celli and I are going to present our case to the judge—" he reached into his satchel and pulled out a document, handing it to me. "This is the answer the Smiths filed. I want you to make some notes in the margins—things I should remember."

"They're probably all in there, already," I groaned.

"Don't let them get to you. You are in the right here. They have to lie to say anything against you, and if they do, they are perjuring themselves and we'll prove it." He reached in his satchel again. "Here is a motion I just received from ABN AMRO's counsel. They are asking the judge to set aside the automatic stay and let them enforce foreclosure—"

"No!" I felt I couldn't take another thing. Hot tears stung my eyes, my heart pounded.

"I think we can defeat this given the way all these characters are acting together," Richard patted me on the shoulder as he spoke. "I know it's upsetting, but you provide me with documentation and I will use it to wipe them out."

During the course of the proceeding Bob spoke up demanding to know what had become of the $20,000 settlement I had received from him. He tried to paint me as some criminal that had conned him into "giving" it to me, and conveniently left out the part about how he *owed* it to me, let alone that he owed more than twice as much. I tried to tell Richard about that in the midst of everything, but he was focused on other issues. As a result, the judge ordered that I provide an accounting of where the money had gone.

By the end of that arduous proceeding wherein I was publicly and shamelessly lied about repeatedly, we at least had accomplished a small win. The bankruptcy judge ordered that the Smiths must let me back in the building to inspect it and to take an inventory of all my assets, as well as see what damages or losses I might have suffered due to them. Evan Tracy had on paper withdrawn as counsel for Bob, and for the Smiths, but they were still represented by the same firm.

FORTY-SIX

What if when evil is exposed, no one cares?
Worse, what if no one recognizes it as evil?

JULY 7TH FINALLY CAME. I met Fred Fiss at the building, but the Smiths wouldn't allow us in. I noted there had been a flurry of activity there in the days leading up to that sunny morning but couldn't figure out what they were doing. Fred tried to reason with them, their lawyer arrived, and even he refused to allow us in unless we had a police escort. Although it was totally unnecessary, I assured Fred that I personally knew a few state troopers who would help us out. I called the barracks and Trooper Eric was happy to oblige.

We went through the shop and my old office first. All my belongings were piled in boxes, many of them broken. I wondered what they had done with the antiques I had on consignment, let alone my personal effects. Several lightbulbs were out, so it was hard to see, and they refused to let me pull things outs of boxes for a better look. I tried to make some notes about what should be there, and what was there as we slowly progressed.

By the time we made our way upstairs to the inn, I was in tears. All my beautiful work was tampered with. I noted they painted over the mural in the kitchen, and the Japanese tea set given to me by my brother was broken in pieces, sitting in a box. Another antique teapot Mimi had given me was gone, and the beautiful gold utensil set Nana gave me was missing from its case. Also missing where family paintings, a French antique spinning wheel from the late 1700s, my beautiful hand-painted tableware, and so much more.

"It's so hard to see in here," I muttered to Fred and Eric through my tears.

"The bastards," whispered Trooper Eric, his eyes soft with concern.

"I am sure that's by design, Karen Marie," Fred replied firmly. He reached out and patted my shoulder, "Are you okay? I know this is really tough."

"It is so hard," I sniffled, wiping away tears. "I put everything into this place, and look what they've done!"

Makeshift sawhorses were set up in various rooms, topped with boxes of my belongings. They appeared to be setting up crude closets of unpainted two-by-fours and plywood in each room and had scuffed the walls and floors badly. I made my way down the hall to the entrance to the studio apartment. There was a note taped to the outside of the door:

REPAIRS HALTED IN MAY DUE TO COURT ORDER.

"Oh my God! What have they done?" I gasped as I opened the door. There was plaster dust everywhere, as well as piles of debris. The load-bearing wall that divided the kitchen from the living area had been taken down, and the ceiling sagged above it. None of the kitchen cabinetry remained, and there was a gaping hole in the wall, covered with plastic, where once had been a window overlooking the river.

"What the hell?" Fred scratched his head as he looked around. "What was this like before?"

"It was a really adorable studio apartment," I told him, tears streaming down my cheeks. I walked into the room carefully, stepping around the debris. "Over here was the kitchen with built-in cabinets that were floor to ceiling, original to the building, 1840. Don Lorry kept asking me for them, but I wouldn't destroy the place. They were more valuable as they were. And here—" I pointed to the area below the sagging ceiling, "this is where the little bathroom was. It was on my list to be updated, but it was perfectly functional for this apartment. They even took out the plumbing in the kitchen."

"For what purpose, I wonder?" Trooper Eric piped in.

"God only knows," I replied sadly. "They kept complaining of a lack of funds, but it seems they were just bent on destruction. They could have rented this out, like I did."

"The more I see how crazy this case is, the more I realize they were out to enrich themselves at your expense. The greed is obvious," Fred stated solemnly. "The destruction is just stupid."

It was a long process. I tried to take pictures, but it was too dark.

The damages were evident in every room. I realized after we left that the flurry of activity was the Smiths moving out of the inn and back into their own home, less than a mile away. In the days that followed, they held a garage sale there, I watched as they sold many of the inn's furnishings and inventory. I called the police, but now they would not get involved, citing that it was not a criminal matter, but rather a civil one. Richard disagreed, as far as he was concerned, they were selling stolen property. That is what was really happening, but no one would get involved, and Richard said I would be reimbursed in the end.

Throughout this time, I had flashbacks to our home in Bakersfield, and of seeing our possessions auctioned off. Fear and feelings of powerlessness plagued me, along with a strong desire to prevent the kind of losses in my children's lives that I had experienced. I struggled to keep a good outlook and prayed for guidance. I wrestled to believe my outcome would be better.

I had strong suspicions that Dave was struggling too, but mainly with porn. Things were difficult, but busy. I spent long hours poring through boxes of documentation, compiling the list of inventory that was missing from the building, getting appraisals on everything from our piano to my diamond ring, and answering the seemingly infinite number of questions Richard came up with as a result of the barrage of papers filed by my enemies in the bankruptcy court. I spoke with Bill Glaberson, the FBI, Judicial Conduct investigators, and even the State Comptroller's investigators as the evidence of corruption expanded. I looked for work, but times were tough, and so far, I had only had about three interviews. Finally, in late November I got another call from Bill Glaberson that he was about to publish a story on Judge Head. He asked if I could convince Vern to talk to him, but Vern wouldn't return my phone calls.

The week of Thanksgiving I interviewed with a local medical practice and was eventually offered the position of practice manager. I was to start the second week in December. The very next day, the *Press Republican* contacted me because of a tip from Bill Glaberson. They planned additional coverage of Justice Head based on the New York Times story to be published. They asked me to come in to their office and be interviewed by the editor and another investigative journalist, Andrea Van Valkenburg. I was a little nervous about the fallout from such public exposure, but I realized it was probably just what I needed to finally see justice ramped up a bit. ABN AMRO's attorney had won his motion and now I had to deal with him again. I would do anything to keep my home for my children's sake. I went in the next day, with much documentation, and told Lois and Andrea my story.

"You have a lot of documentation," Andrea said, eagerly peering at it and sorting it into piles. "Do you have proof that Justice Head is under investigation?"

"I have nothing in writing, just the fact that I communicate with the investigator all the time, and he tells me what he is looking for, what he needs, etcetera." I pulled a letter out of the pile that simply indicated the Commission was reviewing my complaint and handed it to her.

"This stops just short of saying they're investigating," she said sadly as she passed it off to Lois. "Can you get him on the phone maybe? Try to get him to talk about the investigation so we can hear him?"

"I can try, but he's out in the field a lot. I usually fax him or leave him a message and he calls me back." I tried to recall the rules of journalism I learned in college and wondered how I might provide what they needed. "I could . . ." I hesitated a second and it was enough to cause them to look at me keenly. "I could call Glen Michaels, I suppose."

"Glen Michaels? The AGA?" Lois inquired, glasses perched half way down her nose as she looked at me over the top of them.

"Yes. He's been involved since day one. He's the one who told me to file the complaint with the Commission to begin with. I know he is aware of more than I am."

"Please call him," Andrea said excitedly. "Ask him if there's any way he could confirm."

I dialed Glen's office and his assistant immediately put me through as usual.

"Hi, Karen Marie. How are you? Is everything okay?" he asked.

"At the moment," I sighed. "How are you?" Andrea pointed to the phone and then to her ear. I put the volume up and held the phone away from my face so they could hear him, too.

"I'm fine. Just busy. What can I help you with?" he asked pleasantly.

"Glen, I—" I realized that if he knew about Bill's story, maybe he knew what the *Press Republican* wanted. "I suppose you know that the *Press Republican* is going to do a tandem story to Bill Glaberson's?"

"Really? Hmm," I could just imagine his smirk on the other end of the phone. "Are you contributing?"

"Yes, I am. It's a bit scary, but—"

"But don't you think it will help?" he interrupted.

"I hope so. The thing is, I am in their office right now, and they are wondering if you could confirm that the Commission on Judicial Conduct is investigating George Head?"

"Oh, Karen Marie, I wish I could," he said. "But you know how these things go . . ."

"So, you won't confirm that the FBI is investigating either?" I queried, trying to find a way for him to confirm without sanctioning.

"I really hope these investigations end soon and help you put your life back together, Karen Marie. I mean, no one deserves that more than you. You've helped us a lot, and you're helping Justice Head's victims, but you know I can't confirm in any official capacity, right? I wish I could." Glen had just said a mouthful, and I think he knew it.

"Glen, I understand." I sighed.

"When the investigations are over, I'll have a lot more to say," he said professionally. It felt like a pretend conversation, but it was just what Andrea and Lois needed to hear. Andrea put her thumb up, as Lois rushed out of the room.

"Thanks, Glen. I'll talk to you soon."

"You bet. Take care," he said cheerily before hanging up the phone.

"Perfect!" Andrea exclaimed, a smile spread across her face.

FORTY-SEVEN

When ignorance resists truth either for lack of personal knowledge, or a desire to maintain an illusion of utopia, there can be no justice, and the truth-tellers are labeled troublemakers.

"SMALL TOWN JUDGE'S PERSONAL Justice Stirs Concern" read the front page of the *New York Times* on December 14, 2006. Vern refused to go on the record, so Bill Glaberson stopped shy of telling the whole truth, although the article was peppered with insinuation so that anyone open to reality could easily understand what was being inferred. The *Press Republican* ran a front-page story also: "Keeseville Woman Accuses Judge." Andrea detailed how George Head's abuses of procedure left me on the brink of losing my home and had already led to the loss of my business and other assets. I contacted my soon to be new boss to confirm the time he would like me to start, only to be told that he was a "personal friend of Judge Head." No further explanation was needed when he hung up on me.

My Chapter Thirteen bankruptcy protection came to a screeching halt when Richard and Ms. Celli had what appeared to be a falling out. My enemies turned up with new allegations at every turn, all of them false, but needing time and attention. Richard, who had agreed to take the case for a minor fee, now grew tired of the daily onslaught, and didn't seem to keep up with rebuttals. We had petitioned the court for a lower monthly payment under the plan until I could either find work or be restored through the proceedings, and when I drove down to Albany to make the payment in person at the same time as appear for a conference, I was surprised that they would not take my payment. Richard was just as shocked as I. He tried to pull Ms. Celli aside before the hearing and ask why, but she brushed him off. A bit embarrassed, he told me that he would ask the judge about it, verifying that I had cash in hand to make it that very day.

"The payment should have been sent to our Tennessee lock box," the deputy trustee, a scowl-faced woman in her mid-fifties snorted as Richard inquired in open court.

"But my client knew she would be here today for this hearing and in the past has made her payments in person at the same time, with no issues." Richard was openly agitated and seemed more unsure of himself than I had ever seen him. I sat there totally panicked as to why they wouldn't just take my money.

"What is the status of your client's job search? Does she have the means to continue making these payments?" the judge inquired, barely acknowledging me.

"Your Honor, my client has been a witness to judicial conduct and other investigators. When *The Times* and the local newspaper ran a story about it, the job offer she had was withdrawn. She is still actively seeking employment, but she has sufficient means to make the reduced payment until then." Richard looked over at me nervously as he concluded his statement. I nodded in agreement from my seat.

"Your Honor, she should have already sent the payment in to our lockbox," the deputy trustee restated firmly. "That is our normal protocol. We suggest that if the payment is in the lockbox on the due date, then the plan may continue under the reduced payment terms, however, if not, we request that you discharge this debtor." She glared at me from across the room, leaning on the desk as she spoke. Ms. Celli sat nonchalantly nearby but did not get involved as in previous court appearances. My stomach twisted into knots at the thought of what she was proposing. Richard squirmed, shifting his weight from one foot to another.

"Your Honor, I led my client to believe—" Richard choked on his own words, face flushing. "Um, I told her it was okay to make her payments in person, Your Honor. This is nothing more than an oversight. A simple mistake. She will make her payments to the lockbox after this one." The silence that followed his statement was heavy. The judge looked at each of them. Ms. Celli shuffled papers nearby, ignoring him.

"If the payment is in the lockbox by the end of the due day, then the plan will continue. If not, this debtor will be discharged," the judge declared from his elevated desk. "Next case!"

I gulped. I prayed. Once outside the courtroom I asked Richard what that was all about.

"You should have already sent your payment in," he replied quietly.

"But Richard! I sent you three emails and finally called your office twice to determine what to do. Your assistant told me that I could wait and make the payment in person since we didn't know which amount it was going to be. Money is tight," I sighed. "I can't afford to pay more than I have to right now."

"I know, I know. I honestly don't know how you're even eating right now, let alone taking care of your kids." He looked down at the floor, shaking his head and heaving a sigh. "But I should have told you to send it in. Once you get this far into the plan, they expect you to use the lockbox. The accounting is done elsewhere."

"Does it have to be today? Can it arrive tomorrow?" Anxiously I hoped for a solution.

"It might work," he replied. "Can you overnight it?"

I went to the Post Office next, obtained a money order with the cash I had in hand, then to the FedEx store near Richard's office. I sent it by overnight mail to the lockbox and paid for earliest morning delivery. The next day I checked the online resources to see if my payment had posted. Nadda. The day after, it did show on the system, but I was fearful that would not be good enough. When I called the trustee's office to confirm I was informed they only check the lockbox once per day. My payment was considered a day late.

"The people in your area are pieces of shit!" Richard yelled into the phone. I called him to find out what happens next, although I feared I knew the answer. "In my thirty years of practice I have never experienced such bullshit! You're up against fucking thugs!"

"Yes, I really am," I told him, shocked at his language. I had never heard him be anything but professional until that moment, but I completely understood how badly these thugs could get under one's skin. "Why was the judge so harsh?"

"Because it's bad enough you are pitted against another judge, even if he is a town justice, but with those moronic enemies you have parading around in unity with a million false allegations—" he stumbled over his words a second, then continued. "It looks like where there's smoke there's fire!"

Richard said there was no appeal. I don't know if he just wanted to be rid of the aggravation or if that was true. I braced myself for what might come next. I kept searching for work. I fought with the attorney for ABN

AMRO almost daily as we struggled to keep our home. He ultimately agreed that he would not pursue an eviction, but rather he would settle our differences with me. At the same time, I received a letter from the Smiths, through their attorney, asking me if I would take possession of the building once again. Apparently, if I was willing to assume their mortgage, they were willing to walk away. I was stunned. It had been more than a year since they locked me out and destroyed my business, let alone disposed of or ruined most of my assets. I wrote back and asked about the particulars: what had they done to it? What was the status of the mortgage? How would they reimburse me for lost business and all that they had stolen? I never received a reply.

I saw Stephen Johnston and his wife at church one Sunday. As we caught up, he suggested that things had now progressed to the level of a federal law suit and said that if I could convince an old judge friend of his to take the case with him, he would represent me once again. A federal law suit is a lot of work, and making the case would take expertise, specifically under U.S.C. Section 1983.

"That would be so great, Stephen," I told him with sincere appreciation. "I have to admit I was a little concerned when you had Bill Meconi handle that last thing."

"You mean you didn't *ask* Bill to handle it?" he asked with surprise.

"No. He told me that you called him and asked him to handle it, since I was a client of the firm."

"He called me and told me you had changed your mind!" Stephen retorted. "I never did trust him!"

I contacted the retired judge, Dominic, he recommended so highly, and he was amenable to my cause. He indicated a high regard for Stephen, and a need for a little something to do in retirement other than golf. He also claimed to be aware of the abuses of the small town and village court system and had heard rumors aplenty about George Head. He asked me to write up a synopsis of the case, including all parties, and fax it to him.

When I called him to follow up a week later he took great pains to explain to me what had to happen next, including informing me that the statute of limitations was about to expire.

"You see," the old judge said in a genuinely caring professional tone, "you have an action under color of law. These parties—going way back to the beginning—have conspired to defraud you by abusing municipal and judicial authority. They did it in their official capacity, so they are liable. Your losses are quite significant, and you are entitled to damages as well."

"Under color of law, you say? That's a legal term?" I queried, jotting down notes on a piece of paper by the phone.

"Yes. Section 1983 of the US Code says that any person who acts in his official capacity either by ordinance or by custom to cause the deprivation of rights or losses to another person is liable to that person for damages. It is a violation of your guaranteed civil rights under the Constitution. It's harder to go after the judge, but not impossible because he has customarily deprived and abused regulation—we have a pattern. And we can prove that he worked in concert with the Lorrys and the Village officers, so you will be suing not only the town justice, but also the mayor, the Lorrys, the Smiths . . . everybody gets lumped into this."

"That might make it easier to get someone to finally tell the truth," I thought aloud. "I mean, if the pressure is on all of them…"

"That's true," he continued. "But the trick is showing a clear pattern, defining the cooperation between them all. It takes skill, but I can see you can write, and Stephen tells me you have a paralegal background."

"That was years ago," I told him. "And I never worked at the federal level."

"Most attorneys don't work at the federal level. It's intimidating and very tedious." He paused for a moment. "You need to think very clearly, which is hard because you've been so victimized, but when did you first think this was a concerted effort, a plot between all of them?"

We talked a few minutes and he told me of cases to refer to and legal statutes. After about ten minutes, I started to realize that he was coaching me because he probably wasn't going to take my case.

"Sir, I am so grateful for your advice," I finally told him. "Does this mean you and Stephen are going to take my case?"

"Well, now," he sighed into the phone. "I have a good mind to take it, but I didn't make it to retirement only to get divorced for going back to work! I have spoken with Stephen, and I know he has no time to take it unless I help him, but my wife is adamantly against it. She knows I'll be spending too much time working."

"I see," I replied sadly. "Well, I appreciate your time very much."

"Listen to me," he urged. "You have a very compelling case. You can do this by yourself, as a pro se litigant. In fact, you might have more wiggle room since the court has to give you the opportunity to explain and give you the benefit of the doubt in certain ways. This case has the potential to be successful, even though this is one of the hardest types of cases to successfully try in the federal court. You've got facts. You've got obnoxious defendants with blatant wrongdoing."

"I should represent myself? In federal court?"

"Yes. Young lady, you've got what it takes," he said confidently. "And call me anytime, by all means."

"Thank you, sir. I'll think about it." I hung up the phone crying but strangely encouraged.

FORTY-EIGHT

*Do not be deceived, God is not mocked;
for whatever a man sows that will he also reap.*
PAUL THE APOSTLE

WITH NO JOB IN sight, and kids to work around, I started looking for consulting work and trying to refinance the house. Every time we got rejected, we applied somewhere else again. The rest of the time I studied the law to the best of my ability and began drafting my federal complaint.

Judge Dominic pointed out to me in a subsequent call that I needed to include the Village of Keeseville as a municipality as much as each individual officer, the Smiths, the Lorrys, and even ABN AMRO since they conspired with them and particularly with Don. By the time I wrote the caption listing each defendant in the required format, it took up nearly a page. Even that intimidated me, but I knew I had no choice other than to go forward. We had figured that I had until the end of April to file the suit, after that the statute of limitations would be up. I worked feverishly on it and drove the final document, a stack about an inch and a half thick, down to the Albany courthouse for filing. As I left the clerk's office later that afternoon, I felt empowered again, in a way I had not felt in a long time.

It took some time for me to get established as a pro se litigant. There were hoops to jump through I had never even thought of, but by the end of May, I was assured the summons were in the hands of the US Marshall's Office to be personally served upon each defendant.

I heard from Vern that he was about to wear a wire for the FBI and go pay a visit to justice Head. I wondered at the timing and prayed for the best possible outcome. In June, the returns of service started trickling in, and I noted with a keen sense of caution an increase of traffic in front of my rural home. Lorrys' vehicles, the Smiths'—they seemed to be driving by a few times per day. I saw Bob's car a few times at night, along with Buck's. Kat screeched to a halt when she saw me outside in the garden one day, backed up her truck and swung into the driveway threatening me. "I'm gonna take you out! You're goin' down!"

I calmly picked up my cell phone and took a picture, then a video, as she ranted, before walking into the house. She drove around like a maniac for an hour, pounding her horn and waving her middle finger out the window, but I ignored her. Then the phone started ringing. At first, I ignored it, assuming it was Kat, still in a rage. After a few minutes however, I decided to answer.

"Karen Marie!" Julie's voice was rushed. "I thought you might like to know—"

"Julie? How are you? I haven't heard from you since—"

"I know. Don made me do that. He and Carolyn said if I wanted to work for them again I had to say you owed me money in bankruptcy court. I'm sorry," she said wistfully. "I needed a job."

"I know how persuasive they can be," I reassured her, even though I still felt the sting of her betrayal.

"I called because I thought you would like to know that Judge Head just died," she said earnestly.

"What? He's dead?" A plethora of thoughts flooded my mind.

"He got served with your federal lawsuit and sometime soon after he had a heart attack. He already had cancer, and some say AIDs, so he had been in and out of the hospital, but—we all think you scared him to death! His corruption finally caught up with him!" She seemed happy but sober.

"Oh my God!"

"Some of the kids he took advantage of are throwing a party. Everyone around town is saying '*ding dong, the witch is dead.*' Amazing, huh?" She gushed details and I tried to process it all. I especially wondered if Vern had gone to see him yet.

Maybe I was safer from that day on because he was not around to direct retaliation through his network of corrupt troopers, corrections officers, and others. I knew he had still been involved in moving drugs because I saw him and Spike Lorry meeting in the middle of the afternoon in the supermarket just a couple of months previous. The store was virtually empty except for a couple of employees. I had stopped in after a meeting to pick up something to cook for dinner. As I rounded the corner into the middle aisle, they were exchanging something in envelopes. They startled, shoved the envelopes in their respective jacket pockets and each quickly went in a different direction. I noted they pretended to shop, but Spike didn't even have a cart, and justice Head only had a small basket in his hand, empty. I abandoned my dinner mission, went straight to my car and dialed Glen.

"Isn't Spike Lorry a border agent now?" he asked.

"A customs agent," I replied. "Are you going to send someone down here?"

"Are they still in there? Can you see them?" he inquired.

"Yes—plain as day," I told him.

"I'll see what I can do, but I'm sure that you scared the hell out of them and they will be gone by the time anyone gets there. Thanks for the head's up, though. I'll pass this along." When we hung up I wondered if he was getting soft on crime or just being realistic. As I drove away, I noted Trooper Eric in his cruiser heading in the direction of that Peru shopping center.

I started to understand more of how widespread the corruption was when I got a private message from an anonymous source. He told me only that his name was Bill, and that he knew what I was dealing with. He wrote that the network was bigger than I realized and was run by the mob. I wrote back and asked him how he knew this and who was the head of the mob in far upstate. When he finally got back to me days later, he gave me the name of the mob boss and told me that the Lorrys had been playing both sides—the Akwesasne smugglers against the Italian mob. He said that both sides despise the Lorrys, but they know enough to play the middle safely, inferring that Spike's new position as a US Customs agent was profitable for everyone, and acknowledging the sleazy way in which Don operates. With this newfound information, I grew fearful and petitioned the court to appoint me an attorney, pro bono.

Unfortunately, the US Magistrate Judge overseeing my case concluded that I was doing a better than average job of representing myself and declined to assign an attorney to me, however he did leave the door open for me to "ask again" as the case ramped up and got more complicated. At the same time, ABN AMRO ramped up its efforts to take my house. They obtained a local writ of execution, even though the Essex County Judge had signed the foreclosure order before the due date—even before I had the opportunity to respond to the motion in foreclosure. I hoped that the federal court would enable me to prevail but failed to comprehend how reluctant to be involved in state matters they are. I insisted that it was the cooperation of all parties which deprived me of my civil rights, just like Judge Dominic instructed me, but after many months of pleadings and responses, the federal judge finally removed the restraining order against them. This began a flurry of negotiating, *again*.

Just after the new year the attorney for ABN AMRO asked what I wanted to settle the case out of the federal court. We talked numbers from $600,000 down to $350,000. In my legal researching I discovered that ABN had recently paid the largest ever settlement (up until that time) to the Department of Justice, in excess of $40 million, as a result of the Department of Justice's investigation into their mishandling of over 28,000 FHA insured mortgages. Apparently, the DOJ was happy to take the money and let ABN AMRO get away with a promise not to do it again, but no compensation was offered homeowners like me. Not one cent of that money ever made it into the hands of the families they defrauded. I was shocked to find that wasn't even considered in the settlement, and I was one of the 28,000. But, ABN's lawyer handling my case was a smug, wet behind the ears maverick who didn't give a hoot about justice. Realizing that, I finally agreed that I would settle just for the amount owed on the house. He indicated that we likely had a deal, telling me he would check with his client and get back to me in the morning. I went to bed that night relieved and grateful. If they were willing to pay over $40 million, then the measly little balance on my home was nothing to them.

FORTY-NINE

When you make the right choices, and keep your heart pure, there is a tendency to feel entitled to a proper outcome. However, where corruption is rampant, and truth is shunned, outcomes are never guaranteed. Only the reward of an upright conscience is guaranteed.

AFTER JONATHAN WENT TO school the next morning and Dave to work, I sat down to have a cup of coffee. As I gazed out the window at the valley below, I noted a string of vehicles parked on the side of the road, hazard lights flashing. I thought it was curious but picked up my inspirational reading. After a few minutes, I checked the time and got up for a second cup of coffee. As I walked back in the living room I saw those same cars pulling in my driveway, along with a U-Haul truck. Panic seized me. I realized that ABN AMRO's attorney either deliberately lied, or else he failed to put the kibosh on the writ as he had promised. I ran to the phone to call his office, he wasn't in yet. The paralegal I spoke with had no idea of our agreement the day before.

I greeted the sheriff's deputies at the door. As the moving crew waited to get started, I explained that it must be a mistake. I offered them coffee and juice and asked them to please be patient while I contacted the attorney. I called Glen, who said he could do nothing. I called my friends, who got in their cars and began driving toward my home. I prayed fervently, tried to remain calm.

When Dave arrived, we went into my office, closing the door behind us. We got down on our knees and asked God to put an end to this debacle. I trembled, cried, and yet had peace that God was with me. I knew the people assembled there were just doing a job, it wasn't personal, but it was so personal to me. The injustice of it all cut me to the heart. *Surely God couldn't allow this?*

I left another message for the attorney. I even called the federal court clerk asking if there was any emergency proceeding I could bring. Finally, when all my calls were exhausted, the deputies explained that they must begin.

"I am going to keep trying to reach him," I told the one in charge. "I understand you are doing what you have to do, but we just came to terms yesterday." Dave stood by my side, angry.

"I understand, ma'am," he replied. "I am sorry. I hope for your sake this all works out. It's not fun for us either." He turned to the deputy next to him, and the foreman of the moving crew who stood nearby. "Start with non-essentials," he directed. Then, looking back at me he inquired, "Where would be best for us to start if you're sure this is going to be halted at some point?"

"Maybe the basement?" I could hardly believe what was happening. It was all surreal.

They started in the basement, and of course the workshop was chock full, so that took some time. I still had no return calls, and it was getting to be about 1:00. I realized that Jonathan would be on his way home from school by bus soon, and I didn't want him to discover our predicament like that. I started to ask my friend Donna if she would go pick him up but got interrupted by a deputy asking about the barn, and whether I had heard back from the attorney.

"Oh my God! My horses!" Tears escaped my eyes as I tried to grasp what might become of them. Hearing that, Dave started shrieking as the movers began moving boxes of his belongings from the basement. He had a full-blown post-traumatic stress breakdown. My friends came around in awe, I ran to him, cupping his face in both of my hands.

"Dave, Dave," I spoke firmly but lovingly, gazing into his terror filled eyes. "Dave, you are going to be okay. We are all going to be okay. This is not right, but we are. We will be fine." He whimpered and collapsed in a heap on the floor, rocking back and forth. I held him tightly in my arms, whispering in his ear. "I love you. Somehow this is going to work out. Somehow we are going to be all right."

"It's so wrong, so wrong," he cried. "Where is justice? Where is God?"

"He's with us," I whispered. "I guess justice comes in other ways, I don't know. But God is with us, so we will be fine. You are a strong and wonderful man, with a big heart. You've got this." I held him in a strength

I never knew I had. I was hurting, too, and I ached for justice. I longed for my home to be filled with peace and stability. I had my own nagging questions, but somehow, I had comfort in my heart. After several minutes I realized that everyone had stopped working and all eyes were on us. I looked around and saw one of the deputies drying his eyes, and one of the female movers, too. I stood to my feet and Dave stood to lean against the wall, holding my hand, he still trembled, a distant look in his eyes.

"Dave? Do you think you'd like to go to the hospital?" I asked softly. I realized that his breakdown was very real; it scared me.

"No," he whispered. "I am not leaving your side." Just then our friend Blake came over and embraced Dave in a bear hug. Other friends followed suit. We eventually stood in a group hug, and Blake led us in a prayer. The deputies looked on in wonder; later Blake remarked, "They know they're on the wrong side of this one."

I was able to find the anti-anxiety meds the VA doctor had prescribed for Dave when he first got home from combat. He didn't like the way they made him feel, so he never took them after the first few weeks. I asked him to please take them that day and he did. After I gave him the pills I turned to my friend Donna again.

"What time is it? Can you please go get Jonathan? I don't want him to come home to this by bus—"

"Oh no!" Donna exclaimed. "It's 2:45! He's getting on the bus any minute!" There was no way we could be there before the bus departed. We decided to post watch for when it pulled up to the driveway.

Now in addition to everything else, I worried about Dave and Jonathan. Aunt Shirley called and asked what she could do.

"I don't know how to tell Nana," I told her softly, soberly. "She is going to be so upset. I don't want to distress her."

"I'll tell her," she replied. "Are you going to go stay with her?"

"Our friends have offered us to stay with them for a little while. Jonathan needs to be near school—there's no way he could commute from Burlington. I want him to have some stability, but—"

"I know. This is bad," Shirley said somberly. "What can Tom and I do? Do you need anything?"

"Your presence would help immensely. I'm worried about Dave. He had a serious breakdown. Jon's not home yet but will be any minute—" I couldn't say any more for the lump in my throat.

"Did you give him anything for it? Does he need to go to the hospital?" I explained and then she concluded our conversation saying, "We'll be there in a couple of hours."

Donna called me from the front porch: "The bus is coming!"

I ran outside and into the snow-covered driveway without a coat. Sleet was starting to fall and everything was being coated with an icy glaze. As the bus pulled to a halt at the edge of the driveway, Jonathan bolted off the steps and hurled himself toward me, flinging his backpack in a snow bank.

"NO! NO!" he shouted. "NO!" Tears immediately flowed down his gloomy face. I tried to hug him, but in his hurting rage, he ran toward the house. I followed him as Blake came out to greet him. Taking him by the shoulders, Blake spoke calmly to him and then I caught up with them.

To this day this is one of the most painful moments of my life. I struggle to forgive myself for allowing this grievous wrong to affect my children. It was a blessing that at least Katlyn was away at college and didn't have to witness it. I know I did all that I could. I struggle in the raw, gut-wrenching knowledge that I indeed had trusted God for a better outcome, had done everything I could to prevail, and yet lost. I had myself lost home and possessions at the age of sixteen, and now my son was facing the same pain I had vowed to never put him through.

We know that earthly possessions are meaningless, but a home is a gift from God meant to give us a place of solace, rest, a haven of love and laughter, a foundation that is more than physical. It's a launching pad from which we venture into the unknown and return to rest again. At least I knew that we carried home in our hearts but, being subjected to the sheer evil means by which the loss of our house came about struck the familiar chord of powerlessness I had been trying to overcome.

Having lived in that home for over ten years, and having all the theatre gear and props there, as well as horse gear and horses, there was a lot to move. By about 4:30 in the afternoon the deputies came to me to say that they would stop for the day and return at 9:00 the next morning. They gave me a number to call if I was successful in getting the attorney to keep his promise. I did finally reach him at about 4:45 p.m.

"Hello Mr. Case, this is Karen Marie Dion," I said when he picked up the phone.

"Oh! Hello," he seemed surprised to hear from me. "What can I do for you?"

"You can call off this mayhem," I replied quietly. "Did you even tell your client about our agreement?"

"No. I haven't had the chance," he replied. "I was in court all day today."

"You don't plan on it, do you?" I asked him pointedly.

"I'd say it's a moot point now, wouldn't you?" he laughed.

"This is no joke, Mr. Case. In fact, it's not moot. They have not even come close to finishing. You can still make it right."

"Really? They're not done?" he seemed shocked.

"No. My family and I are still here in our home," I paused, trying to garner more strength. "I am respectfully requesting that you relay our agreement to your client for approval. After all, your client is still included in the federal law suit."

"Okay," he said, somewhat awkwardly. "I will relay it, but I'm not promising anything."

With Katlyn away at school, it was just Jonathan, Dave, and me at home that night. Shirley and Tom never came down as promised, heaping yet another disappointment on our day. We talked through what was happening, loving on each other, nibbling on a rotisserie chicken Blake had gone to get us for dinner. Nana called and begged us to "come home to Burlington." We talked about it together, but desperately wanted Jon to have continuity, since he was now excelling in every way academically and athletically. He had been competing at state championships since the seventh grade, and now was being watched by college recruiters. Ultimately, he didn't want to change schools. We discussed everything as a family. We tried to encourage each other.

As night fell, the three of us got on our knees at the foot of our bed. We thanked God for another night in our home and asked for a miracle.

FIFTY

Then Jesus was led by the Spirit into the wilderness . . .
THE GOSPEL ACCORDING TO MATTHEW

IT TOOK EVERYTHING I had to get through the next two days. Nothing miraculous happened. Mr. Case never even called back. Dave was numb. Jonathan was brokenhearted but as respectful and helpful as always. Katlyn worried and wondered from afar. Some of my friends came back every day to help, but I never heard from Shirley again. Months later a mutual friend told me that she had been explaining the incident to others as a tragedy I brought upon myself.

In my soul searching and prayer times that followed, I happened upon the story of Jesus being led into the wilderness to be tempted by the devil. It struck me that *the Spirit* led him into a difficult time. That didn't seem very loving to me, but God is perfect love, so I knew I had to investigate further. It took me many years to fully realize this, but God was trying to answer the prayers I had been praying for most of my life. Pleas for freedom from powerlessness, prayers for a better legacy than what had been left to me, and the persistent cry of my heart for true, reciprocal love and justice were on the other side of my wilderness.

Reading the Gospel According to Matthew simultaneously with the Gospel According to Luke, I noticed that Jesus was led into the wilderness after he had been baptized, after the crowd had seen a dove descend upon him and heard a voice from heaven saying: "This is my Son, whom I love, with him I am well pleased." What a grandiose gesture! What a beautiful picture of affirmation and acceptance and peace, and then, the very next thing that happens is he is *led by the Spirit* into the wilderness to be tempted. He fasts for forty days and is exhausted. He's weary, he is ready for some of that crowd-pleasing, soul-easing voice from heaven stuff again, let alone food and companionship. Instead, he gets tempted. I can imagine him asking *Am I really God's son? If I am, why am I experiencing all this hunger, exhaustion, need?* But when he faced the tempter, he responded with the truth as God said it—regardless of how he felt. And when the devil realized Jesus wasn't buying what he was selling, he left him alone. The next thing we read is that angels attended him, and that he left the dessert *in the power of the Spirit*.

That wilderness experience changed his life from that point forward. He knew his mission, and he went after it. He walked in power and love, doing miracles. I knew I needed that kind of transformation in my life. I didn't understand it as I went through it, but I kept on seeking, trusting, and hoping. Ironically, the dogmatic religious mind-sets of the people around me seemed more and more unloving as I went through this time and yet I felt closer and closer to the heart of God. I came to feel freer to express my disappointments—even in Him—and yet trust that He is good, and that He had my back. Even through the most distressing times, I had a sense of His Presence with me, and peace. On an intellectual level, it made no sense, but spiritually, I developed such an appreciation for the liberty and grace of God which stands in stark contrast to religiosity and strict adherence to doctrine.

We eventually found a beautiful, historic little farm in the high peaks region of the Adirondacks, and due to Dave's blossoming friendship with the elderly blind man who owned it, we worked out a lease-purchase arrangement with him. He had just moved into an assisted living facility, and the house was vacant. We gratefully retrieved our horses from where they were boarded and joyfully moved in to the rambling old house. It needed a lot of TLC, and had many rustic features, but the potential was there, and we couldn't have been happier to move in. We worked hard refinishing the old floors, repairing window jambs and doors, bathroom fixtures, and gardens. As we worked we realized that though we had been told the windows were all brand new, they were in fact original to the house. When we asked the gentleman about it, he insisted he had paid for new windows and sent his caretaker, Russ, over to see what our concerns were.

When Russ arrived, he tried to say that our elderly friend was becoming senile and that there were no new windows. After a few days of back and forth, we were able to determine that Russ had installed the new windows in his own house when he built an addition on it just months earlier. When we confronted him about it, he asked us to give him time to make it right. Not eager to have more trouble, we did. Two days later, the windows were stacked against the side of the house when we got home. We drove by Russ's house a couple of miles away, there were gaping holes where the windows had been.

Issues like this crept up every few weeks, but we held Russ accountable and things got resolved. There was a tenant in the apartment above the big old barn who smoked pot a lot but was generally a quiet giant. We learned to live nearby in peace, enjoying the gardens, having ample trails to ride the horses on, and feeling ourselves heal slowly from our recent wounds. I saw this opportunity as God's reward and I was overflowing with thankfulness.

When Christmas 2008 came, Nana, Papa, and Joseph came over for the day. I had invited Shirley, Tom, and family, but Shirley never got back to me, and I knew by now how jealous she was of my relationship with Nana. Nana and I chatted in the kitchen as we prepared some hors d'oeuvres while Joseph joked and teased the kids and Papa and David talked in the living room.

"Shirley says I don't need to be on blood pressure medication anymore," Nana told me. "I am only on a little bit, but I've been on it since Michael died. What do you think?" she asked.

"Have you talked to your doctor about it? I am guessing you don't need it either, but I also know that if you've been on it so long you have to taper off very slowly."

"I have an appointment to see my doctor in two weeks," she said turning soberly toward me, a solemn look in her aging eyes. "Babes, from now on I would like you to come with me to my doctor's appointments—at least whenever possible, and maybe you could go with Papa to his, too."

"Of course, I will," I replied, somewhat concerned. I realized that she was getting older and had even noticed that she was a little more forgetful lately, but the fact that she was concerned enough to mention it disturbed me. "You know I would do anything for you. I think it's a good idea for someone you trust to be involved as you get older."

"Lately I have been a little forgetful," she confided with embarrassment. "That's why I told you 'if I already told you this just stop me.' I guess it's part of getting older."

"Nana, you are so vibrant in so many ways! Look at you! You drive wherever you want to go, you work out three times a week, you walk every day, you play complicated games and keep your mind sharp. But no one is perfect! My goodness! I forget things all the time!" I hugged her tightly and kissed her soft, wrinkly cheek. "I want to be just like you when I grow up!" We both laughed as she squished my cheeks together in her hand as if I was still only six years old, kissing me.

"Oh! I love you so much, my Karen!" she sighed happily. "I don't know what I'd do without you."

"I don't know what I'd do without *you*!" I told her so honestly that my eyes filled with tears at the thought.

"Well, we don't have to worry about that for a while, now do we?" she winked. "Except sometimes I worry about what will happen to you when I am gone. I mean, I am so disappointed in Shirley and your dad. The way this family is, I feel badly. I kept trying to explain it to Joseph, but he doesn't see it because he doesn't live close by. He just says that Shirley's always been jealous."

"Don't even think about leaving me any time soon! You know how much I hate to talk about that—"

"I know, but it's going to happen someday, in the future, and I want the family to pull together. I am tired of the jealousy and the gossip. I didn't raise them to be like that. It's upsetting." She sat down at the bar stool in front of a glass of rosé I poured for her. "You don't deserve it either."

"I don't like it either, and I love them all, but honestly, Nana," I paused for a second, walked over to the other side of the counter and faced her earnestly. "I feel like if they are going to be so small minded and always stirring up strife then I am better off without being involved. Do I miss them? Of course, but not the way they are now."

"Yes, but they know better," she said softly. "It's sad, but the family tree has a few rotten apples. I love 'em all, but I am disappointed in those two. I keep lovin' them, and pray, and hope they come around."

"I don't expect anything from my dad, as you know. Remember," I paused to reflect. "Remember even Mike said that Dick will never come around. I am at peace with that. I've done all I can."

"I know. I'll tell you something else," she spoke sternly. "If anything ever happens to me, keep Dick away from Papa! There'll be nothing left for anyone. He'll devour it all, and he already has more than his share. We'd have had a much better retirement if it wasn't for all the money we loaned him that he never repaid."

"I know. I am so sorry about that," I told her. "But don't think about that."

"Just hear me out, Babes. You and Joseph get the house, and I have some other things I want you to have. I gave you things I really wanted you to have over the years because I just don't trust some of the family, but there's more to come. But keep Dick away from Papa if anything ever happens. And, while we're on the subject, I told Joseph about an account I opened. If anything happens to me, remind him about it. I don't even trust Papa because he gives in to Dick so easily—even after all these years that Dick's taken advantage of us! So, I have a secret account. You and Joseph are the only ones that I am telling about it."

I understood why she told me these things, and much of the family angst I had been aware of since my youth, but I hated to think of anything happening to her. I listened to her knowing that she was serious, but also knowing what excellent health she was in, realizing these things were at least another ten years away.

As the day progressed, we played card games as a family, enjoyed dinner and barely managed to eat dessert. As the clock neared 5:30, Joseph began ushering Nana and Papa toward the door, reminding them they had promised Shirley they would be at her house by 6:00. It was a beautiful day, but sad that it ended with separate family celebrations.

FIFTY-ONE

*In times of crisis what or who you love most becomes
evident to everyone, including yourself.*

"BABES, I DON'T WANT to put too much on you, but did you remember that tomorrow is my doctor's appointment?" Nana asked sweetly as we talked on the phone in our usual morning routine.

"Yes, of course! It's been on my calendar," I told her. "1:00 in the afternoon, correct?"

"Yes. It would mean a lot to me if you could be there. Shirley keeps insisting that she wants to be there, too."

"Oh, that's fine," I reassured her. "I have nothing against her being there if it's what you want."

"Well, I didn't ask her, she just keeps bugging me about the blood pressure medicine and so I told her I had an appointment to talk to the doctor. She sort of assumed I want her to go, I think."

"It's no problem for me, unless it is for you." I realized that Shirley was a control freak, but I don't let that sort of person bother me anymore, and besides, I still loved her very much.

"It'll be okay as long as you're with me," Nana said. "Do you want to go out to lunch after? Or before?"

"Sure. I can be at your house by 11:30 if you want."

"Okay, honey. I love you so much! See you tomorrow."

"I love you heaps, Nana. See you tomorrow."

We hung up the phone and I went about my day, preparing for the trip to Burlington the next morning. I would have to leave my house by about 10:15 to be at hers by 11:30, depending on which ferry I took across the lake. The weather had been very cold, so I checked and discovered that the Essex-Charlotte crossing had closed due to ice. Realizing that I would be driving right past Shirley's house to go to the northern crossing, I decided to yet again extend the olive branch. I picked up the phone and dialed her number.

"Hi Shirley, how are you?" I asked when she answered.

"Fine. Why?" she snapped. "What do you want?"

"Well, I understand that you want to go to Nana's appointment with us tomorrow. I'm going to be driving right past your house, so I wondered if I might pick you up?" There was a long pause on the other end of the phone. I could scarcely believe how cold she was. "We haven't talked in a long time and I would love to reconnect."

"Um, you're going too?" she seemed surprised. "Uh . . . I have other errands to do in Burlington, but thanks anyway. You know, you don't need to go. I'm the nurse of the family."

"Of course you are," I reassured her. "Nana just asked me to go along a while ago. It's been on my calendar. I wouldn't let her down."

"Oh, I know you wouldn't," she said seriously. "But there's no need for both of us to go."

"Oh well. It's fine either way," I explained. "If you change your mind about riding together just let me know. I have errands I can run in Burlington, too."

"Okay," she mumbled. "Goodbye."

"See you tomorrow. Bye!" I tried to remain polite and loving, maybe that would set the tone for the next day.

The next morning, I telephoned Nana about 10:15 to tell her I was on my way.

"I'm just walking in the door," she said as she answered the phone. "Are you okay, Babes?"

"Of course! I'm just getting in the car. I'll see you soon!"

"But we just came in from the doctor's," she sounded annoyed. "Didn't Shirley call you yesterday afternoon?"

"No. I called her to offer to pick her up, but she wasn't interested," I informed her even as suspicion rose in my mind. "Why?"

"You offered to pick her up?" I heard Shirley protesting in the background.

"Yes. I extended the olive branch, just like you taught me," I replied. "Why?"

"She called the doctor's office yesterday and asked them to change the time so it would be more convenient for her," Nana relayed, even as Shirley continued to speak in annoyance in the background. "She said she would call you and tell you that they moved it up to 9:00 this morning. I knew you wouldn't miss it without calling me."

Once again, jealousy and manipulation had prevailed instead of love. It bothered me, but I also had grown accustomed to it. I honestly think it bothered Nana more because this was blatant, and certainly not the way she raised her children to be. When Shirley left she called me back again to discuss everything in more detail.

"Honestly, my Karen," she sighed. "I am so upset with how Shirley is acting. She's getting worse!"

"Don't let it bother you, Nana. Like you always say, just love her and pray for her."

"Yes, I know, but she knows better. This is going on too long. I love her and she's my daughter, but—" she let out a deep breath as she finished. "Boy! I'm so disappointed in her!"

"Sorry, Nana. Maybe you're just seeing it more clearly now than before," I commented and then wished I hadn't. "Anyway, what did the doc say?"

"I can go off my blood pressure meds by taking a half dose for a month, then a quarter dose, and they will keep checking on my progress. So, I probably won't start until I get back from Costa Rica," she deliberated aloud.

"Good idea. I can't remember what day you're leaving?"

"Wednesday, next week. Put it on your calendar, Babes. We get back on March 10th," she reminded me. "Write it down. Of course, you can always call me on Mimi's phone while we're there, but I think that's expensive. And when did we decide to go have our Spa day in Montreal?"

"I think we said March 19th and 20th. Does that still work for you?" I fumbled for my planner, writing the dates of her trip as I spoke.

"Yes! It will be my treat! Just you and me for a day of pampering! Then shopping the next day before we come home, right?" I could hear her smile through the phone.

"I can't wait!" I told her. "I've never had a spa day and I am really looking forward to it."

The weather was harsh, but as March rolled around, I was comforted by the knowledge that soon Nana and Papa would be returning from Costa Rica, and very much looking forward to our Spa trip. I wrapped up some of the legal pleadings I needed to file in the federal court. Everything was sort of status quo.

On March 9th I placed a call to Nana and Papa's answering machine leaving my customary "welcome home" message so it would be waiting for them when they arrived. That night I went to bed early, around 9:30, and fell asleep quickly. At almost exactly midnight, I awoke with fierce, stabbing pains coursing through the entire left side of my body, and in my head. I must have cried out in my agony, because Dave startled.

"What's wrong?" he asked, lifting his head off the pillow to look at my face.

"I don't know," I sobbed. "I've never had such pain—the whole left side of my body, my chest, my head. Excruciating."

Thoughts of Nana flooded my mind at the same time, but why? I tried to focus on prayer, but the pain gripped me severely. Dave jumped out of bed and ran to the bathroom, returning a minute later with a glass of water and some pills.

"Take this," he ordered. "Where does it hurt most?"

"Even my leg is throbbing," I told him, still crying uncontrollably. "What is it?"

"Aspirin. Let me prop your leg up." He set the water and pills down and lifted me by one large hug into a seated position. Next, he grabbed some pillows and propped them under my leg worriedly. "I've never seen you like this. Should we go to the hospital?"

After gulping the aspirin down, I tried to find a comfortable position, to no avail. Thoughts of Nana persisted along with a growing sense that something was very wrong with her. I breathed a prayer, asking God to send angels to care for her, to make her comfortable.

"Karen Marie!" Dave pleaded with me, stroking my hair. "Should I take you to the hospital?"

"No. This is not normal . . . "

"I know! That's why I think we should go to the hospital!"

"I don't think it's about me. I think something's wrong with Nana. Please pray for her," I cried.

"What? That's crazy! That's just your pain talkin'" Dave replied. "Come on, honey. You need to see a doctor." As he spoke my body seemed to calm down, the pain became duller. I insisted we stay home and kept praying. At some point in the wee hours before dawn, I fell back to sleep. When he got up to go to work, he whispered that he could stay home if I needed him to.

"I'm okay now. Just tired," I mumbled, eyes not wanting to open.

A couple of hours later I got up and made myself some coffee. I sat down wondering about the night before. I had never experienced anything like it. I pulled my bible out to read something reassuring but couldn't focus. I closed my eyes and tried to pray but I couldn't focus on that either. I kept having the thought: *Get your passport in order.* It seemed crazy, but the thought was loud and obnoxious. I found an agency online that could rush it for me and contacted them. They emailed me forms, even a FedEx shipping label, so I began filling it out. As I did, the phone rang.

"Karen!" Joseph cried into the phone. "Honey, something's—"

"Happened to Nana," I finished his sentence, tears silently cascading down my face. "Is she okay? What can I do?"

Joseph explained what had happened as we both wept. At exactly midnight the night before, Eastern Standard Time, she fell and hit her head, which caused a stroke that affected the left side of her body. They were staying at my cousin's place on the Caribbean coast, near the edge of the jungle, so they were four hours away from a hospital. By the time she got to a medic station, she was still alert, but soon after she fell into a coma. Mimi called Joe from San Jose at the hospital a few moments before he called me.

"Honey, Mimi, Papa and I know she would want you to be with her. How soon can you get to Coast Rica?"

My closest confidant, best friend, most loving nurturer, biggest advocate, and best encourager has always been my Nana. Without her I would not have been born alive, and her intercession on my behalf never ceased. She loved me well, always.

The events of the next few months were devastating. It was a harrowing time for me, and especially for her. At first, I had great focus, caring for her and nurturing her, even amid the qualms and doom-saying of others. Eventually, months later when I finally got her home to Burlington by medical evacuation, the most difficult part of the crisis seemed to be navigating the family drama and coming to terms with the fact that the doctors at UVM held out very little hope of a meaningful recovery.

I leave the dramatic and heart-wrenching story of the last few months of her life on this earth to another book. There is simply no way I can do justice to it here. She is worthy of her own time and space; there is much to be absorbed about the love and value of all that she brought to this life.

On her 89th birthday, I sat on her right side and held her hand as she breathed her last. Just hours before, she mouthed "I love you" as she looked deeply into my eyes, searching for permission to leave, it seemed. I know she is with God in heaven, but it has been the greatest loss of my life. To this day, I weep to think of it. I miss her fiercely.

FIFTY-TWO

I will judge between one sheep and another, between rams and goats.
GOD

IN THE BEGINNING OF July 2009, just months after Nana died, we had yet another surprise. Bill Meconi sent us a notice of default on behalf of the old man we were buying the farm from, Mr. Lowe. Since we had paid every payment, I was shocked. I contacted him to let him know there must be a mistake, but he insisted that we were in default and he was going to evict us.

"You cannot evict us, Bill," I said in angst. "We are purchasing the property, have made all our payments on time, and there is no delinquency. This is preposterous."

"I can do whatever the hell I want," he snickered into the phone.

"You know that we have been paying Russ directly, right?" I wondered if there was some confusion between the old man and his caretaker about the payments.

"Yes, and he says you're behind one payment. Case closed!" He jeered.

"Well it's simple enough for me to provide you with proof that we're not," I told him. "Except that the July payment hasn't been cashed yet, but it was mailed out early. As soon as I can access copies of cancelled checks I will fax them over to you."

"Whatever!" he sighed. "Bye."

As if that were not enough, I was at the end of my patience with Dave, too. My spirit was still heavy with grief, I was tired of the fight for justice in my life and had no more patience for his dalliances. Losing Nana distressed me in many ways, but it also sharpened my desire for truth and value, reciprocity, and meaning as well as justice.

I had discovered that while I was at her bedside in Costa Rica, he began using porn again, and I was fairly sure he had an affair. I think he expected me to be as patient and long-suffering as I had been in the past, but I had had enough. One day in my Bible reading and prayer time, I came across a passage in Ezekiel about how God would judge between sheep, the implication being that we each belong to Him, but some of us treat others poorly.

> "Is it not enough for you to feed on the good pasture? Must you also trample the rest of your pasture with your feet? Is it not enough for you to drink clear water? Must you also muddy the rest with your feet? Must my flock feed on what you have trampled and drink what you have muddied with your feet? Therefore, this is what the Sovereign Lord says, I Myself will judge between the fat sheep and the lean sheep. . . . I will save my flock and they will no longer be plundered. I will judge between one sheep and another." (Ezekiel 34:18–20, 22, NIV)

I wept as I read, and then I prayed in desperation that God would judge between me and all those who had harmed me while claiming to be Christians themselves. Tom and Shirley had moved back to Florida; I still prayed for them, and others. But it was especially about Dave that I was perplexed and sorrowful now. I asked God to convict him and release me from my obligation to him, if not. I asked for the grace to accept him if he was sincere. I told the Lord that I was tired of drinking muddy water and being shoved around. After several minutes, I wrote all of this in my journal. As I concluded, I sensed the Lord in my heart asking me to give David one more year. It was very clear and concise. I hated the thought, but I said "yes."

About two weeks later, Dave reached out to Blake, confessing that he had a serious problem, asking for some guidance and accountability. He wrote out a meaningful confession and commitment letter, signed it, and gave it to me. He gave a copy to Blake and kept a copy in his wallet. In my heart, I wanted our marriage to be a success, but I knew this was the beginning of a pivotal year. A year of watching to see if he would do as he said, conquer his demons, or go his own way once and for all.

Nana's death changed me deeply. The family sort of fell apart afterward. I spent a lot of time going to help Papa at the house, teaching him how to heat up dinners I prepared for him, and cook his own eggs. When he wasn't paying attention, I threw out the expired condiments he seemed to hoard. He didn't care for himself well enough at times, especially forgetting to drink water. He told me of how in his Army days the man that came back from an exercise with the most water still in his canteen was rewarded. It struck me how many misconceptions we all carry, and how we need to be open to learn throughout life. I posted little notes around the house: "I love you! Have you had enough water today?"

Also that summer, I ran into a friend who delivered some interesting news. His son and Johnathan were close friends and we occasionally did things together with his family. On this particular day though, we just ran into each other doing errands.

"I guess Bob's news must not have come as a shock to you," he said, watching for my response.

"Bob's news?"

"Yeah. It was quite a surprise to most of us who work with him," he continued as if I understood what he was referring to. "Although it certainly explains a lot."

"The kids and I have not heard from Bob in couple of years or more now," I told him. "I have no idea what his news is, just a guess . . ."

"You mean he told the whole world and didn't bother to inform his kids?"

"He came—"

"He came out as a woman!" my friend exclaimed. "Shocked us all, but the bastard didn't tell you or the kids first?"

"I'm not surprised at either," I told him. "He has always put himself first. Once he couldn't get what he wanted from us and had done all the damage he could do he never looked back." I paused for a moment to let the news sink in. All those years people thought I was being so difficult and cruel to go through with the divorce, the kids didn't even know his secrets, and now, it's in the open. "How did you find out?"

"An email. He sent out an email to everyone affiliated with him through work." He looked at me empathetically. "I still can't believe he didn't tell you first. It's a small community!"

"I'm not. But I'm glad it's out in the open now, except—" I suddenly realized that in such a small community Jon could find out in the worst possible way. "I guess I have to find a suitable time to tell the kids. I don't want them finding out through someone else."

"His email suggested that he has been planning this for a long time. He said it would be a big change for all, but he would expect support and, he insisted that he would remain professional in all of his dealings with us." He let out a long sigh. "You know, he has been a basket case for a long time. I mean, every holiday party he gets drunk and waxes emotional to anyone who will listen. . . . I can see why your relationship didn't work out. Now, we all can. Sorry I had to be the one to tell you."

"I'm glad you told me. I really appreciate it."

In early 2010, virtually all the federal defendants filed motions to dismiss my case, I spent more than fifty hours per week studying, drafting responses, and gathering documentation to refute them. It was me against all their lawyers. I felt like David facing Goliath. I did the best I could but trying to articulate legal concepts beyond me and theories I was still trying to understand was tedious.

At the same time, I fought Bill Meconi to keep our purchase on track. I found out that he was in fact a local boy, and that he and his father were especially good friends with Justice Head. I wished I had known that years previous when I let him represent me. As I let the connections sink in, I realized that he had access to every fax I sent over to Mark, which usually also was information sent to the AG, FBI, and Judicial Conduct investigators.

Once Justice Head died, there was no longer any reason for the Commission on Judicial Conduct to be involved, and Agent Weintraub would not tell me what the FBI was up to except that the investigation extended beyond justice Head, so it probably wasn't closed. Glen Michaels was not as involved either. I was not surprised to discover that Meconi was appointed *guardian ad litem* for many of the young boys that accused justice Head of abuse and molestation. I pointed out to Bill that he had a conflict of interest in representing old Mr. Lowe with respect to me, but he didn't back down, much in the same manner that Evan Tracy didn't. They were not real legal advocates, they were thugs masquerading as legal advocates. I had come to accept what I never wanted to believe was reality: they are part of the syndicate. They abuse the small town and village court system to keep the mob and its friends in business under the guise of legality, but since the town and village justices have no law degree or legal training, and they are put in place by a popularity contest, justice is usually mocked.

On September 2nd, 2010 at about 6:30 in the morning, I checked the federal court docket online and there it was, the forty-page decision that would define my battle going forward. Although I lost some points, I won many others, giving me credibility and focus. The federal judge had declined to exercise supplemental jurisdiction over the Smiths and ABN but stated that I had grounds to pursue them in the state court. Likewise, he upheld my Section 1983 claims, claims for intentional infliction of emotional distress, and claims for breach of covenant of good faith and fair dealing. I wept with relief and joy.

It was Katlyn's birthday, and I got a huge present. I phoned her, still crying.

"Mom! Are you okay?" she said after I wished her a happy birthday.

"Katlyn, I am wonderful! I am winning!" I said, smiling through my tears. "Good things always happen to me on your birthday! First, you were born, making me a mother. You were my first beautiful gift." I sniffled, and she sighed.

"Ahh, Mama, that's so sweet!" she said. "I love you, Mama. But what gift?"

"I love you, sweetie. The federal judge ruled in my favor! I just read his forty-page decision. They tried to get my case thrown out, but he said I have valid claims and facts!"

"Really? That's awesome," she said, starting to cry. "I'm so proud of you, Mama. They are so rotten, but you're staying strong. That's wonderful."

I called Linda next and she was exultant. "Maybe now they'll give you a lawyer!" Jon and Dave were equally thrilled. We all felt as if the tide was turning.

In fact, I did petition the court to appoint me an attorney again, citing the former decision that stated as things got more complicated, I could ask again. I received a call from the judge's law clerk asking me if I had an attorney in mind. I did not, and apparently, they didn't know who to appoint, but were leaning in that direction. Once again, I took to prayer about it, and about a week later had a phone call from an attorney by the name of Gerry Posner. We spoke on the phone at great length. It turned out that he is an expert in the small town and village court system in New York and had for years been advocating for a change in the system. He had been following *The Times* stories and my suit with interest. With my new status as a credible pro se litigant, he knew my case was about to get complicated, and he wanted it.

In sheer retaliation, Bill Meconi ordered his client to stop accepting my payments on the house, just like the Village of Keeseville had done, and initiated a court proceeding in the tiny village court of Ausable—his hometown. I was mortified. The little court didn't have legal jurisdiction over a purchase contract, but that didn't stop Meconi, nor the judge who was totally patronized by him. I petitioned the county court to intervene, but Judge Dawson declined. By now I had learned that he too was vulnerable to intimidation and bribery due to drunk driving and other episodes that had been hastily swept away without much fanfare. It seemed that there was nowhere I could turn that the corruption didn't already permeate. In late September of 2010, in front of the Podunk plumber by day and village justice one night per week, and a "jury" of Meconi's closest friends and allies, we endured a charade of a proceeding. By this time, I was almost assured of defeat at this ruse of courtroom exchange.

Meconi joked with the jury members, had lunch with the judge, and directed the actual court proceedings, citing the fact that he was the only lawyer present. It was a total sham. All my evidence didn't matter. I contacted a lawyer in Albany who promised to handle the case from then on and filed an appeal.

FIFTY-THREE

Intimidation is to fear what promises are to hope.

DAVE AND I MADE the journey down to Manhattan on an early December weekend when Jonathan had an indoor track meet down there. We took in the competition, then met with Mr. Posner in his office on a sunny Saturday afternoon. We lugged the stacks of documentation he had asked for through the tiny hallway, into his many-windowed office and laid them on his desk. After exchanging pleasantries, we sat and talked for a couple of hours, going over the case, and the facts that led to it. He instructed me to write to the federal judge and let him know that he would like to be appointed. I was elated. Finally, things were moving in the right direction, and I would not have to do all this legal work on my own. I had hope that his involvement would mean that even Bill Meconi's shenanigans would be set aside and our home would be secure.

I wrote the judge as directed, giving him Mr. Posner's contact information and waited for the order of approval. After a couple of weeks went by, I called Mr. Posner to see if he had heard from the judge, he brushed me off and said he was sure he would be hearing soon—he had noted my letter on the public docket. But when I couldn't reach him again a week later, I called the judge's law clerk.

"Ms. Dion, have you spoken with Mr. Posner recently?" Scott asked me.

"Yes, about a week ago," I replied. "He told me he was just waiting to hear from chambers."

"Well, we've tried calling him repeatedly this week to verify and he hasn't returned our calls," Scott told me. "This is highly unusual."

I left a few more voice messages for Mr. Posner, then sent him an email. He replied by email saying that he had decided not to take the case. I was distraught when I wrote back and asked him why. In the back of my mind was the information I had about the mob boss that had been given to me surreptitiously. I had to know.

Can you just tell me the truth? Why? You were so excited about my case— even sought me out. Were you threatened?

His reply sent me reeling:

I value my life and the lives of my family. Yes. I was threatened. Watch your back.

Terror gripped me. What could I do now? In the coming weeks, I begged God for a solution. The least little thing sparked anxiety. I looked for a new lawyer for the federal court. At the same time, I looked for a backup plan should Bill Meconi prevail, but the Albany lawyer I hired told me that there was no way the appeal should fail since on its face the whole Ausable town trial was a fraud. Since the amount in controversy was in excess of $3,000 and the basis was a purchase contract, not a lease, the court didn't have jurisdiction. He claimed that Judge Dawson should have taken over, but since he hadn't the appeals court in Plattsburgh had an obligation to get things back on track. I tried to rest in that fact, his assurances, and the promises of God while turning my attention to Christmas.

Katlyn came home for the holidays and we enjoyed a heaping amount of snow. We decorated a live tree and stayed toasty with the woodstove, enjoying each other's company. It was a pleasure to have all of us under one roof, but my nerves were frayed; the least little thing made me jump, a ringing phone, a knock at the door. I tried my best to relax and enjoy the kids, but anxiously awaited the decision of the Third Circuit Court of Appeals in Plattsburgh. The trauma of losing our home in Chesterfield the way we did haunted me. I feared these monsters would do it again, and so did Dave.

Now looking back, I understand a little more the link between fear and the oppression it sets in motion. Fear is powerful. If you allow it, it will trap you in a downward spiral that becomes a self-fulfilling prophecy. It hinders your ability to see reality and especially capitalizes on past trauma. When things go wrong as a result, it perpetuates the myth that your fear was justified rather than exposing the truth that fear is in fact negative goal setting, and advanced fear is a catapult into victimhood.

It's what we do with fear that matters. Do we cater to it or advance in spite of it? I wish I could say that I made forward progress. In some ways, at least spiritually, I believe I did. But in terms of protecting my children from more harm, and keeping my home, I feel I failed.

It was about seven degrees below zero Fahrenheit at 7:30 in the morning. The wind had howled much of the night, leaving snow drifts everywhere. After I put the coffee on, I joined Luke outside for a brief breath of fresh, cold air. As I came back into the house through my office and hung my coat, I noticed through the window and the barren trees beyond a line of cars and trucks parked along the country road beyond our driveway. Panic struck me so violently I trembled from head to toe. I ran to the computer and looked for a notice from the Third Circuit. I had emailed them the day before to inquire as to the status of my appeal. There was nothing in response. I knew the office wouldn't open for a while and wondered what to do next. My lawyer's office didn't answer the phone.

I texted Dave who had gone to work only about an hour earlier. I decided to meet them outside and tell them about the appeal pending. By law, they should do nothing. I paced and prayed for probably about fifteen minutes. It was hard to think clearly, or rather, I knew I was thinking clearly, legally, but the waiting ones outside were not. If they were going to enforce some sort of order, it was not handed down legitimately and there was no way to prove it to these mindless sorts. They just blindly do as they're told by the village justice and attorneys like Meconi. *What should I do now?*

As I watched and paced, an Essex County Sheriff's car moved into the driveway. I put on my coat and headed to the door. In my mind I recalled how empathetic they were at our home in Chesterfield. I prayed for the same cooperation but was rudely surprised.

"Good morning," I said nervously as two deputies got out of the car and approached me. Other cars and trucks followed them into the driveway, going to the end and turning around to park behind them.

"Good morning. We have a writ of execution to enforce today," the taller one said. I recognized him as the kind one when Dave had his breakdown.

"Well, perhaps you are not aware that there is an automatic stay of that writ because of the appeal pending in the Third Circuit," I replied trying hard to be calm and professional. "If you will just allow me to get in touch with Chambers when the office opens in a little while I am sure we can get this straightened out." Shivering, I turned toward the door, Luke sticking close by my side.

"No, ma'am," the other office responded. "We're not getting played for fools."

"I am not trying to be disrespectful, sir," I told him. "I am telling you the truth. The town court doesn't even have jurisdiction in this matter so the whole thing is not right. I am sure we can get it sorted out."

The first deputy approached me, his massive six foot three or four frame, intimidating.

"We're going in there and we're taking everything you own out," he stated threateningly.

"Well, let me go wake up my children," I said, turning toward the door again. At that he bolted in front of me and positioned himself against the door, just as I had put my hand on the handle. I tried to open the door and he slammed it shut again. The other deputy approached from behind.

"We are on to you. Bill Meconi told us that you would try to pull a stunt like this!" He shrieked with venom in his voice, totally beyond anything I had expected. I panicked. I wanted to go and wake up my children myself, before they were traumatized by these thugs in uniform.

"You cannot block me from entering my house! I am going to wake up my children!" I demanded, pulling my cellphone out to take a picture of him blocking the door. He moved as he saw me try to take a picture, and I seized the door handle and went in. They followed me into the office just as Johnathan came down the stairs and around the corner.

"Mom? What's happening? Are you okay?" he asked, still wiping slumber from his eyes. As I went to the house phone, I handed him my cell.

"This is so wrong, honey. Call David, and Blake. I will call the court." At that, the deputies motioned the others with them to start taking everything in the office. I had boxes and boxes of documentation of the corruption and evidence of how they abused the judicial system. I didn't want to lose it and lose my means of proving my case. One person grabbed the fax machine and tried to yank it out of the wall, so I placed my hand on it and asked him to stop.

"Bill Meconi told us to take everything in the office first!" The deputy shouted at me. "Do you want me to arrest you for obstruction of justice?"

"I am not obstructing, sir," I told him. "I need this to fax the court.

And he doesn't need to damage it by breaking the connection. Can you just let me fax the court in order to get to the bottom of this please?"

"No! Arrest her!" he shouted to the other deputy. I could scarcely believe my eyes and ears. "Get all of this stuff out of the office. Everything! File cabinets, phone, boxes, computer! Don't give her any way to get out of this!"

"Mom! Stay calm!" Johnathan yelled at me, looking at my cell phone to find Blake's number. I shook uncontrollably as they grabbed my arms and pulled them tightly behind my back. Katlyn came down the stairs at all the noise, freaking out as she saw what was transpiring. They led me out of the house and put me in the back of a patrol car like a common criminal. As they did, I felt my heart convulse, physically. I quivered uncontrollably for a few minutes, feeling pain then numbness in the left side of my face and down my left arm. Jon came out and talked to me through the window, which was part way down. "What should I do, Mom? Dave and Blake are on the way."

"Umm," I could barely speak. I felt like I was moving in slow motion and my mouth wouldn't cooperate. "They are going after the evidence. Can you lock it up in my car? I'm so sorry, honey…"

"It's going to be okay, Mom. We'll take care of it," he said with authority beyond his years.

I don't know how long I sat there. My shoulders ached from being pulled so tightly back, and my wrists hurt from how tightly they locked the cuffs. Due to a flurry of radio activity wherein I heard them describe me as some threat to society, a couple of state troopers had arrived, one of them a female. She opened the back door of the car I sat in and asked me if I needed anything.

"Could you loosen the cuffs, please?" I asked her, trying not to cry. "They hurt."

"I don't even know why they put you in cuffs!" she clucked, disgust in her voice. "Let me see what I can do." She walked away, leaving the door open as she did. I turned and saw Katlyn and Jon carrying the remaining boxes of documents that had been left in the snow and putting them in my Mountaineer. Jon put his arm on Katlyn's shoulder as they wiped tears from their eyes. *What have I done? How could I let my children go through this again?*

FIFTY-FOUR

If your enemy can find nothing wrong with you, he will create something, hoping others believe it, and you might, too.

AS WE PULLED OUT of the driveway, tears rolled down my cheeks. There were already piles of our belongings in the snow. Mark, another friend, was just pulling in, and I noted Ben had arrived and was helping the kids put boxes in his car. The ride to Elizabethtown was a long one. I asked the female state trooper on the way, where they were taking me as I shifted uncomfortably in the seat.

"Give me the key to these cuffs," she said to her partner reaching to the front. He handed them back to her and she motioned for me to turn in my seat. She quickly unlocked the cuffs and took them off completely. "Bastards!" she murmured as I rubbed my red, marred wrists.

"You're no criminal! Jeez!" Then she settled back in the seat. "I told your son that you will be taken to the county jail in Lewis, but first we have to take you to court in Elizabethtown."

"The county court?" I knew I had done nothing wrong, but my head was spinning that this could even be happening. I also knew that the county court was for major infractions of the law.

"No, the town court. You will have to appear before a judge and he will either let you go—depending on the judge—or set bail."

"Bail?" I hadn't thought of that.

"Listen, I don't know what you have on these guys, but play it cool. Be polite and courteous to the judge. Just answer 'yes' or 'no' and don't say more than you have to. When we get there, I'll see if I can sneak a minute to let you call someone to help you. Don't tell anyone."

I didn't know why she was gracious to me, but I was grateful. I could barely form words and felt as though I was in a dream like state. At any minute I thought I would wake up and all of this would have been just a nightmare. Twenty minutes later when we pulled up in front of the little courthouse, she pulled the cuffs out again.

"Sorry I have to do this, but I will leave them loose," she sympathized. My shoulders burned from being pulled back so tightly for so long, but I began to lean forward in the seat and put my arms behind my back dutifully. "No! Just put them in front of you. I'm sure you're sore."

"Yes. Thank you," I breathed, tears again falling. *Lord, where are you? Help me!*

Once inside they ascertained that the judge had not yet arrived. Pulling me to a little side office area that was empty, the friendly trooper pointed to an old desktop rotary phone. I realized I couldn't call Dave because he would be a nervous wreck or might become violent and make things worse.

"Um, my son has my cell phone with everyone's numbers in it. . ." I said in a whisper. She nodded and winked, standing at the entrance, where she kept looking to see if anyone was approaching. Awkwardly, I picked the receiver off the cradle and put it down so I could dial, then picked it up again to hold it to my ear. "Jonathan? Can you get me Blake's number?"

"Mom! Are you okay? Where are you?"

"I can't talk, I am about to go into court but—"

"Don't worry, Mom. I've got it. Ready?" I realized I didn't have a pen. I glanced over to the side of the desk and saw paper. The female trooper realized my dilemma, pulled a pen from her pocket and made a motion as if to write.

"Jon? I'm ready," I told him. He rattled off the number and I repeated it so the trooper could write it down. "Thank you, honey. I'm so sorry about this. I love you." I wept as I hung up the phone.

The door opened and the other trooper came in from outside announcing that the judge had arrived. I nervously watched the two troopers whisper to each other, then the female trooper came over and patted my shoulder.

"We're going into court now. You'll get to make a call at the jail." She guided me out of the office area and into the spacious, empty courtroom.

When it was all said and done, the troopers did nothing to corroborate the charge of obstruction of justice. They informed the judge they arrived after the fact and stated that I had been completely courteous and cooperative, even that the deputies were a bit zealous in their execution of the writ. It seemed they were trying to get him to see this must be a ruse, but in the car afterward they told me they had hoped for a different judge. I was ordered to jail until bail in the amount of $1,000 was posted.

Once in the car again, the cuffs were mercifully removed. When we pulled into the garage sort of entrance to the jail, I heard the male trooper tell the intake officer "this is a bad collar. She's no criminal," as the female officer helped me out of the car.

"What is she here for?" the intake officer asked.

"Obstruction of justice," the female trooper stated tersely. "She's a college-educated mom with no record who happens to have dirt on people *we know* cross the line. . . . You figure it out." I was stunned that they knew. Why couldn't they do something about it?

After I was finger printed, I was told I could make my phone call. I called Blake from the payphone near the intake station. He was on his way to my house but said he would stop at the bank and come post bail. Gratitude for his brotherly love and friendship was like a bit of comfort in that cold dark place. I was led to a cell near the center of the room, very close to the big work station in the middle, which was manned by a solitary officer—the one whom they addressed when they first brought me in. Trauma still had a grip on my body, and my mind. I sat down on the bench and fully expected the officer to close the cell, but he didn't.

"Don't worry," he said gently. "You don't belong here, I'm not going to make it any harder than it already is."

"Thank you," I barely spoke as the tears tumbled down my face again. I was worried about my kids, about Dave.

"You've got someone coming to post bail?" he asked. "Are you hungry?"

"Yes. I have. Thank God." I wiped my eyes. "Yes, I haven't eaten."

"I'll order some food for you. I know this sucks, but try to relax. You won't be here long." He turned and went to the desk, leaving me alone with feelings of betrayal, abandonment, and utter grief.

God, how could you allow this?

I heard nothing in my heart. My mind raced. Suddenly I realized that I needed to get a grip on myself, but how? I thought for a few moments. I couldn't seem to pray. I mustered all my willpower to sing.

No matter the circumstance, I will praise You. You are bigger, Your ways are higher, and Your love endures forever. I don't understand it now, I can't find the good, but I will trust You. No matter the circumstance, I praise You. Jesus be near me, Spirit come guide me. You are all I need. You are worthy no matter the circumstance. I praise You. Thank You for loving me. I thank You that You are working all things out for good. No matter the circumstance, I will praise You.

I wasn't loud, in fact, it was barely a whispered song, but it was a song of praise that helped me to focus again. They could take my belongings and throw them in the snow, take my house, try to give me an unearned reputation, and get me out of the way, but they could not take my heart or break my spirit. Sure, I hurt badly, but I am alive, and I am on the right side of truth. I didn't sell out. I didn't compromise, and what they say about me doesn't matter.

My friends really rallied, and I am eternally grateful. As Blake arrived so did Jonathan, with Mark's son. They informed me that others had already begun the process of moving some of our things into storage and others to Mark's house where we were being welcomed to stay. I had nothing left to give that day. I still had numbness in parts of my body, and especially my mind. But I was grateful for the support. At the end of the day when darkness was falling and we could do no more, Mark's wife ordered massive amounts of Chinese takeout and opened a couple of bottles of wine as we all gathered to share a meal together at their house and rehash the events of the day.

I felt the stigma of being arrested try to creep up on me, but it immediately dissipated as Blake and Mark asked how it came about.

"So, they said you were jumping up and down and then screaming, jumped onto the back of one of the deputies to stop him from going in the house," Blake laughed out loud. "And I said, 'You better get a better story 'cause anyone who knows her knows that's not what happened!'" The room erupted in laughter.

"They said that?" I was dumbfounded.

"That's what they said. Come on! No one believes that!" Blake remarked, still laughing.

"All she did was ask them not to tear the fax machine out of the wall and ask if she could use it before they took it," Jonathan stated. "They're not supposed to lie."

"That's it? Wow. Well, at least you know it'll get thrown out of court. Have some wine," Blake poured a red into a glass and handed it to me. "Are you okay?"

"I need to eat first. They gave me chicken nuggets and corn—full of gluten, so I only drank the grape juice." I let out a deep breath. "It's good to have all of you around tonight," I sniffed back more tears. "Thank you."

"You're up against sheer evil, if you ask me," Mark said as he handed me a plate and I helped myself to a portion of Massaman.

"I heard one of the deputies ask another one about your appeal." Blake swirled the wine in his glass studiously. "They said they called the court and the court said they were going to eventually rule against you anyway so not to worry."

"That's not right!" I fumed, with what little energy I had left. "Seriously?"

"I overheard them. That's what they said. It's total corruption. Shake the dust off your feet."

Just then Mark's youngest son appeared with a bowl full of fortune cookies.

"You get two, Aunt Karen," he said with a grin.

"Oh sweetie, I can't eat them anyway—"

"You don't have to eat them! You just have to get the fortune!" he pleaded.

I grabbed one and he handed me a second one. Opening the first one brought tears to my eyes again. It read, "You will enjoy good health and be surrounded by luxury."

"Wow!" I exclaimed. "Do you think—?"

"Yes!" Blake replied before I could finish! "Yes, sometimes God has to use a fortune cookie because we're so traumatized, we can't hear Him! What does it say?"

I handed it to him and he read it aloud to the hoots and smiles of others.

"Read the next one!" He gleamed. I opened it and collapsed in sobs. Blake took it from my hands and read it aloud: "You will move into a beautiful, spacious home within the year."

FIFTY-FIVE

God is a loving friend who both upholds you and creates freedom within you. What you believe has everything to do with what you experience.

BY SPRING, DAVE AND I had moved to Saranac Lake, closer to his work. I searched for work there but wished I could move back to Vermont. To say I was fed up with New York, particularly upstate, would be a giant understatement. The shenanigans in the court had only cemented my hunches into foundational beliefs. I know that seems ridiculous given all I discovered up to that point, but I now understood that it was not just the small town and village courts that were corrupt. The way the county and appellate court allowed that sham of a trial in Ausable to stand was blatant abuse. I had even gone to look at the docket in the county to see why Judge Dawson ignored so many facts. I found whole pages of my pleadings completely missing from the file.

As the federal proceeding was at a standstill until a suitable advocate could be found for me, I worked on the state case against the Smiths. In fact, they had deeded the building back to the mortgage company and sold most of my assets. I was led to believe my things were still in the building, and a year had dragged on where the mortgage company promised to let me in to retrieve them. The new owner, Wil, who subsequently bought the building from the bank, contacted me. He asked if we could meet to discuss the situation and I asked him about my assets.

"What do you mean? There were some boxes of things that apparently hadn't sold when the Smiths were here, but Evan Tracy told me that I could not sell them, they had to be donated."

"Evan Tracy? Did he represent you in the purchase?" I knew this couldn't be good.

"Yes, he was recommended to me by the Lorrys," Wil continued.

"Anyway, now I am having the worst troubles with the Lorrys and I realize that all of the stuff they told me about you was probably wrong and all the stuff I heard about what they did to you is probably right!" He sighed loudly into the phone.

"I am so sorry for you," I told him earnestly. "When can we meet?"

Wil and I met the next day by the lake. We sat and talked for two hours. A delightful, kind, black man from Hollywood, he had a gentle demeanor, though he was not spineless. I recognized in him the same unwillingness to accept the evil intentions of others that I had grappled with for so many years; it kept me from protecting myself early on, and he had fallen into that trap, too. Now, he was scraping by as the Lorrys claimed their lease (the one drafted by Evan Tracy years earlier between me and them,) was still valid and refusing to pay for heat or air conditioning as well as other costs. They had continued to cause damages and Evan Tracy pretended to represent Wil's interests, telling him the Lorrys were right and there was nothing he could do. But they weren't right, and Evan was a wolf in sheep's clothing.

"So now they are offering to buy the building back from me, but they only want to pay a pittance!" he whined. "It's absurd! I am filing to evict them instead."

"It's what they've wanted all along," I reassured him. "They never wanted to sell to begin with. They just wanted someone else to take on the cost and headache of doing the renovations after the fire and then take it back by hook or by crook. I'm so sorry you got conned, too."

"Maybe knowing this will help your case and we can help each other out," Wil looked at me sideways, arching one eyebrow as he spoke.

"For sure. Absolutely."

In the next few months Wil and I collaborated a lot, but Dave and I barely spoke to one another. I kept praying about our relationship, reminding God that I was trusting Him. I was awakened in the night many times by Dave attempting some lewd act on me while I slept. I had finally asked him to sleep in the other room if he wasn't going to respect my personal boundaries. I also found a lot of evidence of porn use—DVDs in his lunch box, magazines in his truck. I didn't really need the evidence because I already knew by his behavior what was going on. I had become an expert.

I had also begun writing about my experiences. One afternoon while

I was working in my little office area off my bedroom, Wil called. He was so distraught that at first, I could scarcely understand what he was saying.

"I'm a fully-grown man and they've got me wanting to curl up in a ball and sob in a corner!" he shrieked into the phone. "I don't know how you've made it up to now!"

He filled me in on the latest and then I asked him if he had faith in God.

"Yes, I do," he said. "All I can do is pray about this and try not to go crazy, I guess. But I just can't believe the corruption here . . . the lawyers, the judges . . ."

"It's something, isn't it? The only way I've gotten through is the grace of God," I replied. "I would not have stayed sane without God."

"You need to write that book and expose this stuff," Wil urged. "Expose this!"

When we hung up the phone, I threw myself on my bed and cried. *God, if you will let me move home to Vermont and live in the country, I will write that book.*

That night Dave was obnoxious. I went to my kickboxing class in tears and came home wiped. He was sitting in the living room watching porn, but hastily turned off the DVD player as I approached.

"How was your class?" he feigned interest, face red and eyes darting.

"It was great. Just what I needed," I told him. "How was your porn?"

"I guess I'm not foolin' ya am I?"

"Not one bit," I replied calmly, sitting across from him. "So, what's the plan?"

"I guess I have just decided I'd rather do what I want. I mean, the pull is so strong. It's not anything against you. And when I see you, I feel so guilty . . ." He stood to his feet, walked toward me and reached out his hand. I wasn't sure what to think, but I gave him mine and he pulled me to my feet, hugging me. "You don't deserve this. I need to be better for you, but I can't."

"Can't or don't want to?" I asked.

"You are the best woman I know. You're my best friend. I love you so much," he began to cry, looking me long in the eyes. "I want you."

"But you love porn more," I whispered, meeting his gaze with tears of my own. "And other women . . ."

"No, that's not it," he sighed, his bright blue eyes still fixed on mine.

"It's bigger than me. An' I feel so bad because you deserve better, but I don't have it in me to stop. I don't want to hurt you anymore."

"Do you want to divorce?" I asked, honestly hoping he would say 'yes'.

"No, I don't," he pounced. "Do you? I mean, I guess I couldn't blame you if you did."

"Let's talk tomorrow," I said, pulling away. "I need some time to think and pray."

The next morning, I waited until I heard him leave for work before I went downstairs for coffee. There was a note on the counter, "I'm so sorry. I love you." The thing is, I know Dave does love me, but I know as long as he believes porn is more powerful than him, it will be. He has always struggled to stay with his convictions and makes most decisions on a sheer feeling basis.

I took my coffee to the living room to read and pray. Nothing earth shattering came to me, but I did pray to be open and to have understanding. *How much more do you expect from me? Remember those sheep and goats?*

I went on with my day, responding to professional job postings, and talking with the lawyer who was finalizing the obstruction of justice charge. Apparently, the deputies were all prepared to say that I jumped on the back of one of them kicking, clawing and screaming. I could not believe it, but Blake had overheard the same thing, so my lawyer suggested I agree to adjournment in contemplation of dismissal. "Otherwise it's your word against theirs," she had said. That was six months ago and now the charges were finally being dropped, my bail money was being returned (I paid Blake back a couple of weeks after the whole incident,) and according to the court if I am ever asked if I have been arrested, I am legally allowed to say "no." Funny, they think they can just make things disappear and there's no harm?

I exhausted all the local job postings, sending out resumes, and thought about looking at postings in Vermont, but decided against it. Going to my closet to grab the dirty laundry I suddenly heard in my heart "It's okay now. You are released."

"God? What?"

"I asked you to give Dave another year and you did. He didn't respond well, that's not your fault. I do remember." It was crystal clear inside of me. I slumped down alongside the wall and sat for a moment, allowing myself to cry and release all the pent-up emotions.

"This is for real, isn't it?" I whispered. "And Vermont?"

"You are free to go. Remember my promises." Crystal clear, deep down in my heart. There was no denying the Voice.

"I was thinking a lot today about what we talked about last night," Dave cleared his throat nervously, sitting down to watch me prepare dinner. "Did you think about it?"

"Yes," I exhaled anxiously, sadly. "What are your thoughts?"

"Well, I think the best thing for me to do is go back to Tennessee." He paused and let out a long sigh. "I mean, I can't expect you to put up with this anymore, but I think we'll always be great friends, right?" He looked at me with that telltale quivering jaw, tears brimming his eyes.

"I hope so, Dave," I told him earnestly. "When it was good, it was wonderful."

"I know," he cried openly now. "It was, and it's all my fault. I take full responsibility."

I shed a lot of tears that night, too. Even so, I was grateful that God had not forgotten me. I worried about the kids' reactions, especially Jonathan. I knew Papa would be upset, too. But for the next few days and weeks things between Dave and I were actually great. We talked and helped each other plan. We filed our own divorce papers, and we made plans for how to tell Papa and the kids together.

FIFTY-SIX

Sometimes the best beginning is an ending.

THERE WERE PLENTY MORE jobs in Vermont. I eagerly applied to many, then started looking at housing. The phone began ringing with interview requests and I began setting my plans in motion. I planned on going home to Burlington, but one of the positions that appealed to me the most was in Saint Albans. It had been many years since I had been in the workforce outside of hospitality or my own consulting business. I was feeling like a washed up has been with all the losses I suffered, so I wasn't very confident about high powered positions, and I knew I needed to make time to write. When I saw the part time medical practice manager position, I knew it was mine. They called me the day after receiving my resume and we set an interview for Monday of the following week.

"Hello?" I answered the phone cheerily.

"Is this the woman who called about the rental in Fairfield?" A tickly, high-pitched voice on the other end of the line inquired.

"Possibly. Um, I called quite a few places. Who is this?"

"My name is Bonnie," she said warmly. "I am trying to help rent a doctor's house in Fairfield. You called about it the other day, but I didn't get your name."

"I'm Karen Marie," I told her. "Which house?"

"It's five bedrooms, four bathrooms—a big Victorian style farmhouse. Are you still interested?"

"Oh! No, I remember the listing now. I'm sorry; I cannot afford that rent."

"Well, how many are in your family?" she inquired in an upbeat voice.

"Well, my daughter is out of the house and my son is away at college most of the year, so it would just be me and my old golden retriever and my cat," I said, smiling into the phone.

"Oh! Then why were you interested in such a big house?"

"I used to have a B&B. I thought I might do so casually once I get home to Vermont. I plan on working about thirty-two to thirty-four hours per week, and writing, and I thought it would be good, but the rent is too high for me right now."

"You're from Vermont?" She seemed a little nosey, but I was up for a friendly chat. We spoke for a while and exchanged information. However, I hung up the phone, expecting I would never speak with her again.

I found a few apartments to look at in Saint Albans, which were much cheaper than Burlington and yet only twenty minutes away. Not wanting to lose the opportunities, I made appointments to see them Monday, trying to cram it all into one day. Dave had given his notice at work and expected to leave New York by the end of October. With the change in divorce laws that had just taken effect before we filed, ours was handled in record time—less than nine weeks and it was official.

"I want to help you get settled in Vermont before I leave," Dave said sweetly Sunday evening. "I've been thinking about it and I can rent an SUV from Burlington and drive down from there just as easy as here. Besides, I want to make this as easy on you as possible."

"Well, that's nice of you," I replied. "I guess I hadn't thought about the moving part yet."

"Just let me know what you decide after your interview and apartment hunting. I don't want you to have to handle all this by yourself."

The next day I set out early for Saint Albans. I decided to drive straight over Route 3 and across the top of Lake Champlain, crossing the bridge along the Canadian border between Rouses Point, New York and Alburgh, Vermont. It was bright and sunny and though I was nervous, I was excited to be making this drive. The interview went so well it lasted an hour longer than anticipated. I knew when I left their office I had the job but waited for a phone call and an offer. I went to see a few rentals, mostly rundown apartments that had been made out of big old stately houses. I feared the heating bills would be high and wasn't sure about the utilities. My income was limited, and my savings was even more so, barely a couple of thousand dollars. Of course, Bob was not helping me with the kid's education expenses either.

I had filed yet again to collect all the back medical expenses Bob owed me, in excess of $10,000, but had not had any success yet. When I went to court, the judge thought we were a lesbian couple fighting over adopted kids. I very pointedly assured him that despite his new appearance, this was in fact my children's biological father. The judge found it very amusing, and Evan Tracy once again got the case thrown out on a technicality. My lawyer asked for more documents and receipts in order to refile.

Monday afternoon, I saw a larger apartment off Lincoln Avenue; realizing it had plenty of room for Jon and was priced reasonably, I had all but made up my mind. The gaudy 70's wallpaper and paneling, let alone all the carpeting really bothered me, but I asked the owner if she would allow me to make some changes. She indicated she might, and I told her I would get back to her in the next day or so. The thought of that apartment was the only downside to my day, but it was the best I could find. I headed toward Burlington to visit with Papa.

I answered my cell as I pulled into his driveway. They offered me the position, and the beginning salary I had requested. I was to start the following Wednesday. I begrudgingly called the owner of the 70's house and told her I would take the apartment. We set a time to meet Thursday afternoon to sign the lease. Wednesday morning as I was packing, I got a phone call from Bonnie, my new acquaintance.

"We would like you to come see the house," she must have been grinning into the phone because I heard it in her voice.

"I'm sorry," I was a bit exasperated. "Like I said, the rent is not right for me."

"It's not about the rent, it's about the person!" She insisted. "We looked you up. You have a wonderful reputation, and the doctor is more concerned with keeping the house lived in and clean than the amount of rent. So why don't you come see it?"

"Well, I am supposed to sign the lease on another place Thursday afternoon, and move this weekend! I—"

"Perfect, I can meet you Thursday morning and let you see it before you regret it!"

I met Bonnie at the Maplefield's plaza on Route 104 at exactly 12:00 noon. We chatted as she drove up Fairfield hill and toward the mountains. I hadn't been there since high school. Memories came flooding back. After turning off the main road, and then onto a dirt road for a couple of miles we finally pulled into the long driveway. As we passed the huge trees at the end and the house came into sight, I tried not to gasp. It was big and beautiful, the type of country home I had always wanted. It was at that moment I remembered my fortune cookie: *You will move into a beautiful, spacious home within the year.*

"What do you think?" Bonnie asked excitedly.

"I already love it," I replied somberly, admiring the Victorian flair and oversized porch with built-in gazebo area.

She showed me around the plentiful rooms with tons of natural light, large kitchen and living room, study.

"Do you like it? Want to move in?" she quipped. "Let's call the doc!"

We went down to the hospital and met the doc in one of the conference rooms. He asked me what I had planned to pay for rent in the 70's house and offered to match it—everything included. He had a place for me to store the furnishings I wouldn't need in the house and was prepared to let me move in on Saturday. After calling the owner of the other place and apologizing, I waited for the lease he had his lawyer prepare and we signed it a few hours later. He gave me a key right then and there and I wrote him a check for the first month plus security.

It was about 7:00 pm when I started the three-hour journey back via the ferry across the lake and back roads through Ausable, Saranac, Lake Placid, to Saranac Lake. The moon was full, looming large on the horizon, and though I was tired, I was overcome with gratitude. Dave was worried about me and had been packing while waiting for me to arrive. As I pulled in after 10:00 PM he met me on the sidewalk.

"You should have called me," he whined. "I still care about ya! I was worried!"

"Sorry, Dave," I exhaled deeply. "Long, wonderful day."

Saturday it took us most of the day to load up the U-haul and car, but we finally pulled out of Saranac Lake around 3:00. We drove along the top of the lake and I honestly sensed the biggest weight lift off my shoulders and chest as we came across the bridge into Vermont. As prearranged, I called my new landlord, Doc, on his cellphone and he set out to meet us at the house.

"Wow, this is beautiful!" Dave exclaimed getting out of the truck. "You're gonna love it here!"

"I know! God is so good to me," I told him. Luke waddled around sniffing things and I put Pepper in a bedroom so she wouldn't get lost. Doc wanted to show me how to handle the outdoor wood burning furnace, and a few other necessities before we went into the house together.

"So, this is your *ex-husband*?" His eyebrows arched in surprise.

"I'm David," he reached his hand out to shake. "Nice to meet you."

"Nice to meet you. I hope you don't mind my saying, but I can't imagine you two being so friendly and you're just divorced."

"No point in holding onto bitterness," I said, "Forgive and move on."

"We'll always be friends," Dave told him as Doc ushered us inside. We went up the stairs to the second floor and I pointed to a blue bedroom in the front of the house with a queen bed in it.

"Will you be okay in this room, Dave?" I asked, noting Doc's astonishment showed on his face even more.

"This is great," Dave said.

"Seriously? So, you're not even friends with benefits?" Doc asked a little too intrusively. "Wow."

We unloaded the Uhaul and then took the remaining items down the road a quarter of a mile to the sugarhouse belonging to the three-hundred-and-eighty-acre maple farm where I was told I could store them on the second floor. It was a long, back-breaking day, I could not have done it without Dave's help.

He stayed about six days, tidying up the loose ends of our not even seven years together. We spent a lot of time apart in the first few years due to the military, dealt with trauma after trauma, the loss of my precious Nana, the loss of not one but *two* homes. Some have asked me if it had not been for the trauma, would we have made it. I don't really know. The traumas didn't help his addiction, for sure, but I am not looking back and second-guessing.

It was an odd but pleasant transition. We spent our days pursuing what we had to separately, but took turns making meals for each other in the evening and sharing a glass of wine before going to our separate bedrooms and closing the doors.

At the same time, I was appointed an attorney to handle the federal case. That weight was lifted, too. I was getting nowhere in the state court, and no one seemed to care anymore about the one and a quarter million dollars' worth of losses I had by now accumulated. Bill Meconi never returned our purchase money in escrow. Don and Carolyn never paid a dime, the Smiths battled me cruelly, and I began to alter my idea of justice.

I made preparations to open my little part time B&B on Airbnb, I called it *The Sugar Farm, where life is sweet.* Before long I was taking in my first guests. I was reunited with old friends and slowly began to grow my circle of new friends and acquaintances. Bonnie went through a divorce and ended up renting a room from me, thus we established a sister-type of bond.

Time marched on, and I began to heal. I enjoyed time and space in the countryside and nurtured my soul and body back to health as best I could. Dave called every few weeks and we chatted, he was already asking for advice about women, and before long was seeing two of them without each other knowing. A while later I found myself in love again, which was not what I expected or sought after. By the grace of God, I ended up with a beautiful and spacious home of my own that also happens to be a bed and breakfast.

Though what you have read seems harsh, I am not embittered, rather I am empowered. I told you this true story, including my mistakes and heartaches, but the person I am now is not the weak, confused and easily manipulated young woman that started this journey. No, the journey through the wilderness prepared me; it trained me. My senses are sharper, my joy is fuller, and my peace is deeper than I ever knew before. I am so grateful, even though the legal battles ended wrongly, and I lost everything, because what I gained is far more precious. The wilderness trained me for a better life.

So, you see, my friend, God keeps His promises and loves to restore what's been lost. This is not the end of my story; there is so much more to tell, but this is where I stop for now.

When *you* finally come out of *your* wilderness, make sure you've got the power that comes from standing strong in trials and believing in the goodness of God despite what appearances are. I want to remind you to have hope, and don't lose faith when all around is wild and bleak. What you believe influences outcomes. Keep your heart open to hope and dream.

It may not be an ending, but a beginning.

www.ingramcontent.com/pod-product-compliance
Lightning Source LLC
Chambersburg PA
CBHW071301110526
44591CB00010B/731